LIVING BEACHES
of Georgia and the Carolinas

A Beachcomber's Guide

LIVING BEACHES
of Georgia and the Carolinas

A Beachcomber's Guide

Blair and Dawn Witherington

Pineapple Press, Inc.
Sarasota, Florida

To our parents

Front Cover

Background: Little Cumberland Island, GA
American oystercatcher
Knobbed whelk
Atlantic ghost crab
Seaglass
Royal sea star
Beach morning glory
Hatchling loggerhead sea turtle
Variable coquina clams
Boneyard oak

Back Cover, Willet

Front Flap, Boneyard cedar

Title page, Little Cumberland Island, GA

P. 1, Swash zone ripple marks
P. 51, Ring-billed gull
P. 229, Seaoats, saw palmetto, live oak
P. 285, Coquina formation, Ft. Fisher, NC
P. 295, St. Simons Island, GA, lighthouse
P. 328, Sanderlings

Inquiries should be addressed to:

Pineapple Press, Inc.
P.O. Box 3889
Sarasota, Florida 34230

www.pineapplepress.com

Library of Congress Cataloging-in-Publication Data

Witherington, Blair E., 1962-
  Living beaches of Georgia and the Carolinas : a beachcomber's guide /
Blair and Dawn Witherington. – 1st ed.
      p. cm.
  Includes bibliographical references and index.
  ISBN 978-1-56164-490-2 (pb : alk. paper)
  1. Seashore ecology—Georgia. 2. Seashore ecology—North Carolina.
3. Seashore ecology—South Carolina. 4. Beaches—Georgia. 5. Beaches—North
Carolina. 6. Beaches—South Carolina. 7. Beachcombing—Georgia. 8.
Beachcombing—North Carolina. 9. Beachcombing—South Carolina. I.
Witherington, Dawn. II. Title.
  QH105.G4W58 2011
  578.769'909756--dc22
                              2010050606

First Edition
10 9 8 7 6 5 4 3 2 1

Design by Blair and Dawn Witherington
Printed in China

Contents

CONTENTS

Acknowledgments and Photo Credits

For their contributions and reviews we are greatly indebted to Troy Alphin, Dean Bagley, Mike Blanchard, Dale Bishop, Betsy Brabson, George Burgess, Sarah Dawsey, Carly DeMay, Mike Durako, Mark Dodd, Kevin Edwards, Bill Frank, Danny Gleason, DuBose Griffin, Shigetomo Hirama, Terri Hathaway, Harry ten Hove, Kim Mohlenhoff, Bill Neal, Nellie Myrtle Beachcomber Museum, Jo O'Keefe, Ed Perry, Orrin Pilkey, Steven Pinker, Jennifer Slayton, St. Catherines Is. Sea Turtle Conservation Program, Jerry Tupacz, Chaz Wilkins, and John Willson.

Photographs and illustrations are © Blair and Dawn Witherington unless listed.

Page 41 top, Google Earth
Page 44 top/center, NOAA
Page 45 top, NOAA
Page 45 bottom, © Don Bowers
Page 46 Google Earth
Page 47 all, Google Earth
Page 48 Google Earth
Page 50 top/center, Google Earth
Page 137 center, © Carly DeMay
Page 141 top, © Hans Hillewaert
Page 172 2–5, © George Burgess
Page 178 bottom, © John Willson
Page 179 bottom, © Shigetomo Hirama
Page 181 bottom, © Shutterstock
Page 193 bottom, © Jim Fenton

Page 194 center/bottom, © Kevin Edwards
Page 214 bottom, © Kevin Edwards
Page 221 top, © Shutterstock
Page 222 top, © Steve Johnson
Page 222 center, © Shutterstock
Page 223 top, © Steven Pinker
Page 225 bottom, © Gale Bishop
Page 226 center/bottom, © Tom Pitchford
Page 227 top, © FFWCC
Page 227 bottom, © Jennifer Slayton
Page 242 bottom, © Jo O'Keefe
Page 301 center, US Army Corps of Engineers
Page 317 top, © Americasroof
Page 320 second, Google Earth

Top Fifty Living Beaches of Georgia and the Carolinas

Each of our beaches has life, but some beaches stand out as vibrant examples of natural processes free to run their course. These are not beaches devoid of humans; many are among our most visited shores. But these do tend to be beaches where our influence has been more casual than insistent. In geographic order the list includes:

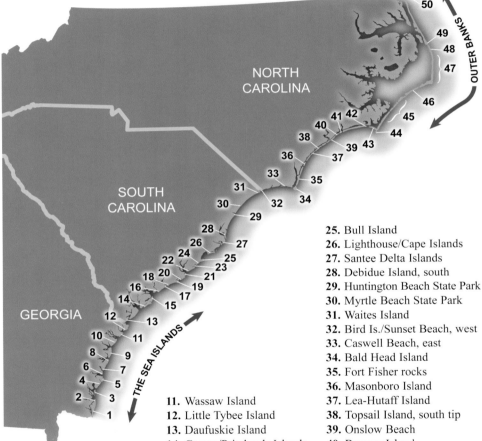

25. Bull Island
26. Lighthouse/Cape Islands
27. Santee Delta Islands
28. Debidue Island, south
29. Huntington Beach State Park
30. Myrtle Beach State Park
31. Waites Island
32. Bird Is./Sunset Beach, west
33. Caswell Beach, east
34. Bald Head Island
35. Fort Fisher rocks
36. Masonboro Island
37. Lea-Hutaff Island
38. Topsail Island, south tip
39. Onslow Beach
40. Browns Island
41. Bear Island
42. Fort Macon State Park
43. Shackleford Banks
44. Cape Lookout
45. Core Banks
46. Ocracoke Island
47. Hatteras Island
48. Pea Island
49. Bodie Island, south
50. Corolla, NC/VA state line

11. Wassaw Island
12. Little Tybee Island
13. Daufuskie Island
14. Capers/Pritchards Islands
15. Hunting Island State Park
16. Edisto Beach State Park
17. Botany Bay Beaches
18. Seabrook Island, north
19. Kiawah Island
20. Folly Beach, N and S tips
21. Morris Island
22. Sullivans Island, south
23. Dewees Island
24. Capers Island Preserve

1. Cumberland Island
2. Little Cumberland Island
3. Jekyll Island, N and S tips
4. Sea Island, south
5. Little St. Simons Island
6. Wolf Island
7. Sapello Island
8. Blackbeard Island
9. St. Catherines Island
10. Ossabaw Island

The Beaches Are Alive!

Yes, our Southeastern beaches are alive. Some of this vitality is obvious. Stroll onto the beach, sink your toes in the sand, and look around you. On the dune-front, gulls glide above flagging sea oats. On the open beach, crabs toss sand from their burrows. And at the tide line, shorebirds busily poke and turn the clumps of seaweed.

Look closer and you'll see even greater evidence of life. The seashore is vibrant with dozens of dune-plant species; a diverse array of seashells; birds that dive, run, wade, and soar; and the wrack—that ever-changing line of formerly floating drift-stuff from faraway.

Clearly, beaches attract, foster, and collect life . . . and the testament of life. But in an important way, beaches are also alive themselves. Beaches and dunes grow, diminish, evolve over years, and shift with the seasons. To pulsate with change is the very nature of a sandy sea coastline. This change is the essence of what makes beaches so fascinating.

In the long term, beaches are tumultuous, even dangerous places. Yet, a short-term visit allows a pleasant acquaintance with the beauty generated by all that turmoil. Our beaches are the easily accessible margins of a spectacular wilderness—the sea. To visit a beach is to peer into that wilderness and even examine it closely, for much of the sea's mysterious nature ends up on its beaches.

We hope that this book will provide some helpful interpretation for the curious seashore visitor. In part, it is a guide to critters, plants, formations, and stuff that might be puzzling enough to go nameless without a little assistance. But an additional aspect of this book is to share the mystery and intrigue of many things that are easily identified but little known. From the elegant to the plain, from the provocative to the mundane, everything on a beach has a story to tell.

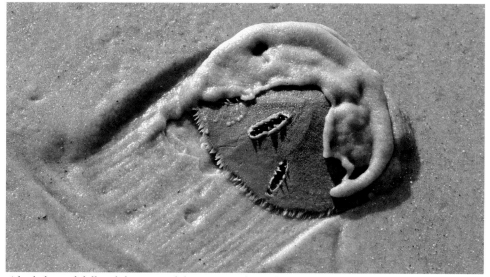

A keyhole sand dollar slides seaward during a receding tide

How the Story Unfolds

This book is in sections dividing categories of beach stuff—*Beach Features, Beach Animals, Beach Plants, Beach Minerals,* and *Hand of Man.* Within each section, related groups presented together share an identifying icon at the top of the page.

Most items have a map showing where and when one might find it on a beach. These ranges pertain specifically to an item's beach distribution, which may be different from the places it occupies when not on a beach. For example, many of the plants that produce drifting seeds known as seabeans live far away within inland tropical rainforests. Yet, the plants' floating seeds show up on our Southeastern beaches at particular places and times (due to rivers, ocean currents, and weather). Coastal lines on the maps are **red** if they describe a warm-season distribution and **blue** if they describe a range during cooler months. **Purple** lines pertain to all seasons and an open **black** line indicates brief passage during spring and fall migrations. Each line is solid where an item is relatively common, and is open where relatively uncommon. Because the range maps are not absolute, a gap may indicate either rarity or uncertainty. Some items that occur in isolated locations have individual dots showing their distribution.

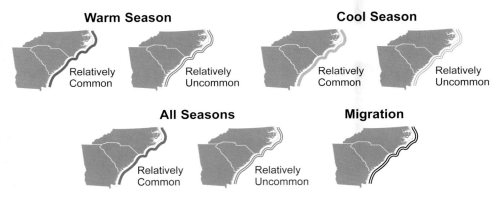

Warm Season		Cool Season	
Relatively Common	Relatively Uncommon	Relatively Common	Relatively Uncommon

All Seasons		Migration
Relatively Common	Relatively Uncommon	

Because this is a guide to beach-found things, all the depictions are of things found on a beach. That is, some are likely to show a beach-worn look. Although we've tried to represent the living elegance of creatures, some are merely deceased lumps and blobs by the time they reach the shore.

Note that where an item's size is given, the measure refers to its maximum dimension unless otherwise indicated. Also note that a few featured items hold the potential for an unpleasant encounter. These will have a watch-your-step or don't-touch symbol 🚫 🚫, which we hope you will see before you engage the thing with your bare feet or put it in your pocket.

Rather than simply set the scene, introduce a cast of characters, and leave you hanging, we've tried to end with the motivation for an endeavor, or as we refer to them, quests. These target a selection of rare, beautiful, or otherwise compelling hope-to-finds that can provide a blanket excuse for beach adventure.

Blair and Dawn Witherington

BEACH FEATURES

What is a Beach Feature?

The features of a beach are its life-signs. These signs reveal a beach's relationships, growth, withdrawal, and restless movement (yes, beaches move). Although much of this book describes beach things, this *Beach Features* section deals mostly with processes and the evidence they leave.

Beach features help describe the relationship between land and sea. Although some may see this relationship as a battle, another view sees an association with mutual exchange. Whether harsh or congenial, this land-sea relationship depends on sand. The land stakes claim to former sea bottom blown into mounds (the dune) and covers its claim with pioneering greenery. But this sand is just a loan. In the economy of sand, this currency shifts between land and sea, between undersea features, between beach elevations, and between adjacent beaches. The dynamics of this bustling economy can be read in a beach's features. To an educated eye, beach features are both evidence of history and indicators for prediction.

The give-and-take between land and sea also involves energy. As you'll see, beach features include exchanges of heat, wind, waves, and biological material that further define the beach economy.

To a true beach aficionado, an otherwise pedestrian pile of sand offers a host of signs revealing a beach's beating pulse. Sensing that pulse is basic to understanding what beaches are all about and can add wonder and intrigue to a coastal visit.

A breaker pounds foreshore sands in the continual movement that defines a beach

Beach Anatomy

Each visit to the beach is unique. No two beaches are exactly alike, and at any given beach, every day is different. But despite their dynamic forms, beaches tend to share a common anatomy that is predictable based on location and season.

You may have noticed that our Southeastern beaches have a lot of sand. Most of this sand is quartz, once part of the Appalachian Mountains. Shell bits make up much of the rest of our beach sands, in addition to variable amounts of feldspar and heavy minerals like metal oxides (p. 288). Sand character varies between beaches, seasons, and the parts of a beach's anatomy. Finer and lighter grains are found on beaches with the lowest wave energy, during calm summer months, and in dunes. Coarser grains are found on steep, rough beaches, during winter, and on the lower beach.

Within each beach, anatomy is laid out relative to elevation above the sea. These beach zones range from high, dry, and occasionally wave-washed (the **dune**), to frequently wave-washed (the **backshore**), to the constantly wave-washed zone between high and low tides (the **foreshore**). Further seaward are two zones critical to the beach (and formerly beach themselves): the **nearshore** and **offshore** zones.

Within each zone are the lumps, bumps, dips, waves, and wave-washed stuff that further describe a beach's structure. The **dune scarp**, if present, marks the elevation where recent storms have swept away dune sands. Between the dune base and the daily high-tide mark lie one or more **wrack lines**, the piles of marine organisms

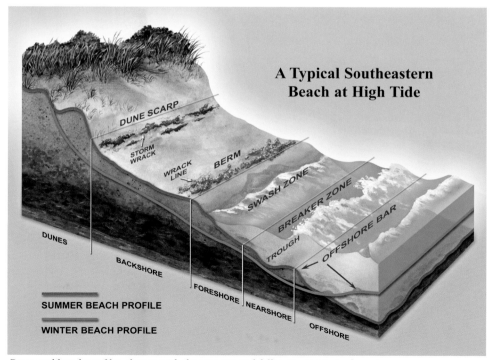

Dune and beach profiles change with the seasons and following events such as storms

A fisherman aims for productive surf waters

Black skimmers read the surf to fish between waves

Numerous treasures cluster in predictable patterns

(mostly marsh reeds or seaweed) that in their death bring life to the beach. The highest average tide generally reaches the **berm**, a sandy platform between the flat backshore and the sloped foreshore. Beach meets sea at the **swash zone** (p. 26), where waves rush the sandy incline and wash back into the following breaker. Often, this final pounding of wave energy creates a step-down into a **trough** landward of the **breaker zone**. The breakers begin where the **offshore bar** presents a rise shallow enough to trip incoming waves.

All of this anatomy changes between winter and summer, storm and calm. Compared to a summer beach fronting calm seas, winter and storm beaches tend to be flatter with a narrow berm and a distant offshore bar. Artificially nourished (man-made) beaches begin with an engineered anatomy but equilibrate over a period of years as the sea sculpts the foreshore, then backshore, then dune.

A beach's profile varies with tidal range and wave energy (p. 6). Big waves make dissipative beaches that are flat with a wide breaker zone within extensive offshore bars. Smaller waves allow reflective beaches that are steeper, narrower, and have most of their sands within the upper beach and dunes. Our Southeastern beaches are intermediate between dissipative and reflective, but they shift toward dissipative profiles when winter's rough seas pound and when stormy weather strikes. Some Southeastern beaches with coarse sands may remain more reflective, and some fine-sand beaches may remain dissipative, regardless of wave conditions.

A beachcomber who knows a little beach anatomy and coastal weather often finds the best beach stuff. The ocean scatters its varied treasures in different beach zones depending on its mood (sea conditions).

Combing the swash zone (**A**) at low tide is the best way to find small and delicate seashells. When a stiff onshore wind is blowing, this is also the place to find blue animals (oceanic drifters). The recent high-tide line at mid-beach (**B**) is normally the best place to find large or fluttery shells, buoyant items like sea-beans (pp. 269–277), and invertebrates like sponges and soft corals. Keep in mind that the high-tide wrack from previous days may have been higher up the beach (**C**), where drift treasures can be found if they have not been covered with sand. The largest waves during the highest tides sweep up the beach to the storm wrack (**D**), which is often at the base of the dune but may extend into overwash areas (p. 12) between the dunes. Although wrack-hunting is fruitful for almost anything immediately after a storm, even months-old storm wrack yields persistent, storm-stranded items like big shells, driftwood, and lost cargo. Storm wrack on infrequently combed beaches is filled with rare finds.

Beach anatomy becomes less esoteric and more real to visitors who experience features forming before their eyes. **Aeolian** (wind-driven) **transport** of sand is but one of these watchable developmental processes. To experience sand flowing over a beach on a breezy day is to witness the origins and pulsation of many beach features. As sand rolls across the beach, some features are exposed, others are buried, sand ripples march with the wind, and the growth of a dune from seed begins at a seaweed clump that has drifted at sea for hundreds of miles.

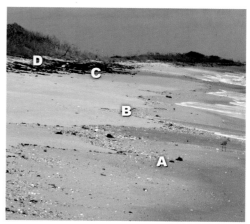

Lettered areas show where to find beach treasures

Waves and currents assemble a patch of shells

Aeolian transport of sand

5

A wide, flat, wave-dominated beach, Outer Banks, NC

Low-tide terrace, tide-dominated beach, SC

A steep, coarse-sand beach, SC

Beach Profiles

Wave-dominated

Tide-dominated

WHAT ARE THEY? Wave energy, tidal range, and sand coarseness dictate the slope of a beach's profile. **Wave-dominated** beaches, exposed to big waves and a modest tidal range, are flatter and wider. **Tide-dominated** beaches, with lower wave energy and higher tides, are typically steeper at high tide but have a wide, flat terrace at low tide. Coarse sands allow steeper beaches.

HOW COME? Big waves move sand to and fro in the swash zone, flattening the beach. Fine sands contribute to a flat beach because they do not drain well. Waterlogged sands allow waves rushing up the beach to rush back down instead of soaking in. This backwash carries sand with it. High tidal range (p. 38) creates sandbars that reduce wave energy to the upper beach at low tide. The small waves push coarse grains up and soak into the beach before washing sand back down the steepening beach.

FOUND: Outer Banks beaches tend to be wave-dominated, and Georgia's Sea Islands tend to be tide-dominated. Many beaches are intermediate.

SEASONS: Each beach type widens with the reduced erosion of summer and narrows during the tumultuous winter.

DID YOU KNOW? Beaches either dissipate or reflect wave energy. On this scale, our beach profiles are dissipative or intermediate, but not truly reflective.

Beach Lifespans

Circles of life turn at varied rates. For some features and associates of a living beach, only seconds pass between birth and death. Others may persist for a century or more. But in comparison to lifespans elsewhere on our planet, very little on beaches ever gets old.

Even the least patient among us have attention spans that would allow us to witness many generations of some beach features. For example, walk through the wet sand of the swash zone (p. 26), then look behind you. Within a few seconds a wave will end its life by crashing onto the beach and rushing up the slope in a froth-margined sheet of water. The final energy of the wave's life is spent suspending the sand that fills your **footprints**. As the leading edge of the wave wash reaches its peak, a **swash mark** is born where grains floating upon the water's surface tension come to rest in a tiny ridge. The wave-wash then slips back into the surf, leaving streams of bubbles from air forced out of the beach as water soaks into the sand. The escaping air leaves **bubble holes**. These are either obliterated by the next wave or remain during a falling tide until a rising tide replaces them with a different set of bubble holes.

The incoming tide also marks life's end for **sandcastles**, some **scarps** (small cliffs), **cusps**, and other topography of the beach berm. On the open beach, ghost crabs take diurnal refuge in burrows that may last only until the next high tide. But burrows in the dune may allow overwintering crabs to remain protected for months above the wash of winter storms. As testament to storm tides, **wrack lines** pushed high on the

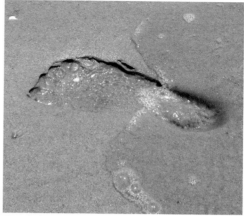

Beach footprints fill quickly

Sandcastles seldom survive high tide

The Outer Banks house from Nights in Rodanthe

beach may remain for the weeks it takes for component seaweeds and marsh reeds to decompose. Just above this recent high-water mark, **sea turtle nests** become unrecognizable following a few days of wind or rain, although a successful nest will contain viable eggs for about two months until their hatchlings escape.

On the **dune**, life is at the mercy of periodic storms. For many pioneering dune plants, life strategies anticipate annual catastrophes. These same events define the useful lives of all things near the dune crest, including our own buildings and our efforts to defend them from the sea. Only well behind the dunes does one find lives lived for more than a decade or so. But mighty **oaks**, **houses**, and the **barrier islands** on which they stand are inevitably swept away in their own time. Nothing near beaches is permanent.

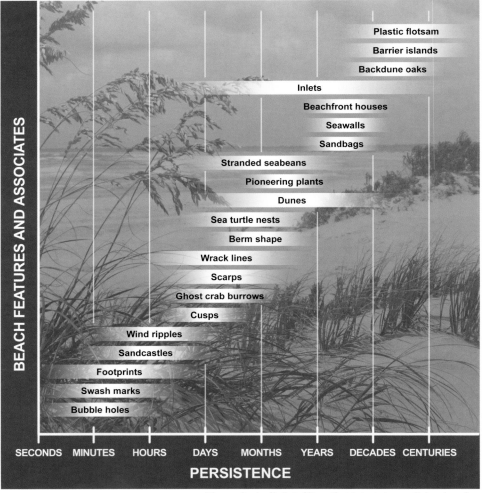

The geologically brief lives that intertwine on living beaches

Dunes

WHAT ARE THEY? Dunes are piles of windblown sand stabilized by fast-growing, salt-tolerant "pioneer" plants. Although the primary (most seaward) dune may be swept by storm tides every few years, more stable back dunes often support woody vegetation. Dunes are part of a sand "banking" system within which the beach makes continuous deposits and withdrawals. See artificial dunes (p. 321).

SIZE: Small mounds to promontories more than 30 ft (9 m) high. Stretches of Outer Banks dunes average 18 ft (5.5 m) and Georgia dunes average 10 ft (3.0 m) above sea level.

HOW COME? Dunes begin when windblown beach sand comes to rest within the sheltered "wind shadow" in the lee of old wrack lines and vegetation. Pioneer plants colonize these sand piles, roots keep the sand from migrating, and the dune grows into a shore-parallel ridge of individual mounds.

FOUND: All sandy beaches, although some dunes are without plants and very low (pp. 14–16). Large dunes form where there is a strong sea breeze, extensive sand supply, and unfettered plant growth.

SEASONS: All year. Rapid erosion and formation can occur during storms.

DID YOU KNOW? Ancient dune formation has made much of the coastal high ground we see today along the southeast US.

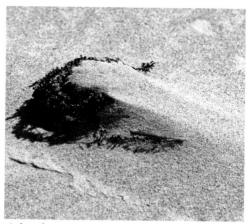

A dune begins in a seaweed wind shadow

Seaoats often foster discontinuous dune mounds

An eroding dune bluff, Little Cumberland Island, GA

9

The slipface of an active dune

Dune swales are low troughs behind a fronting dune

A freshwater swale behind a Georgia dune

Slipfaces and Swales

Slipfaces

Swales

WHAT ARE THEY? Slipfaces are the steep, downwind sides of active dunes. **Dune swales** (also called dune slacks) are low, marshy flats behind the dunes.

SIZE: Slipfaces are relative to dune size. Swales are variable, to as wide as a football field.

HOW COME? Dune slipfaces mark "active" (moving) dunes, which slope toward the prevailing wind and are steep (34°) to the point of slippage on the leeward side. Wind blows sand up to the crest, which periodically collapses down the slipface like a slowly breaking wave. Swales can form during backdune erosion from blowouts (p. 12). When this erosion lowers the elevation to the water table, or where impervious sediments such as mud or peat lie, fresh water collects from rain. Moist sands and protection from salt spray (p. 13) allow a unique coastal ecosystem to thrive.

FOUND: Slipfaces form when directed winds blow. Swales are scattered where large dunes sit on old marsh.

SEASONS: All year, but dune faces slip most during dry days with persistent high winds. Swales are prettiest with the blooming flowers and green vegetation of summer and early fall.

DID YOU KNOW? Dunes can become active if their vegetation is removed and will march landward over swales and many other things in their path.

Sand Layers and Lag Deposits

Sand Layers   *Lag Deposits*

WHAT ARE THEY? Sand layers show up as horizontal lines containing sands of different colors or consistencies, often seen in eroded dunes. **Lag deposits** are layers of shells and stones.

SIZE: Sand layers range from paper thin to the depth of an entire dune. Lag deposits can be one or many shells thick and may be exposed over flat areas as large as a football field.

HOW COME? Layers of sand mark events when wind or water moved sands of similar makeup into the upper beach or dune. Light-wind events move fine sands, fresh breezes move coarse sands, and the heaviest, dark-mineral sands are brought by stiff winds or flowing water. Lag-deposited shells were pushed onto the upper beach by waves and were later exposed as wind blew away surface sands. The exposed shell "pavement" prevents further wind erosion.

FOUND: Sand layers occur in all dunes. Lag deposits are most common on the Outer Banks south of Cape Hatteras.

SEASONS: All year.

DID YOU KNOW? Layers tell the history of a dune, including when human visitors have left artifacts. Nearly all the bivalve shells (e.g., clamshells) paving lag deposits rest concave-side down. In this most hydrodynamic orientation, they were least likely to be resuspended by the flowing water that brought them.

Sand layers in an eroded dune

Dark mineral layers laid down by strong winds

Shell-lag deposits exposed by wind

11

Evidence of overwash behind an Outer Banks dune

An overwash gap on a Georgia Sea Island

Blowouts leave only the highest seaoat tufts

Overwash and Blowouts

WHAT ARE THEY? Overwash occurs when waves push water through dunes, creating overwash gaps. This water flow often crosses entire islands. **Blowouts** are dune gaps created by wind.

SIZE: The smallest gaps are a few yards (meters) wide; the largest span hundreds of yards of former dune.

HOW COME? Offshore shoals focus wave energy toward particular beaches where low dunes allow wave-water to push landward. On thin islands, storm tides (p. 44) can flow overland to the backing estuary, creating fans of former beach/dune sand behind the island. Blowouts begin as small vegetation gaps that focus winds as they widen.

FOUND: These features are most common on wave-dominated barrier islands (p. 46) but form any place storms strike.

SEASONS: Overwash flow and blowouts take place during storms, but traces of these processes persist for years.

DID YOU KNOW? Coastal geologists struggle to predict where major overwash will take place based on models factoring wave height, storm surge, and dune elevation. Often, overwash past is a prologue for both future overwash and inlet formation (p. 49). Overwash flow is essentially a short-lived inlet. Tidal flow after passage of the storm surge can keep the passage open. Evidence for past overwash events includes layers of shells and mineral sediments.

Salt Pruning

WHAT IS IT? Salt pruning describes the trimming effects of salt spray. This process creates dune shrubs and trees with a sloping-hedge appearance.

SIZE: Salt spray can sculpt century-old live oaks into wavelike forms that are knee-high on their seaward side and well overhead on their protected side.

Seaward dune face, Little Cumberland Island, GA

HOW COME? Salt spray from breaking waves settles on the outer foliage of dune plants. Evaporation of this spray concentrates salts that can enter leaves through abrasions caused by wind-whipping. The salt gradually kills the most exposed, windward leaves. This trimming stimulates extensive branching, which produces dense, windward canopies. Salt pruning results in shrub-sized bonsai forms that lean away from the sea. Like bonsai, the beautiful forms of salt-pruned dune shrubs are acquired over decades.

FOUND: Beaches with mature dunes and woody vegetation. Picturesque examples of salt pruning can be found on most Southeastern beaches and in landward dunes far from the ocean.

A lone live oak, Outer Banks, NC

SEASONS: All seasons, although most of the actual pruning occurs during the driest months when there is little rain to wash salt from exposed leaves.

DID YOU KNOW? Salt-spray resistance dictates which plants exist on the dune. Survivors of this torture benefit by having few plant-competitors.

Bear (originally Bare) Island, NC

13

A boneyard-beach live oak, Hunting Island, SC

This mature forest was once far from the beach

Salt-tolerant cabbage palms die only after they fall

Boneyard Beaches

WHAT ARE THEY? Boneyard beaches (inaccurately called driftwood beaches) occur where the sea has eroded through the dune into the mature forest, killing the trees with salt water and leaving their sun-bleached woody "skeletons." These beaches are where the barrier island is literally sinking.

SIZE: The tallest pines and broadest oaks have left their bones on these eroding beaches, which can extend for three miles (5 km) or more.

HOW COME? Boneyard beaches are a consequence of beach retreat (p. 48). On most islands with boneyards, longshore currents (p. 41) driven by the strongest winds (typically from the north) carry sand from northern beaches to southern beaches. An island's northern beaches can erode into boneyards when a channel or inlet (p. 49) steals replacement sand that would have flowed from the island neighbor to the north.

FOUND: Most common on the northeastern ends of Georgia's and South Carolina's Sea Islands.

SEASONS: All year.

DID YOU KNOW? Oaks provide the most conspicuous boneyard skeletons. Their flat root mats allow them to tip over and persist. The vertical roots of pines snap, allowing timbers to roll away with the tides. Salt staves off insects and fungal rot, but trees in the water succumb to various wood-chewing marine animals.

Saltmarshes and Peat Outcroppings

Saltmarshes

Peat Outcroppings

WHAT ARE THEY? Saltmarshes are the grassy estuaries backing many Southeastern barrier islands. **Peat** is compacted, partially decayed marsh plants. **Peat outcroppings** are from old saltmarsh or freshwater swales formerly behind the beach. Their presence is evidence for island migration (p. 48). Exposed clay layers lie under the peat.

Oysters and Spartina *grass in a back-beach marsh*

SIZE: The most extensive coastal marshes span more than six miles (9.6 km) between the mainland and the barrier island. Peat outcroppings can extend for hundreds of yards (meters) down the beach but are generally only about two feet (60 cm) in thickness.

HOW COME? Saltmarsh grasses (p. 235) require protected waters that have a brackish blend of fresh and salt. Sandy barrier islands provide the protection, and coastal rivers provide the fresh water. Saltmarsh and swale plants live, die, and accumulate faster than they rot away in the oxygen-poor bottom. Dead plants plus mud make peat. As our sea level has risen, ocean waves have pushed sand over peat-lined marshes and freshwater swales. The

Beach oysters mark a former saltmarsh channel

landward-moving barrier-island sands roll like an immense tank tread over a bed of peat, which is revealed where the supply of sand is too low to cover the island's path. Shelves of peat and the underlying clay remain because they erode more slowly than sand. Channels of softer peat erode first, producing ridges in the outcropping.

Grass remnants in peat, Botany Bay Beach, SC

Peat from a freshwater swale, Barden Inlet, NC

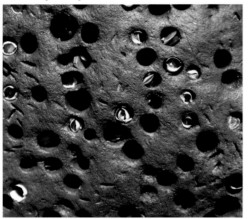

Atlantic mud-piddocks in old saltmarsh peat

Peat erodes to reveal reddish and bluish clays

FOUND: Most Georgia and South Carolina Sea Islands are backed by salt-marsh. This grassy ecosystem is thin or absent from the backs of North Carolina's Outer Banks, which have large open estuaries (sounds) between them and the mainland. Layers of peat, clay, and/or mud underlie most Southeastern beaches. These layers are exposed at specific sand-starved locations, often where updrift inlets have been dredged by man and lined with jetties (p. 317).

SEASONS: Saltmarshes are green in summer, golden in fall, and brown in winter. Peat outcroppings are more commonly exposed in the winter and spring and following storms.

DID YOU KNOW? Although underlying clay layers exposed at low tide may be thousands of years old, surfaces of most peat outcroppings are only a few hundred years old. This younger peat indicates the pace of island movement, which can be as rapid as an island-width in one human generation. Peat formations contain the plants and animals that called the former marsh home. Tegelus clams (p. 124), **Atlantic mud-piddocks** (p. 131), and other burrowing bivalves have their old shells within conspicuous pits in the muddy peat. Exposed beds of eastern oyster shells (p. 112), still anchored in their growth position, mark channels of tidal flow through the old marsh. These shells are from estuarine mollusks that would not have lived in exposed ocean waters. Intact stems of *Spartina* grass are common covering the surface layers of saltmarsh peat, whereas freshwater plants and tree stumps reveal peat from **freshwater swales**. Peat, mud, and clay exposed offshore can erode into clay- and mudballs (p. 291).

Wrack Lines

WHAT ARE THEY? Wrack lines, or strand lines, are lengthy piles of floating stuff that has washed in with the tide. Wrack is largely composed of uprooted seagrass, algae, and marsh plants. Much of this book contains descriptions of the elements and occupants of wrack.

SIZE: Although knee-high piles are common following rough weather, under calm conditions a beach may be starved of wrack for weeks.

HOW COME? Wrack lines are the ocean's bathtub ring, collecting all things that float or are pushed by waves. Much of this accumulation has a local origin, but some items have drifted at sea or tumbled along the sea bottom for years, with origins many leagues away.

FOUND: All beaches, although the components of the wrack vary by region. Georgia wrack is commonly *Spartina* reeds, whereas drifting *Sargassum* is most frequent in the Outer Banks. Wrack lines indicate where the tide has reached. Old wrack may remain high on the beach for weeks before disappearing under sand.

SEASONS: Wrack lines can be extensive in fall and spring following storms.

DID YOU KNOW? At the end of their life's journey, the plants and animals that wash onto beaches provide the base of an important beach food web. Many of the beach's most appealing animals would be absent were it not for the lowly wrack.

Fresh eelgrass and algal wrack

Spartina *reeds are common in wrack near inlets*

A ruddy turnstone shops the wrack for groceries

A dark sand layer partially covered by lighter sand

A patch of shell hash, Hatteras Island, NC

Dark Sands and Shell Hash

WHAT ARE THEY? Dark sands are thin layers (called placers) containing the heaviest (densest) mineral grains on the beach (p. 288). **Shell hash** describes surface patches of mollusk shell shards.

SIZE: Dark sand layers are typically less than a coin's thickness. Shell hash is up to a few inches thick and can cover thousands of square feet.

HOW COME? Dark sands often appear following storm erosion. Sands appear "dirty," but are perfectly "clean" minerals that make up a tiny fraction of the beach's sand grains. The mineral grains are mostly iron and titanium oxides, the heaviest on the beach. They tend to settle together in layered sheets (p. 11) and are last to suspend in wave-wash. Shell hash forms from mollusk shells broken into shards. Rounded, polished pieces of all sizes exist on the beach. After a period of rough surf, the largest shell shards settle out first in patches that are often concentrated in the upper swash zone (p. 26) at low tide.

FOUND: All beaches, although lighter beach sands contrast dark-sand layers most clearly, and the shelliest beaches do have the most shell hash.

SEASONS: All seasons, but most common during calm periods after storms.

DID YOU KNOW? Dark sands contain tiny grains of semi-precious gemstones (p. 288). Shell hash often contains seaglass (p. 303).

Gravel Beaches and Shell Beaches

Gravel Beaches

Shell Beaches

WHAT ARE THEY? Gravel beaches have extensive patches of coarse sediments including pebbles and "pea gravel" (p. 290). **Shell beaches** have a wide layer of shells covering other beach sediments.

SIZE: By definition "gravel" is coarser than sand and finer than cobbles, with grain sizes spanning 0.08–2.5 in (2–64 mm). Shell beaches are frequently covered with finger- to hand-sized oyster-shell. Each type of beach may stretch for many hundreds of yards (meters).

HOW COME? A beach's makeup reveals its history. Gravel beaches likely sit where there was once a river channel that polished pea-sized rocks as it cut through the coastal plain during the last ice age (20,000 years ago), when sea level was much lower. Shell beaches sit where abundant oysters once grew in shallow estuaries. Both pea gravel and oystershell remain in patches because of the way that water moves similar shapes in similar ways.

FOUND: Most gravel beaches are found north of Hatteras Island. A few marsh-backed, sand-starved beaches in South Carolina seem to be the shelliest.

SEASONS: All year.

DID YOU KNOW? Although gravel beaches are steeply sloped, wind cannot push the coarse grains into dunes. Much of the gravel is highly polished quartz of varied colors.

A pea-gravel beach, Nags Head, NC

Closeup of a gravel beach largely of coarse quartz

An oyster shell beach, Botany Bay, SC

19

Wind ripples, with arrow showing wind direction

Coarse brown grains linger on a set of ripple crests

Ripples in the fine sand of a wind shadow

Wind Ripples

WHAT ARE THEY? Wind ripples are elongate miniature dunes arranged perpendicular to the wind that formed them.

SIZE: Remarkably, sand ripples, crest to crest, are almost always about the length of an index finger.

HOW COME? There is much debate. A widely accepted explanation is that ripples are formed and spaced by how far a sand grain can leap. Wind moves sand by saltation—sand grains leaping, bouncing, and jostling other grains that further leap, bounce, and jostle others. The horizontally leaping grains are more likely to land where there is a slight rise, and these rises gain sand. The "wavelength" between rises is about how far grains can leap over the wind shadows between crests. As crests get too high, their exposed grains leap to the next ripple. Ripples move slowly downwind and change their orientation quickly when the wind shifts.

FOUND: All medium- to fine-grained beaches, in dry sand.

SEASONS: All year when winds are more than 15 knots and sands are dry.

DID YOU KNOW? Ripple crests tend to have larger grains, which occasionally give contrasting colors to crests and troughs. Finer grains are typically quartz and accumulate as white sand drifts behind wind shadows. In light wind, these wispy sands ripple whereas underlying wet or coarse grains do not.

Pedestals and Harrow Marks

WHAT ARE THEY? Pedestals are mushroom-shaped sculptures of sand with a rounded head atop a narrower base. **Harrow marks** are similar but with an elongate base and narrow head topped by a shell shard or seaweed scrap.

SIZE: Pedestals are ankle to shin high and are commonly isolated. Harrow marks are locally abundant, with the size of each structure determined by the shell-bit topping it; the smallest are capped by a single fragment of sand-grain size.

HOW COME? Each occurs where concentrated salts remain from evaporated wavewash. The brine lightly cements sand grains together in a mix called "salcrete." Because upper layers receive more salts, top salcrete layers are more resistant to wind erosion. As winds carve the salcreted sand pile, the stiffer salcrete remains together as a larger cap supported by a more easily carved base. Harrow marks occur in wetted sand, which persists during strong winds only in the wind shadow of a solid object like a shell.

FOUND: On the backshore and in overwash areas (p. 12).

SEASONS: Any windy, dry weather that follows high tides.

DID YOU KNOW? Pedestal "mushrooms" look like their namesake when variable winds make a more rounded cap and stalk. Aerodynamic shapes of harrow marks clearly show wind direction.

A mushroom pedestal carved by directional wind

Harrow marks formed from winds left to right

21

An arc showing a 360° swing in wind direction

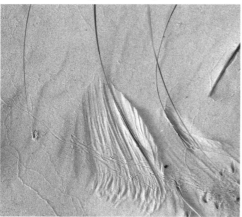

Detail of a plant arc from light, uniform winds

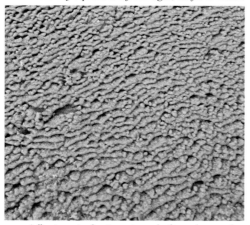

Adhesion ripples in wet sand after a breezy day

Plant Arcs and Adhesion Ripples

WHAT ARE THEY? Plant arcs are the tracings of leaf tips that surround a windblown plant. **Adhesion ripples** are warty surfaces in wet sand.

SIZE: Plant arcs have the radius of the plant inscribing them. Adhesion ripples are only 0.25 in (6 mm) tall but can cover the entire wet beach.

HOW COME? Plant arcs are traced when limber plants, especially grasses, wave in variably directed winds for many hours. Adhesion ripples form when strong winds blow sand from the backshore and dunes onto a water-saturated beach. There, the dry transported sand sticks to the wet sand surface. Each sand grain adheres, then wicks water by capillary action, allowing additional dry sand to stick. The irregular ripples are tiny versions of the dribble sandcastle spires made by dripping a slurry of seawater and sand.

FOUND: All beaches.

SEASONS: Formation of adhesion ripples generally requires a strong land breeze, which is more common following the passage of weather fronts in fall and spring. The same seasonal weather results in wind shifts that can produce the longest plant arcs.

DID YOU KNOW? Plant arcs occur at a wind speed that is just enough to move grass blades but not enough to erase the delicate sand markings.

Antidunes, Crescent Marks, and **Rhomboid Ripples**

Antidunes   Crescent Marks   Rhomboid Ripples

WHAT ARE THEY? Each mark is composed of swash sand separated by density and color. **Antidunes** are low, parallel ridges with their steepest face landward. **Crescent marks** are isolated V-shapes with an apex at a shell or other object. **Rhomboid ripples** occur in an extensive regular pattern of similar Vs.

SIZE: A foot's length separates most antidune bands, and is the width of the average crescent mark. Rhomboid ripples are most often 4 in (10 cm) long with a landward angle of 45°.

HOW COME? Water flow during a wave's backwash is not uniform. On flat forebeaches, sheet flow of backwash is interrupted by standing waves creating the bands of turbulence that form antidunes. Crescent marks form due to turbulence from an object in the swash zone, especially shells. The creation of rhomboid ripples is a mystery of fluid physics, except that they form in the last moments of backwash along spaced wave-interference zones.

FOUND: In swash zones (p. 26). Flatter forebeach shows antidunes and steeper swash displays rhomboid ripples.

SEASONS: All year.

DID YOU KNOW? The steepest side of an antidune faces into the backwash current, opposite the orientation of dunes to the wind.

Antidune ripples inscribed by a falling tide

A crescent mark trailing a sand collar (p. 81)

Rhomboid ripples point into the former backwash

23

Mild-current ripples, crests separated by inches

Swift-current sand waves, crests separated by feet

Flat-topped ripples

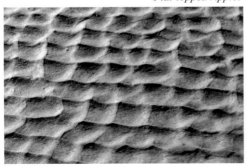

Ladderback ripples show two current directions

Current Ripples

WHAT ARE THEY? Current ripples are similar to wind ripples (p. 20) but are formed in sand by flowing water. Ripples are occasionally outlined by dense, dark mineral sands (p. 288). Current ripple ridges vary from low and parallel to large and irregular. **Flat-topped** ripples have flattened tops and **ladderback** ripples have perpendicular sets.

SIZE: Most ripple crests are separated by about 3 in (8 cm), but strong currents can pile up much larger **sand waves**.

HOW COME? Assembly of ripples by flowing water is similar to the process described for wind ripples. Swift, deep, turbulent currents create undulating sand waves that are similar to dunes. As current flow ends, parallel ripples still under water erode first at their crests, making them flat-topped. Ladderback ripples begin as parallel ridges, and receive superimposed ridges when a new flow direction is perpendicular to the original current.

FOUND: Anywhere water moves over sand, especially in runnels (p. 29) and tidal flats near inlets (p. 49).

SEASONS: All year.

DID YOU KNOW? Like wind ripples, current ripples are not static. They move continually in the direction of water flow until the tide drains the water away. The ripple forms are briefly suspended in time for us to admire until the next high tide arrives.

Rills and Rivulets

WHAT ARE THEY? Rills are marks etched by water flowing out of the beach. **Rivulets** are ephemeral flows that drain tidal lagoons behind the beach. Long, shore parallel rivulets are runnels (p. 29).

SIZE: Rill channels have thin, pencil-width branches but may connect in tree-sized systems originating up the beach. Most rivulets can be jumped across. Larger semi-permanent rivulets could be considered inlets (p. 49).

HOW COME? Rill marks form where groundwater seeps from saturated beach sands and the flow is enough to erode fine sands from tiny channels. Rills form where the water table intersects with the foreshore. Most often, this flowing water is salty, but following wet weather it may be fresh. Rivulets form where water pushed into temporary lagoons and runnels during high tide finds its way back to the ocean. A rivulet may last only one tidal cycle and re-form along a slightly different path each falling tide.

FOUND: Rills form as the edge of the water table is exposed at low tide. Rivulets form most prominently during bi-monthly spring tides (p. 38).

SEASONS: All year.

DID YOU KNOW? Sands saturated with water often seep where shells or stones have primed a flow by wicking water through capillary action. The shell produces a tiny spring and the flow erodes out a miniature river delta.

A set of tree-form rill channels at low tide

Shells mark the origins of a set of beach rills

A rivulet draining a tidal lagoon, Jekyll Island, GA

25

Swash flows up the beach

A sheet of backwash flows into a standing wave

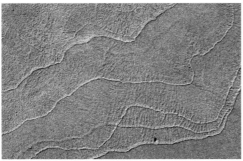

Swash marks from multiple incursions

A closeup of grains cresting a swash mark

Swash and Backwash

WHAT IS IT? **Swash** and **backwash** are the sweeps of water from spent waves. Within the swash zone, swash rushes up the beach and backwash flows down. Often, the two flows meet in a stationary, **standing wave**. This wave-lapping moves sand, brings material from the sea, and defines a home for a variety of beach animals.

SIZE: From a few feet (about 1 m) to over 100 yards (100 m) wide. Swash marks are several sand grains across.

HOW COME? The distant energy that produced a wave is finally spent in the swash zone. The most landward travel of each swash also leaves tiny, ridgeline **swash marks** from sand grains and shell particles that rode up the beach floating on the water's surface tension. Swash-zone sands have unique properties. Seawater soaking into the porous beach transforms the sand into a liquidlike medium giving animals like mole crabs (p. 150) and coquina clams (p. 121) a momentary opportunity to sand-swim.

FOUND: All beaches.

SEASONS: All times, but the widest swash zones are when waves and tidal ranges are highest.

DID YOU KNOW? The swash zone is not quite land and not quite sea, but it is the liveliest part of the beach. See the *Beach Animals* section for tracks, burrows, and other evidence of these swash-zone critters.

Bubble Holes, Blisters, Pits, and **Volcanoes**

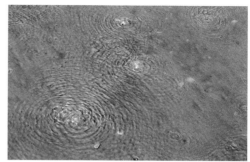

Air bubbling out of a fluffy beach

WHAT ARE THEY? All are perforations in the middle beach above the swash. Simple **bubble holes** are punctures, **blisters** are bumps over air pockets, **pits** are holes within a depression, and **volcanoes** are bubble holes surrounded by a tiny rim.

SIZE: These air outlets are pin- to nail-sized holes. Blisters are coin-sized.

HOW COME? Sand pushed up the beach by wavewash drains at low tide to leave air trapped within a mushy matrix. When the tide returns to the upper beach, the swash surges over the fluffy sand in sheets of water that drain into the sand to force out air. The air bubbles out in simple holes or may erupt forcefully to produce a tiny volcano of watery sand. Air trapped beneath a skin of salcrete (p. 21) may merely push up a sandy "blister." If the swash erodes away this blister, a pit remains.

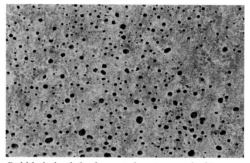

Bubble holes left after swash waters soaked in

FOUND: All beaches, typically in the beach berm at the upper reach of the recent swash.

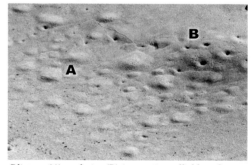

Blisters (A) and pits (B) in an air-puffed beach

SEASONS: All seasons, although these holes form most during dry weather. Look for these features forming on a rising tide and remaining after a falling tide.

DID YOU KNOW? These holes are commonly mistaken for animal burrows. Most critters in this zone sand-swim rather than construct persistent homes. The fortified tubes of ghost shrimp (p. 147) are an exception.

A volcano bubble hole shows forceful air expulsion

27

Beach cusps on an Outer Banks beach

Swash reaching an eroded scarp at high tide

Cusps eroding into scarps

Beach Cusps and Scarps

Beach Cusps

Beach Scarps

WHAT ARE THEY? Cusps are waves in the sand on the lower beach, cresting and dipping at regular intervals. The rises (horns) contain the coarsest sands, and the valleys have finer sands. **Scarps** are cliffs in the beach marking the recent line where erosion has taken away sand.

SIZE: Cusps and scarps are generally 1–6 ft (0.3–2 m) high. Scarps following severe storms can be 12 ft (3.5 m) or more.

HOW COME? Cusps form mysteriously, but most agree on how they are maintained. The horns of coarse sand divert incoming waves into adjacent valleys, carry finer grains with their flow, and wash some of the valley's sand back to sea. Scarps form due to rapid erosion (p. 32) following a period of sand accretion (p. 33).

FOUND: Cusps are most pronounced on wave-dominated beaches (p. 6). Artificially nourished (p. 321) beaches commonly form scarps as the beach equilibrates from an unnaturally accreted profile.

SEASONS: Cusps are common in summer as beaches are building and scarps are common in the stormier fall, winter, and spring.

DID YOU KNOW? Cusps move slowly in wavelike fashion down the beach. Large storm-scarps in the dune can persist for years.

Sandbars, Ridges, and Runnels

An exposed sandbar during a spring-tide low

WHAT ARE THEY? Sandbars are underwater linear mounds just off the beach (inner bar) or offshore (outer bar). Bars can migrate landward to become beach **ridges**. Exposed ridges breached by high tides contain linear **runnels** or troughs that are filled with water at high tide and may linger as "beach lagoons" through low tide.

SIZE: Sandbars and ridges may be up to hundreds of feet wide. Runnels may be equally wide and up to 6 ft (2 m) deep.

HOW COME? Each of these features describes a beach in transition. Inner sandbars become beach ridges when they have swelled with sand from an eroded beach. Runnels are the troughs formerly carved by longshore currents (p. 41) or by water-flow after flooding tides. Ridges often trap water from the high-tide swash. This water may persist when muddy sediment slows drainage through the sand. Some ridges grow into wide beaches, and some runnels persist as isolated lagoons.

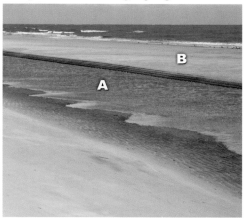

A beach runnel (A) and ridge (B) at low tide

FOUND: These features are most prominent on wave-dominated beaches (p. 6).

SEASONS: Sandbars occur closest to the beach in summer. Ridges and runnels form following storms and on accreting beaches during spring tides.

DID YOU KNOW? Runnels that persist as lagoons trap invertebrates and small fishes that attract shorebirds.

Resting seabirds on a beach ridge at high tide

29

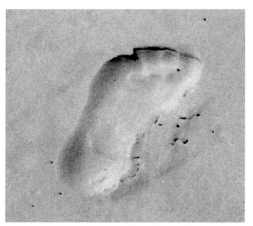

Squeaky backshore sands

Strong surf roar can be heard for more than a mile

"Pops" come from uniformly breaking waves

Squeaks, Barks, and Roars

WHAT IS IT? Beach sounds include **squeaks** and **barks** from footsteps in powdery sand, and **surf roar** from the rolling crash of breaking waves.

SIZE: Sounds are measured by pitch. Sand squeaks are a high pitch heard (and appreciated) best by children. Surf roar is a deep bass sound, which can be heard at great distances.

HOW COME? Each sand grain rubbing past another makes a sound. Compound this action by many thousands and you have a footstep squeak. More forceful steps make barking sounds. These sand sounds require dry, fine, clean, uniform (well-sorted) sand. Wave crash is loudest in plunging breakers (p. 36), where wave energy is explosively released in a downward-directed water mass that traps air and bursting bubbles within a resonating sound barrel. When waves arrive parallel to the shore, lengthy barrels break all at once (lower image), creating loud, staccato pops.

FOUND: Squeaks and barks can be made in the upper beach and dunes of natural (non-artificial, p. 318) beaches. Strong winds bring continuous breaking waves that produce a constant roar.

SEASONS: Any time of year when the sand is dry and waves are large.

DID YOU KNOW? Underwater surf noise on a rough day can be as loud as a jackhammer an arm's length away.

Hard and Mushy (Bubbly) Sand

Prints on a hard wet beach

WHAT IS IT? Hard sand is more compact, and **mushy sand** has more air in it. These features are easily recognized by **footprint depths.**

SIZE: Prints in hard sand barely scuff the surface, but steps in mushy sand can sink down to the knee.

HOW COME? Sand hardness varies with how the sand was packed (wet or dry, wave-fluffed or not). In wet sand, water films surrounding each grain form surface-tension bridges linking grains together. In dry sand, only grain-to-grain friction keeps a foot from sinking. Mushy sand has air spaces within a matrix held by weak salt-bridges. This forms where sand piled by airy wavewash drains of water without the air escaping through bubble holes (p. 27). These sands can have air as a third of their volume. Although not quite the "quicksand" of movie fame, mushy sands can partially swallow vehicles. Some dry beaches are very hard where fine, poorly sorted grains are wet-packed during artificial nourishment (p. 321). With poor sand sorting, smaller grains (silts) fill the air spaces between larger grains.

FOUND: Typically the hardest sand is on the lower foreshore and mushy sand is near the high-tide line.

SEASONS: All year.

DID YOU KNOW? Footprints on wet sand are lighter because detached quartz grains are free to refract incident light. Wet sand absorbs light within the beach.

Dog pawprints in mushy upper-beach sand

The beach at Hunting Island, SC erodes landward

A flat, narrow eroded beach at high tide

Erosion of a dune bluff

Sand Erosion

WHAT IS IT? Erosion is beach-sand loss, indicated by the line between wet and dry sand. The sand isn't really lost. It just goes someplace else. The term "critical erosion" is used to describe sand loss that threatens buildings on the dune.

SIZE: It is common to lose 1–2 ft (30–60 cm) of sand depth after a moderate storm. During hurricanes, 10 ft (3 m) of sand can disappear in a matter of hours.

HOW COME? Erosion comes from waves and currents. Waves suspend sand, and currents carry it away. Erosion is constant, even on growing beaches. When accretion (facing page) outpaces erosion, beaches become flat and narrow. Erosion occurs rapidly during storms that drive rough surf and strong longshore currents. Chronic erosion occurs where inlets and jetties intercept the longshore flow of replacement sands.

FOUND: All beaches. Net erosion can "sink" beaches at the ends of barrier islands (p. 14). Where erosion intersects the dune, beaches move landward. Where erosion intersects with buildings or coastal armoring, beaches disappear.

SEASONS: Most erosion occurs late fall through winter. Profound erosion can occur during intense storms.

DID YOU KNOW? Sand that erodes from beaches generally goes no farther than the offshore bar. After severe storms, this bar widens to become exposed beach at low tide.

Sand Accretion

WHAT IS IT? Accretion is beach sand build-up. Accretion and erosion (facing page) are the yin and yang of beaches. Their dynamic balance maintains beaches as open and sandy places.

SIZE: Beach accretion is noticeable when things on the upper beach get covered with sand. Logs and other large items on the lower beach may be buried in sand within a single tidal cycle.

HOW COME? Accreting sand comes from eroding up-drift beaches (up the long-shore current stream) and from the eroding offshore sandbar. Accretion is typically more gradual than erosion. During calm periods, breakers suspend sand and carry it up the beach-face where the sand falls out of suspension. As an accreted berm dries, its sand can be blown into the upper beach and dunes by aeolian transport (p. 5).

FOUND: All beaches. Some beaches, such as those up-drift from inlets, may experience years of net accretion (more accretion than erosion). Accretion is also favored where gaps in offshore sandbars refract waves to spread out their erosive energy.

SEASONS: Most accretion occurs gradually during summer. Rapid accretion can occur during or after intense storms.

DID YOU KNOW? Although beach erosion makes headlines, accretion takes place in obscurity. Judging only by news reports, our Southeastern beaches should have long ago disappeared.

An accreting upper beach around a dune mound

Beach grasses covered by accreting sand

A sign of accretion

33

Tawny sea foam during choppy surf

White foam rolled up the beach by onshore wind

A willet navigates particularly sudsy sea foam

Sea Foam

WHAT IS IT? Sea foam is the white, greenish, or brownish froth brought to the beach by breaking waves.

SIZE: Sea foam comes mostly from diatoms, which are microscopic single-celled plants in glasslike capsules. The foam they generate in the wave wash is generally the consistency of a good stout beer, but airy sea foam can occasionally roll from the swash in thick suds rivaling any bubble bath.

HOW COME? Most sea foam originates from planktonic (small and drifting) plants and animals. Wind and surface currents bring billions of these tiny organisms to the surf where their cells are pulverized and their fat is whipped into suds. Brownish foam may also come from organic sediments.

FOUND: All beaches.

SEASONS: Sea foam is generated when there are nearby "blooms" of plankton and when local sea conditions are rough enough to whip the plankton into froth. Summer and fall tend to have the foamiest surf, especially when there are strong onshore winds.

DID YOU KNOW? Bursting sea-foam bubbles during a red-tide event (rare in Georgia and the Carolinas) can release algal toxins that severely irritate the nose and throat. However, most sea foam is harmless. In fact, this intertidal foam is an important food source for a local species of hermit crab (p. 149).

Water Color

WHAT IS IT? From the beach, seawater may appear blue, emerald, mint-green, tea-colored, or gray-brown.

SIZE: Algae that tint seawater green are smaller than sand grains. Suspended silt particles can be even smaller.

Sky reflection can make any water appear blue

HOW COME? Pure shallow seawater is faint blue, but coastal water tends to have extra stuff in it. Some of this stuff includes algae, which color the water green. When turbidity is low, these single-cell plants give shallow waters over light sand an emerald color. On coasts with high waves, suspended particles reflect a pale gray into the mix, giving hues ranging from turquoise to "seafoam" (mint) green. The surf downstream from an estuary inlet may receive tidal water stained by tannins steeped out of saltmarsh plants, giving the water a tealike, red-brown color. Red-brown plus turbidity equals gray-brown water. The color of clear surf water is also influenced by sand color, which is seldom completely white.

Tea-stained inlet water contrasts with offshore blue

Algae and low turbidity make surf waters green

FOUND: Cape Hatteras can receive clear, light-blue, or emerald waters, but like most other beaches, mint-green is most common. Due to numerous inlets, Georgia and South Carolina surf is often tealike following rainy weather.

SEASONS: The bluest and greenest waters are in spring and early summer. Rough winter waters tend to be mint-green or gray-brown.

Light shines through a mint-green wave

DID YOU KNOW? Fish living in deep, clear waters have a visual sensitivity only to blue light, whereas fish in shallow, tea-colored waters see best in the yellow portion of the spectrum.

Clear waters show through to tawny sands

A spilling breaker

A plunging (barrel) breaker

Shorebreak conditions attract skimboarders

Waves and Surf

WHAT ARE THEY? Waves bring energy to the beach from far away. Waves that enter shallow water trip into breakers and become **surf**.

SIZE: From 1–12 ft (0.3–3.5 m) in height (measured base to crest). A typical 3-ft (1-m) wave offshore with a 10-second swell-period will evolve into about a 4-ft (1.2-m) breaker.

HOW COME? As a wave enters shallow water, it drags the bottom and slows down. This drag causes waves from many directions to gradually turn parallel to shore (to refract). At a water depth about 1.3 times its height, a wave breaks. Breaking occurs when the entire length of a wave piles into the shallows. Waves slow down, and become higher and steeper before breaking. The wave crest slows last and pushes ahead of the breaker. Wave crests identify three kinds of breakers: **spilling**, **plunging**, and **surging**. Spilling breakers have frothy crests flowing down the wave-front and occur when waves advance on a gentle nearshore slope. Plunging breakers have crests that curl over to crash before the wave-base and occur when large waves enter shallows with a moderate nearshore slope. **Shorebreak** occurs when a wave plunges directly onto the beach. Weak shorebreak gives surging breakers with crests that just begin to spill when the leading wave-base slides rapidly up the beach. Surging breakers are rare and occur when the beach approach is steep.

FOUND: All beaches have some surf from time to time. Outer Banks beaches tend to have the highest surf. Offshore bars mark significant "breaks" where bigger surf occurs.

SEASONS: Summer has calmer surf than the other seasons, but nearby or distant storms can bring high surf at any time. A storm's "fetch," or the distance wind blows over water, is important to the height of the waves it makes.

DID YOU KNOW? Wavelength (distance crest-to-crest) greatly determines surf height. A long wavelength as indicated by a 20-second swell-period can mean that waist-high offshore waves become surf as tall as a single-story house.

SURFSPEAK: To fully appreciate surf, it helps to speak the language. Parts of the awesome wave in the top photo include the **face**, the **lip**, and the **curl**. In the middle photo, a **grom** (grommet, or young surfer) misses a left-peeling tube. In the bottom photo, a dude gets boosted and **throws chunks** (spray) as the wave closes out into soup (whitewater). Other surf descriptions include **blown out** (windy and choppy conditions giving crumbling waves not good for surfing), **clean** (waves with smooth, glassy faces), **gnarly** (intimidating), **ground swell** (long swell-period waves from distant sources producing big surf), **mushy** (slow, low-power waves), **set** (an approaching group of rideable waves), **peak** (tallest wave-point where a breaker forms and peels in both directions), and **rippin'** (to shred, to make the most of available surf, including cutbacks, slashes, airs, tailslides, 360s, chop-hops, and floaters).

Wave anatomy

A grom on a clean wave

A surfer throwing chunks

37

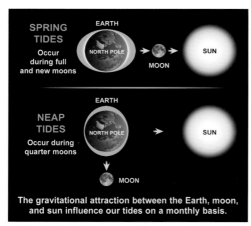

The highest tides occur when sun and moon align

Tidal cycles are linked to moon phase

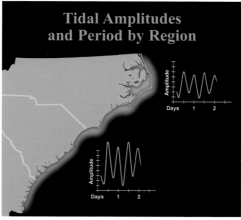

Southerly beaches have the largest tidal range

Tides

WHAT ARE THEY? Tides are periodic changes in local sea level. Astronomical tides are those produced by our sun and moon.

SIZE: Average amplitudes between high and low tide vary: 7 ft (2.1 m) in Georgia, 6 ft (1.8 m) in South Carolina, and 4 ft (1.2 m) in North Carolina.

HOW COME? Astronomical tides can be predicted from Earth's position relative to the sun and moon. Their celestial gravity pulls out a bulge of water, slightly offset from the equator, that travels around the planet's oceans. Our tides are **semi-diurnal**, meaning that every 24 hours sees two sets of high and low tides. But because the Earth-circling bulge is offset from Earth's spin, there is also a small **diurnal** component, with one low and one high tide dominant each day.

FOUND: All beaches. Beaches near the GA/SC border are at a focal point in the curve of our Southeastern coastline and as a result get the largest regional tides.

SEASONS: All seasons. **Spring tides**, when highs are highest and lows are lowest, generally occur near full- and new-moon periods. **Neap tides** have the smallest amplitude and typically occur during quarter-moon periods.

DID YOU KNOW? Tides come and go based on the lunar day, which is longer than an Earth day because the moon orbits the same direction Earth spins. So, high and low tides occur about 48 minutes later each day. Low barometric pressure and onshore winds can create storm tides higher than normal.

Beaches at Night

WHAT HAPPENS AT NIGHT? Some beaches are splendid places to see nature's subtle glow. Nighttime glow-shows include **bioluminescence**, the **stars** and **planets**, and **meteor showers**.

SIZE: Glowing bacteria and dinoflagellates are microscopic. Luminescent comb-jellies are walnut-sized. Brilliant as they are, most meteors are the size of sand grains. The universe is boundless.

HOW COME? Bioluminescence on darkened beaches is visible in the surf from dinoflagellates and comb-jellies that glow green when disturbed. In the swash zone, parts of mole crabs (p. 150) and other animals have a greenish glow from a coating of luminescent bacteria. Many barrier-island beaches are distant from large, lighted cities. These beaches are some of the last convenient vantage points where urban glow has yet to bleach the heavens.

FOUND: Beaches preserved as public land or backed by sparse development with glare-managed lighting.

SEASONS: Consult astronomical charts for seasonal night-sky features. Perseid meteors fly in mid-August, and Leonid meteors can be seen on clear nights in mid-November.

DID YOU KNOW? To protect nesting sea turtles, many beaches enforce light-control ordinances, which also enhance star-gazing.

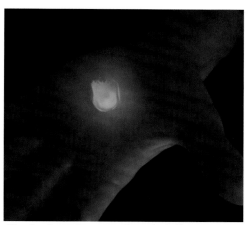

Glowing bacteria on a mole crab shell

Perseid meteors give a midsummer night's show

Our Milky Way galaxy

39

Offshore Currents

Many will be surprised to learn of links between Southeastern US beaches and faraway events. The coast is at the margin of the **North Atlantic Gyre**, a clockwise swirl of surface currents spanning the New and Old Worlds. These currents are pushed by easterly tropical tradewinds and include a continuous flood into the Gulf of Mexico between Yucatan and Cuba. This head of water drives the **Loop Current**, which connects with eastward flows to squirt out of the Gulf as the **Florida Current**. After veering left and rushing due north past Georgia, this ocean river evolves into the **Gulf Stream**. Examples abound showing how these ocean currents link local beaches with distant places and processes:

A) Gulf Stream eddies spin into the Labrador Current to create upwellings. These conditions bring food for swordfish, caught by fishermen using lightsticks (p. 312), later discarded, that drift the Atlantic before stranding on a Southeastern beach.

B) Buoyant, stone-hard seabeans from Central American vines (pp. 273–274) plop into rivers, float to the Caribbean, and eventually strand on Southeastern coasts.

C) Airy pumice rocks (p. 292) blown from volcanoes in the Windward Islands bob at sea for months or years before making a Southeastern US landfall.

D) Fallen tropical hardwood trees (pp. 283) washed out by Amazon rainforest floods are swept into ocean currents that allow an arrival on local beaches after a long, circuitous journey.

E) Waters surrounding the Azores host nursery-age, current-riding, loggerhead sea turtles (p. 176) that first scampered to the surf as hatchlings off Georgia and the Carolinas.

F) Nearly five million plastic LEGO-toy pieces spilled off Land's End, England, in 1997, and began a voyage that would end for many in the hand of a curious local beachcomber.

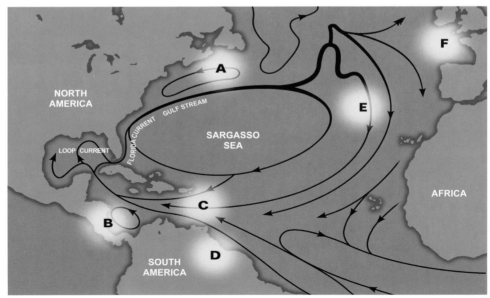

The North Atlantic Gyre and associated currents

Nearshore Currents

WHAT ARE THEY? Nearshore currents include the **longshore current**, which flows parallel to the beach, **rip currents**, which flow perpendicular to the beach, and **tidal currents**, which flow through inlets.

SIZE: The longshore current runs for many miles along a beach. Rip currents run only a few hundred feet (about 100 m) into a plumelike head just outside the breakers. Tidal currents run for many miles through inshore channels. Each current can flow at a swift walking pace.

HOW COME? The longshore current runs inside the surf and is driven by waves striking the beach at oblique angles. Longshore currents typically run with the prevailing wind direction. Rip currents come from waves driving water into the trough between the beach and the offshore bar. This water rushes away from the beach along short-lived rip channels through the bar. Rip currents are strongest when large swells arrive near low tide. Tidal currents are driven by tides (p. 38).

FOUND: Longshore and rip currents are strongest on wave-dominated beaches.

SEASONS: All are strongest during high waves and spring tides (p. 38).

DANGERS: Rip currents and the panic they induce cause many drowning deaths. To save your life, do not swim into a rip back toward shore. Swim parallel to the beach until you exit the rip or until it subsides outside the surf.

Location of the longshore current inside the bar

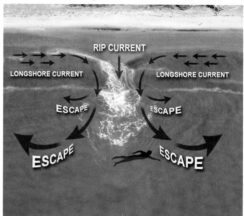

Escaping a rip current

A strong tidal current exits an inlet channel

Sea breezes develop after the mainland warms

Visible salt-spray aerosol drifts inland

Beach Weather and Seasons

WHAT IS IT? Beach weather, described by temperature, humidity, wind, rain, and sunshine, is often different from mainland weather because of a beach's closeness to the sea.

HOW COME? In warm months, inland surface air heats and begins to rise around midday. This rising air is replaced by cooler air rushing in from the ocean's surface. In summer, this pleasant **sea breeze** often makes beach air cooler than inland sites by 5° F (2° C) or more. The sea-breeze front is where cool and warm air masses meet, and where puffy cumulus clouds form. By afternoon, some of these clouds will darken with rain and rumble with thunder. At night, when the sea is warmer than the land, a weak land breeze (reverse sea breeze) can form, often just before dawn. In winter, the ocean's high heat capacity moderates beach temperatures, making beach areas less prone to freezes. In summer, **offshore winds** can drive out warm surface-waters, which are replaced by cold water from the depths. These upwellings bring a clammy chill to what would normally be sultry summer weather. **Salt spray** is unique to beaches and is a highly localized form of weather. This briny aerosol mist is formed during high humidity and rough surf. **Sunshine** really is brighter on the beach. Reflection from the sea and sand can intensify the ultraviolet light we receive. Similarly, an open horizon and reflecting sea can enhance our visual experience at dawn, orchestrating more vivid **sunrises** than those over land.

FOUND: Sea breezes, land breezes, salt spray, and sunshine occur on all beaches. Wave-dominated beaches have occasionally dense salt spray.

Clouds can either enhance or extinguish sunrises

SEASONS: To every beach thing there is a season. The graphic below shows how some conspicuous beach features vary throughout the year. Sea-breeze seasons are late spring through summer. Except for their moderated temperatures, beaches are most like the mainland in the winter. Fall through spring, passing cold fronts can make for spectacular sunrises.

DID YOU KNOW? Beachside plant species tend to be less cold-tolerant and more salt-tolerant than their landward neighbors. Some species common in the Caribbean are at home on beaches in Georgia and the Carolinas. Cycles of plant flowering, seeding, and dormancy are closely tied to beach weather.

DANGER: Sunburn increases skin-cancer risk, which kills about 2,000 Americans each year. Wear a hat and sunglasses and enjoy the beach at dawn and dusk. **Lightning** is a danger due to the electrical exposure of an open beach. Take shelter when thunder is heard.

Most beach plants are dormant in winter

Beaches are hotspots for dangerous lightning

JAN	FEB	MAR	APR	MAY	JUN	JUL	AUG	SEP	OCT	NOV	DEC
					Hurricanes and tropical storms						
Nor'easters										Nor'easters	
High erosion, accretion, overwash							High erosion, accretion, overwash				
Narrow berms, distant sandbars				Wide berms, close-in sandbars					Narrow berms		
Infauna offshore				Abundant beach infauna				Infauna migrate offshore			
Plant dormancy									Plant dormancy		
			Flowering								
			Annuals grow								
					Seeds dispersed						
Big surf				Calm surf				Variable surf			

Seasonal changes make each beach visit a unique experience

Hurricane Isabel strikes North Carolina, 2003

Isabel's surge divides Hatteras Island with an inlet

Paths of 68 hurricanes striking land, 1851–2009

Tropical Cyclones and Nor'easters

Tropical Cyclones

Nor'easters

WHAT ARE THEY? Tropical cyclones are counterclockwise-spinning low-pressure systems with a cloud-free central eye. These cyclones include **tropical storms** and **hurricanes**, which originate in warm seas between Africa and the Caribbean. These tropical systems spin over long distances, generally traveling through a great clockwise hook before dissipating between the northeastern US and the North Atlantic. **Nor'easters** are low-pressure cyclones that typically arise from a southern low-pressure system pushed north to intersect with a polar air mass. Nor'easters affecting beaches the most form offshore, where warm, moist air from the Gulf Stream is pulled toward cold northern air in a counterclockwise sweep. Unlike a hurricane, a nor'easter's strongest winds are not near its center. Nor'easters are named for the winds they give our Atlantic coast—from the northeast. Each storm's greatest effects on beaches come from waves on top of storm tides, which are elevated sea levels during storms.

SIZE: Disturbances from each of these storms can occupy an area larger than multiple states. In 1989, Hurricane Hugo brought storm tides 20 ft (6 m) above normal to some South Carolina beaches, along with sustained winds of 135 mph. Tropical cyclones begin as an "organized" depression with winds less than 38 mph, and may increase intensity to tropical storm (39–73 mph) or hurricane (>73 mph) status. A nor'easter's strength is measured by its central pressure, and by the anecdotes of oldtimers in coastal coffee shops.

HOW COME? These intense storms are fueled by heat energy from a warm ocean. The energy is released from water vapor as it condenses and/or freezes, which drives the movement of moisture and air upward, creating low air pressure at the surface. Outside surface air rushes into the low after spiraling in with a vortex spin following the Coriolis Force. This spin is counterclockwise in the northern hemisphere. A storm tide is elevated sea level brought about by astronomical tides (p. 38), plus the push of water by wind, plus the carry of water by waves, plus the pull upward by the storm's low pressure center. These storm-tide levels are much higher where ocean water surges into shallow or constricted bays.

FOUND: Tropical cyclones have struck all Southeastern beaches, but are most frequent on North Carolina's Outer Banks, which also bear the brunt of most nor'easters in the region.

SEASONS: Most hurricanes occur August to October. Nor'easters occur between fall and early spring.

DID YOU KNOW? These storms are merely punctuation in the perpetual process of coastal change. Assaults by storms set back the advance of land plants, shift sands between land and sea, cut islands in two, and foster some stunning, rugged scenery. Plants and animals that rely on beaches take this geological uncertainty into account by having strategically brief life cycles. For us, the profound effects of coastal storms make beaches beautiful and wondrous places to visit, but scary places to live.

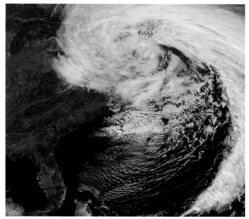

The classic comma-shaped profile of a nor'easter

NC Hwy 12 is overwashed by a 2009 nor'easter

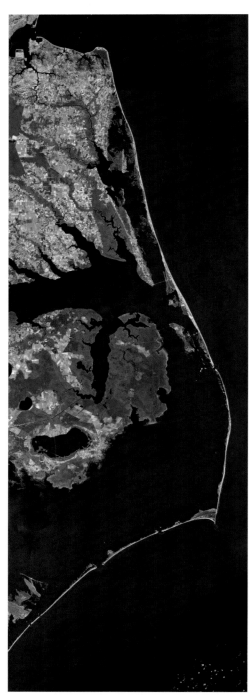

Wave-dominated Outer Banks barrier islands, NC

Barrier Islands and Island Shapes

Thin Islands   *Drumstick Islands*

WHAT ARE THEY? Barrier islands are ocean-fronting, elongate piles of sand that are isolated from the mainland by intervening estuaries or marsh. These islands often have their highest ground along a dune ridge immediately behind the beach. Geologically speaking, barrier islands are short-lived, although most have portions that have been above the sea long enough to support woody plants. **Island shapes** are of two kinds, determined by the wave- and tide-dominated processes that continually act on them (p. 6). **Wave-dominated** barrier islands are slender with frequent overwash fans (p. 12) revealing past ocean breaches. Inlets separating these thin islands are narrow, short-lived, and migratory in the direction of longshore currents (p. 41), typically north to south. **Tide-dominated** islands experience high tidal amplitudes (p. 38) and tend to be shaped like stout chicken drumsticks. They are separated from adjacent islands by broad, stable inlets with extensive, offshore tidal deltas (p. 50). These deltas may evolve into small islands themselves, like **Little Egg Island**, Georgia.

SIZE: Some delta shoal islands with important nesting seabird colonies may be only a few hundred yards (meters) long. Our largest tide-modified islands are Cumberland Island, GA (19 mi, 31 km), and Hilton Head Island, SC (13 mi, 21 km). Our largest wave-dominated barrier island is Hatteras Island, NC (54 mi, 87 km).

HOW COME? We owe our currently extensive chain of Southeastern barrier islands to a momentary stall in rising sea level, which has allowed sand to assemble into islands over the last few thousand years. This assembly took place in at least four ways, 1) from longshore currents that carried abundant mainland sand down lengthening spits that broke away from the mainland, 2) from the slow drowning of mainland beach dunes, 3) from submerged offshore bars that gained enough sand to rise from the sea, and 4) from delta shoals that similarly became land. In all cases, footholds by dune plants helped sand retention and dune building. Evidence of the former mainland and of recently lengthened sand spits can be seen in the Sea Islands of Georgia and South Carolina. These tide-dominated islands often occur as partially fused old- and new-island pairs. An example is **St. Catherines Island**, GA, which has a northern, old-mainland end (the wide end of the drumstick), roughly 30,000 years old and eroding, and a southern, recently accreted end, just a few thousand years old.

FOUND: The regional trend is for short and stout barrier islands in the south and long, thin barrier islands in the north.

SEASONS: All year.

DID YOU KNOW? Our Southeastern coast is almost completely fronted by barrier islands, but these sandy ribbons make up only 13% of the world's coastline. These barriers allow estuaries to exist, along with their valuable inhabitants, including our seafood. The momentary slowing of sea level rise seems to have ended, which means big changes are in store for our barrier island beaches.

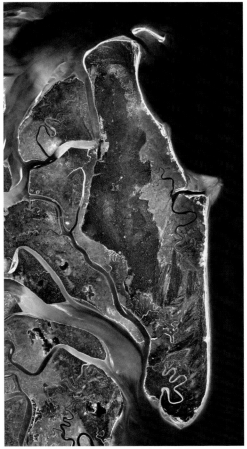

Tide-modified St. Catherines Island, GA

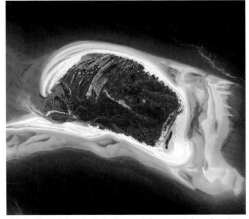

Little Egg Island, GA, formed from a delta shoal

47

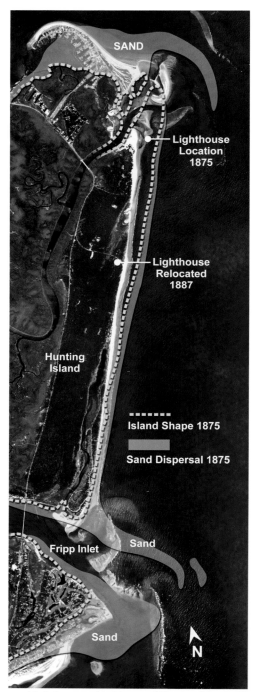

A brief geographic history of Hunting Island, SC

Island Migration and Shoreline Retreat

WHAT IS IT? Island migration is movement of an entire barrier island, and **shoreline retreat** involves only the beach. These days, nearly all island migration is transgressive, or toward the mainland. Some island beaches are retreating on one end and growing on the other. Comparing old and new maps of these islands gives one the impression that the islands are rotating. Recent sand movement at **Hunting Island**, SC, has contributed to the growth of adjacent islands, with an effect similar to a balloon squeezed in the middle.

SIZE: Shoreline change at the dynamic Outer Banks is about 15 yards (14 m) landward each decade.

HOW COME? Sand-supply is small relative to sea-level rise, so islands tend to move landward. In geological slow motion, such a transgressing island appears to be rolling over itself. The rolling takes place during storm overwash (p. 12) and the landward blowing of sand. Shoreline retreat occurs when sand is stolen by an adjacent inlet or by changes in sand-transporting longshore currents. In the case of Hunting Island, these changes come from shoals that bend incoming waves, resulting in localized erosion or accretion (pp. 32–33).

FOUND: Outer Banks islands tend to migrate. Georgia's and South Carolina's Sea Island beaches tend to retreat.

SEASONS: All year.

DID YOU KNOW? It's all connected. Dams on some rivers contribute to migration and retreat by halting sediment that would build islands ahead of rising seas.

Inlets

Wide Inlets

Narrow Inlets

WHAT ARE THEY? Inlets are channels through or between barrier islands that allow flow into the barrier-protected embayment or marsh. Some inlets occur where rivers empty into the ocean.

SIZE: Widths range from leaping distance for small cuts, to about seven miles wide spanning Bulls Bay, SC. Natural inlets are 3–20 ft (1–6 m) deep. Major rivers and dredged inlets may be over 40 ft (12 m) deep.

HOW COME? These passages have been recently cut by man or by storm tides, or have flowed as rivers for thousands of years. They are dredged, or naturally maintained (kept open) by tidal currents. Natural inlets fill with sand when a newly formed inlet into a shared bay "steals" some of the local tidal current. Narrow inlets tend to fill with sand from the longshore current (p. 41) and migrate in the current's direction. Because of this, some inlets that serve boat traffic have a sand-blocking jetty (p. 320) on either side of the opening to the sea. Wider inlets are more stable and the widest are simply broad openings in estuaries (sounds and bays).

FOUND: Hundreds are found throughout coastal Georgia and the Carolinas.

SEASONS: All year.

DID YOU KNOW? Inlets provide the critical ocean connection between coastal estuaries and the sea.

Topsail Inlet, NC, moves south ~ 85 ft (30 m) per year

A shrimp boat plies St. Simons Channel, GA

A narrow cut through a South Carolina Sea Island

49

Cape Hatteras Point, NC

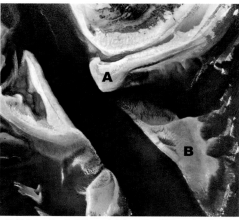

Bull Island spit (A), and delta (B) off Price's Inlet, SC

Seabirds rest on an exposed delta shoal

Capes, Spits, and Tidal Deltas

Capes

Spits and Deltas

WHAT ARE THEY? Each is a temporary pile of sand. **Capes** (cuspate forelands) are triangular landforms that extend seaward. Sand **spits** extend from island ends. **Tidal deltas** are fans of sediment washed by the flows of a tidal inlet or river. This flow pushes sediment into ebb shoals outside the inlet, and into flood shoals inside the inlet.

SIZE: Can be miles in length and width.

HOW COME? Capes and spits form due to the longshore current (p. 41) acting in an area of abundant sand. Spits form where this current carries sand to an island end. Capes form where longshore currents in opposing directions converge, sculpting sand outward. One theory has it that capes originated from ancient river deltas. The sediment in deltas and shoals was carried down rivers from the eroding piedmont, but may have been washed in and out of tidal inlets for thousands of years.

FOUND: The most prominent capes are in North Carolina. Georgia has the most extensive tidal deltas and shoals. At Outer Banks inlets, flood shoals are larger than ebb shoals, with the opposite true for the Sea Islands farther south.

SEASONS: All year.

DID YOU KNOW? Cape Hatteras marks the northern influence of the Gulf Stream on shelf waters and serves as a barrier defining the northern and southern range of many marine animals.

BEACH ANIMALS

What are Beach Animals?

This section highlights animals whose paths lead to the beach. For some animals, this means living near, on, or inside the beach. For others, a beach visit is a brief stop during a grand life journey. And for many, the beach is reached only at life's end.

Figuring out what is and isn't an animal—or what used to be one—can be tricky. Although most folks can place a bird, crab, or fish into a general animal category, some of the simpler critters can be a puzzle. A wide variety of beach animals bear similarity to plants, rocks, blobs, trivial specks, or visitors from outer space. Some of these mystery items are what they seem (and are featured in other sections of this book), but others may be animals, colonies of animals, or their lingering parts.

As a rule, live animals often twitch when prodded, and dead ones smell worse than rocks or plants. But the sniff test may fail to identify an animal's mineral remnants, and among these there may be impostors. A spongy branching thing may indeed be a sponge or a bryozoan (both are animals), but also could be an alga (which is a plant). Quivering jelly, soft lumps, and gobs of goo are generally animal in nature but could be either tunicates, jellyfish relatives, or a host of other invertebrates.

This section also includes tracks, burrows, and other evidence from some familiar but elusive beach animals. Beach sands can provide an elegant record of animals that are rare, nocturnal, or shy. Note that we've placed fossils from animals in the *Minerals* section and that human traces are in the *Hand of Man* section.

The unblinking, blue-highlighted spire of a shark eye, a common predaceous snail of intertidal sands

Swash Meiofauna

RELATIVES: Meiofauna include distantly related, invertebrate groups.

IDENTIFYING FEATURES: Swash meiofauna (MY-o-fawna, meaning "lesser animals") are tiny animals that live within a beach's sands. They include **water bears** (tardigrades, **A**), **ostracods** (tiny crustaceans, **B**), **nematodes** (**C** and **D**) and **polychaetes** (**E**). By definition, these miniscule animals can pass unharmed through a 0.5–1 mm mesh. There are many meiofaunal species for each one of the larger conspicuous species described in this book.

HABITAT: Swash meiofauna live between the wet sand grains and are part of the psammon (SA-mon) community, comprising the tiny plants, animals, and fungi that live inside the beach.

DID YOU KNOW? The meiofauna have an important role in a living beach. These little critters consume detritus and bacteria, hunt each other, and provide a food link to familiar larger animals. This animal assemblage is most diverse on beaches least altered by humans. Water bears shrivel at low tide but reanimate when waves return. Remarkably, a water bear can wait on the next wetting tide for many years by replacing its cellular water with sugar. The psammon community is amazingly diverse, with 22 major groups (phyla) discovered so far. This diversity in major-groups surpasses our tropical rainforests.

Meiofaunal invertebrates live between sand grains

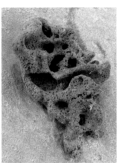 

Some sponges can't be identified by shape and color

A branched demosponge from a Georgia beach

This red sponge faded to brown after stranding

The spongin skeleton of a beached demosponge

Sponges *(Unidentified)*

RELATIVES: Sponges are in the phylum Porifera. The varied forms shown here are related to bath sponges (class Demospongiae).

IDENTIFYING FEATURES: These demosponges are spongy, and most forms washed onto beaches are firm but flexible. Beyond this generality, demosponge forms vary widely in shape, texture, and color. To frustrate identification, there is often more of this variation within a species than there is between species. For dozens of species found stranded on Southeastern beaches, growth form and color are determined by water currents and turbidity, which means that different species growing together may be more similar in appearance than members of a single species growing separately. The most species-consistent parts of sponges are their spicules. These microscopic elements of a sponge's skeleton are used by scientists to make definitive species identifications.

HABITAT: Beached sponges have been torn free from hard bottom or shell beds.

DID YOU KNOW? Sponges are simple animals without brains or other organs. They have persisted for about 500 million years and were probably Earth's first multicelled animals. Sponges grow in place by filtering organic particles from the water. These bath-type sponges are spongy because of a plumbing network supported by **spongin**, a fibrous protein.

Sponges *(Yellow Boring, Crumb-of-Bread, and Vase)*

RELATIVES: These are in the class of bath sponges (class Demospongiae).

IDENTIFYING FEATURES: Most specimens are identifiable by their color, shape, and texture.

Yellow boring sponges *(Cliona celata)* are given away by their habit of penetrating hard substrates. Beached sponges have enveloped the item they washed in with, typically shells, rocks, coral, or other sponges, and leave them riddled with characteristic holes (p. 133). Color in fresh sponges is generally bright yellow. Other species of *Cliona* vary from gray to red-orange.

Crumb-of-bread sponges *(Halichondria bowerbanki)* have a breadlike texture with numerous extending tassels. Color is typically gray/yellow in winter and beige in summer, but occasionally orange.

Vase sponges *(Ircinia campana)*, 2 ft (60 cm), are vase-shaped and smell really bad after being beached.

HABITAT: Boring and crumb-of-bread sponges grow on other things in harbors and estuaries. Beached vase sponges have been torn free from offshore hard bottom.

DID YOU KNOW? Boring sponges are important producers of calcareous sands and shell rubble. These sponges provide habitat for myriad invertebrate species.

Yellow boring sponge within shell rubble

Crumb-of-bread sponge

Vase sponge

Club-finger sponge

Redbeard sponge

Brown finger sponge

Sponges *(Club-finger, Redbeard, and Brown Finger)*

RELATIVES: Bath sponges (class Demospongiae).

IDENTIFYING FEATURES: Each of these sponges is relatively soft and squishable, even when dried. Their shape and color vary, but all turn brown after drying. Because their shapes vary with growing conditions, identifications are certain only after a microscopic look at each sponge's skeletal spicules.

Club-finger sponges *(Desmapsamma anchorata),* 16 in (40 cm), grow with a stout stem and thick branches. They are generally orange or salmon-colored.

Redbeard sponges *(Microciona prolifera),* 8 in (20 cm), beach as bouquets of slim, velvety red branches.

Brown finger sponges *(Axinella pomponiae),* 12 in (30 cm), tend to have erect, flexible, tapering branches with occasional lumps. The branches often fuse together.

HABITAT: Club-finger and brown finger sponges grow on sandy hard bottom. Redbeard sponges grow on nearshore shell bottom and dock pilings.

DID YOU KNOW? Redbeard sponges are used in laboratories to study cellular reaggregation: the reassembly of disembodied cells back into a functional organism. After they are turned to soup in a blender, these sponges can eventually find themselves and rebuild their structure with correct cellular placement.

Cannonball Jelly

RELATIVES: Jellies (jellyfish) are in the phylum Cnidaria, class Scyphozoa.

IDENTIFYING FEATURES:

Cannonball jellies *(Stomolophus melea-gris),* 8 in (20 cm), have a thick, dome-shaped bell with no marginal tentacles. The bell is a cloudy beige in life, with brown around the margin. Beneath the bell are mouth folds with short oral arms. Stranded cannonball jellies get pounded by surf until only the toughest parts remain (cylinder of mouth folds and interior mesoglea, p. 59).

HABITAT: Estuaries and nearshore ocean waters.

DID YOU KNOW? A group of jellies is a "smack," also called a swarm or bloom when jellies are super abundant. The largest cannonball jelly smacks occur during midsummer. Cannonballs feed on tiny zooplankton. They have symbiotic relationships with several fishes and with the longnose spider crab (p. 152), who uses the jelly's bell for protection and feeds from the jelly's mouth folds. Cannonball jellies do not sting humans, but they do feed us. Local waters contribute to a commercial fishery for this species, with many tons of this animal sold to markets in China and Japan. Salted cannonballs add a crunchy texture to "sea salads."

Cannonball jelly

Varied remnants of stranded cannonball jellies

A midsummer cannonball smack reaches the beach

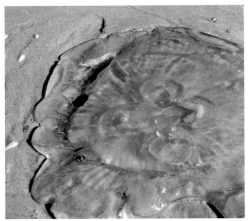

A beached male moon jelly

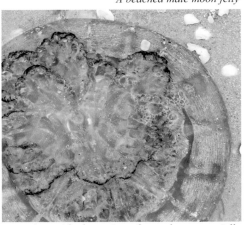

An upside-down view of a mushroom cap jelly

Sea nettles

Jellies
(Moon, Mushroom Cap, and Sea Nettle)

Moon Jelly and Sea Nettle   Mushroom Cap

RELATIVES: Jellies (jellyfish) are in the phylum Cnidaria, class Scyphozoa.

IDENTIFYING FEATURES:

Moon jellies *(Aurelia aurita),* 12 in (30 cm), have a saucerlike bell that is clear except for four lobe-shaped gonads that are violet-pink (in males) or yellow (in females). Moon jellies have hundreds of short, marginal tentacles and four oral arms that are frilly and colorless.

Mushroom cap jellies *(Rhopilema verrilli),* 20 in (51 cm), have a whitish, transparent bell and a limp central cluster of brown-fringed oral arms.

Sea nettles *(Chrysaora quinquecirrha),* 10 in (25 cm), have rusty radiating stripes and long tentacles. A bay (sound) form lacks the stripes and is milky white.

HABITAT: Nearshore and open ocean.

DID YOU KNOW? Moon jellies have a detectable sting, which is a mild burning for most people. Sea nettles can deliver severe blistering stings even after they are dead. Each of these species is an important predator of zooplankton. Swarms of jellies can decimate populations of these drifting animals. Blooms (population booms) of jellies are linked to nutrients from agricultural runoff and overfishing. The jellies benefit from nutrient-fertilized plankton and replace commercially caught fish as marine predators.

Sea Wasp, Ovate Comb Jelly, and **Mesoglea**

Sea Wasp

Comb Jelly and Mesoglea

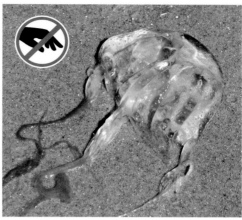
Sea wasp box jelly

RELATIVES: Sea wasps are box jellies (phylum Cnidaria, class Cubozoa). Comb jellies are phylum Ctenophora, distantly related to jellyfish.

IDENTIFYING FEATURES:

Sea wasps *(Chiropsalmus quadrumanus),* 5 in (12 cm), have a cube-shaped bell with handlike appendages streaming tentacles at four corners of the cube. A similar box jelly, *Tamoya haplonema,* has four spatula-shaped appendages.

Ovate comb jellies *(Beroe ovata),* 4.5 in (11 cm), have pinkish egg-shaped bodies with eight comb rows of iridescent cilia.

Mesoglea (mez-o-GLEE-a), to 12 in or more (>30 cm), is the "jelly" in jellyfish and comb jellies. It washes in as lumps of clear, nonsticky jelly. This substance is the gelatinous support of a jelly's swimming muscles.

An ovate comb jelly shows its iridescent combs

HABITAT: Sea wasps live offshore and ovate comb jellies live in coastal waters.

DID YOU KNOW? The sea wasp is our most venomous jellyfish, requiring hospitalization for some sting victims. Ovate comb jellies feed on sea walnuts *(Mnemiopsis leidyi)*—smaller, lobed comb jellies that are voracious predators of fish larvae. The mysterious pulses of light seen in the nighttime surf are likely from bioluminescent comb jellies disturbed by waves (p. 39).

Mesoglea beached. In its former glory (inset)

59

Portuguese man-o-war, retracted tentacles (arrow)

The pneumatophore of a beached man-o-war

A man-o-war sailing on a starboard tack

Portuguese Man-o-War

RELATIVES: These are hydralike animals, class Hydrozoa, in the phylum Cnidaria. They are siphonophores, which are distantly related to blue buttons and by-the-wind sailors.

IDENTIFYING FEATURES:

Portuguese men-o-war *(Physalia physalis)* look like blue-tinged balloons with pink-crested sails and trailing tentacles. The float-sail (pneumatophore) is 1–10 in (2.5–25 cm) long. Tentacles can be 6 ft (2 m) on the beach and reach 150 ft (46 m) when fully extended at sea.

HABITAT: The wide-open sea, except at the end of their voyage when they are found in the wave wash and wrack line.

CAUTION! Their tentacles sting and cling. If stung, remove tentacles without rubbing (scraping with a credit card works) and rinse with seawater, not fresh water. For symptoms other than localized pain and redness, seek medical attention.

DID YOU KNOW? Apparent individual man-o-war animals are actually colonies of many polyps (float-sail, stinging, feeding, and breeding). As a group, siphonophores have the highest division of labor between zooids (individual members) of all colonial animals. Right- and left-handed men-o-war sail in different directions, and those on the same "tack" beach together. Beachings are most common December through May.

Blue Button
and **By-the-Wind Sailor**

RELATIVES: These are hydralike animals, class Hydrozoa, in the phylum Cnidaria. They are chondrophorines, distantly related to siphonophores like the Portuguese man-o-war.

IDENTIFYING FEATURES:

Blue buttons *(Porpita porpita),* 1 in (2.5 cm), have a small disklike float, surrounded by blue-green tentacles.

By-the-wind sailors *(Velella velella),* 2 in (5 cm), have an oval float bearing a crestlike sail and deep blue tentacles beneath.

HABITAT: These animals float on the surface of the wide-open sea, except when beached. Their cellophane-like "floats" linger in the wrack for weeks.

DID YOU KNOW? Neither species is a jellyfish. Like the Portuguese man-o-war, they are colonies of many individual animals. Blue buttons and by-the-wind sailors feed on small animals captured by their tentacles, which are composed of individual animals called zooids. By-the-wind sailors have mirror-image forms that are either right-sailing or left-sailing. Because of these directional tendencies, beaching events usually involve only one form. Their sailing efficiency is such that they are able to sail 45 degrees to the downwind direction.

Blue button

By-the-wind sailor

Freshly beached sailors. Old "float" (inset)

Snail fur hydroids covering a sharkeye snail

Plumed Sargassum *hydroids*

Red stick-hydroids

Coquina hydroids on a coquina clam

Hydroids

RELATIVES: These are colonial hydrozoans like the Portuguese man-o-war, blue button, and by-the-wind sailor.

IDENTIFYING FEATURES:

Snail fur *(Hydractinia echinata)* forms a fuzzy tan coating on marine snail shells. The "fur" is composed of stiff spines that project between the individual hydroid polyps.

***Sargassum* hydroids** (order Hydroida), 0.25 in (6.3 mm), add a sparse tan fuzz to varied drifting items within the open-ocean *Sargassum* community. About 27 species are known.

Red stick-hydroids *(Eudendrium carneum),* 5 in (12 cm), have irregular tree-like branches bearing pink-orange polyps.

Coquina hydroids *(Lovenella gracilis),* 0.8 in (2 cm), are brown tufts growing from the posterior end of coquina clams (p. 121).

HABITAT: Snail fur hydroid colonies mostly grow on gastropod shells occupied by long-wristed hermit crabs (p. 149). *Sargassum* hydroids grow on ocean-drifting objects of all kinds, especially *Sargassum* algae. Red stick-hydroids grow on bottom rubble. Coquina hydroids grow only on coquina clams.

DID YOU KNOW? *Sargassum* hydroids feed on plankton and are themselves food for young sea turtles. Coquina hydroids slow a coquina's burrowing escape, but protect their host by stinging would-be predators.

Sea Pansy

RELATIVES: Sea pansies are related to corals and anemones (phylum Cnidaria, class Anthozoa) and are in the order Pennatulacea, family Renillidae.

IDENTIFYING FEATURES:

Sea pansies *(Renilla reniformis),* 2 in (5 cm), look like a purplish, thick, leaf-like pad on a purple stalk called a peduncle. At low tide, sea pansy colonies look like small hearts covered by a thin silt layer.

HABITAT: Sea pansies live in intertidal sands, especially on current-swept flats near inlets.

DID YOU KNOW? Sea pansies are a collection of polyps. The largest of these is the peduncle, which anchors the colony in the sand and can be distended for a better hold when waters get rough. Anemone-like feeding polyps cover the purplish pad, which also has specialized pumping polyps (white dots between the feeding polyps) for deflating at low tide and inflating when flooded at high tide. Sea pansies flash a green glow when disturbed. The light comes from a green fluorescent protein, which is currently being used as a tool in biochemical and medical research. Sea pansies feed on particle-size plants and animals and are fed upon by sand-burrowing striped sea slugs *(Armina tigrina).*

Sea pansies, underside (left), topside (right)

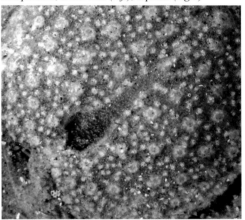

Beige rings are retracted sea-pansy polyps

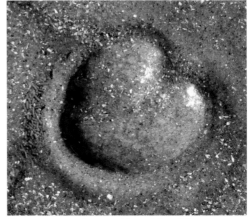

Sea pansy on an exposed bar at low tide

63

An exposed onion anemone

Onion anemone retracted. Partially buried (inset)

Warty anemone at low tide. In water (inset)

Sea Anemones *(Onion and Warty)*

RELATIVES: Sea anemones are related to corals and sea pansies, class Anthozoa.

IDENTIFYING FEATURES:

Onion anemones *(Paranthus rapiformis)*, 3 in (7.5 cm), have short, thin tentacles and anchor themselves in the sand using a small basal disk. Anemones eroded from the sand assume the appearance of a cocktail onion.

Warty anemones *(Bunodosoma cavernata)*, 4 in (10 cm), are green-brown "flowers" made up of about 100 stubby tentacles blooming from a warty column. At low tide these anemones pucker up into what looks like black globs of jelly at the sand's surface.

HABITAT: Onion anemones burrow into sandy bottom just below the low tide. Warty anemones are most common where sand covers intertidal rocks, to which they anchor themselves.

DID YOU KNOW? Warty anemones do not stay in one place and frequently move between temporary anchoring points where they aggressively compete for space with other anemones. They feed on a variety of invertebrates including scorched mussels (p. 105), which are common in its rocky habitat. Onion anemones have a similar diet, but are supplemented with food by symbiotic algae (zooxanthellae) that live within its tentacles.

Hermit Anemone

RELATIVES: Sea anemones are related to corals and sea pansies, class Anthozoa.

IDENTIFYING FEATURES:

Hermit anemones *(Calliactis tricolor),* 2 in (5 cm), have a fringe of fuzzy tentacles and a purple-and-yellow tinted column with dark spots at the base. Their column commonly has distinct stripes, or in the contracted anemone, radiating rays. The mouth is most often tricolored with yellow, red, and purple.

HABITAT: Hermit anemones live on bottom debris and on gastropod shells occupied by hermit crabs (p. 149).

DID YOU KNOW? Hermit crabs and their anemones have a cooperative agreement to trade travel for stinging protection. Hermit crabs with anemones growing on them suffer fewer octopus attacks. Apparently, hermit crabs value their protection enough to take their anemones with them when they upgrade to larger shells. Hermit anemones defend themselves by extruding stinging orange or white filaments, called acontia. When not used in defense, the filaments line the gut and help to subdue swallowed prey. This anemone can reproduce by dividing lengthwise, producing two new anemones.

Hermit anemone showing tricolored mouth

Retracted hermit anemones on skate eggs (p. 171)

Stressed hermit anemones expel orange acontia

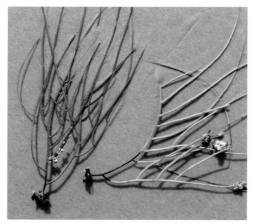

Colorful sea whips

The gorgonin skeleton of a sea whip

Regal sea fan

Soft Corals

RELATIVES: These soft octocorals are in the class Anthozoa, order Gorgonacea, and are only distantly related to stony corals.

IDENTIFYING FEATURES: All may be found simply as a core of tough, woodlike branches.

Colorful sea whips *(Leptogorgia virgulata),* 3 ft (1 m), have long, bending branches attached to a thin base. They are most commonly purple or yellow, but also can be red or orange.

Regal sea fans *(Leptogorgia hebes),* 9 in (23 cm), grow as densely branched fans. They are most commonly orange, but also can be purple or red.

HABITAT: Soft corals grow anchored to the bottom on reefs and rubble less than 100 ft (30 m) deep.

DID YOU KNOW? Soft corals are colonies of polyps, each with 8 tentacles (hence their name: octocorals). Unlike most stony corals, soft corals do not need symbiotic algae (zooxanthellae) to survive, so they can live in waters with less light. There, the polyps feed on tiny plankton. Soft corals are branched rods of a flexible hornlike protein (gorgonin) surrounded by polyps bound to each other by a matrix of glasslike spicules. Color variation in sea whips is genetic, and many areas may have more than one color growing. A unique barnacle (p. 143) grows only on the branches of sea whips.

Stony Corals

Northern Star Coral

Compact Ivory Bush Coral

RELATIVES: Stony corals are in the order Scleractinia.

IDENTIFYING FEATURES: All are white or stained when beached.

Northern star coral *(Astrangia poculata),* 2 in (5 cm), is a lone ball or an encrusting dome with tight, deep, 0.2-in (5-mm) cups.

Compact ivory bush coral *(Oculina arbuscula),* 12 in (30 cm), has pencil- to finger-thick branches with widely separated cups.

HABITAT: Northern star coral colonies grow on a wide variety of nearshore bottom rubble. Compact ivory bush coral grows anchored to hard bottom farther offshore. Each occurs in waters less than 100 ft (30 m) deep.

DID YOU KNOW? These corals survive turbid and dark conditions. Some colonies of northern star and ivory bush corals receive food from photosynthetic zooxanthellae, but others are able to grow under low-light conditions without these symbiotic algae. Their polyps gain most of their nutrition from feeding on tiny animal plankton. Tropical corals get about 95% of their organic carbon from sugars produced by zooxanthellae, and would starve without ample light. Northern star coral's ability to grow in cold, dark waters allows it to extend into New England waters, farther north than any other stony coral.

Northern star coral colony on shell rubble

Northern star coral, closeup of cups

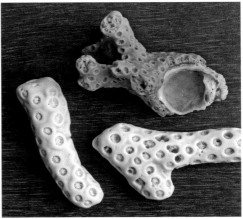

Fragments of compact ivory bush coral

Shelled Mollusk Anatomy

Seashells are the protective or supportive skeletons of mollusks (phylum Mollusca). The most common shells are from snails (with one coiled shell) and **bivalves** (with two hinged shells). Snails are **gastropods**, as are sea slugs and sea hares, which have an internal shell or none at all. Other shelled mollusks include tusk shells and some squids.

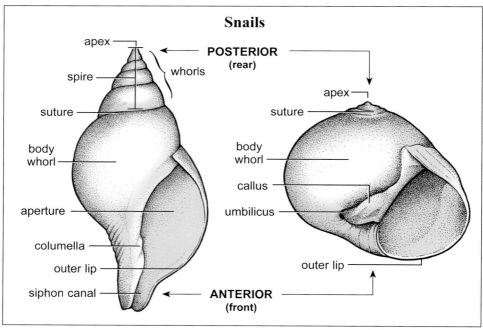

Snails

apex — spire — suture — body whorl — aperture — columella — outer lip — siphon canal

whorls — POSTERIOR (rear)

apex — suture — body whorl — callus — umbilicus — outer lip

ANTERIOR (front)

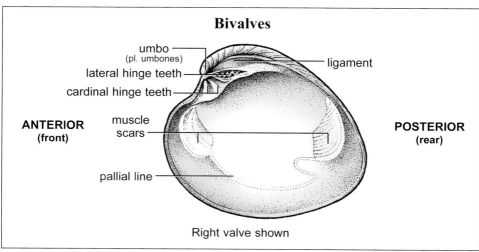

Bivalves

umbo (pl. umbones) — lateral hinge teeth — cardinal hinge teeth — muscle scars — pallial line

ligament

ANTERIOR (front)

POSTERIOR (rear)

Right valve shown

Limpet, Falselimpet, and **Wormsnail**

Keyhole Limpet   Falselimpet   Wormsnail

RELATIVES: Keyhole limpets (family Fissurellidae) are not directly related to falselimpets (Siphonariidae). Wormsnails are in the family Turritellidae.

IDENTIFYING FEATURES:

Cayenne keyhole limpets *(Diodora cayenensis)* are shaped like oval-based volcanoes with a keyhole opening offset from center.

Striped falselimpets *(Siphonaria pectinata)* have a limpetlike shell with radiating brown stripes and no top opening.

Florida wormsnails *(Vermicularia knorrii)* grow wormlike after reaching about 0.5 in (1.25 cm), but also may grow in masses of many intertwined snails. These snails are generally brown with a white spiral tip.

HABITAT: Limpets and falselimpets live on rocks. Limpets are in shallow water, and striped falselimpets are in and above the wave splash. Florida wormsnails live in sponges near shore out to 360 ft (110 m).

DID YOU KNOW? Limpets and falselimpets feed on algae using their rasping, tonguelike radula. Limpets anticipate low tide and return to resting spots before the water leaves their rock. Their top hole passes exhaust from their gills. Falselimpets are pulmonate snails (they have lungs and breathe air) and can be found above the tide on jetty rocks.

Cayenne keyhole limpet, max 2 in (5 cm)

Striped falselimpet, max 1 in (2.5 cm)

Florida wormsnail, max 3 in (8 cm)

A knotted mass of Florida wormsnails

Sculptured topsnail, max 1 in (2.5 cm)

Chestnut turban, max 2 in (5 cm)

Common sundial, max 2.5 in (6.4 cm)

Topsnail, Turban, and Sundial

Topsnail

Turban and Sundial

RELATIVES: Topsnails are in the family Trochidae. Turban shells are in the family Turbinidae. Sundials are in the family Architectonicidae.

IDENTIFYING FEATURES:

Sculptured topsnails *(Calliostoma euglyptum)* have a dark-tipped apex and rounded whorls with beaded cords.

Chestnut turbans *(Turbo castanea)* have rounded whorls like a knobby turban and have a circular aperture. They are occasionally bright orange.

Common sundials *(Architectonica nobilis)* have a deep umbilicus and a spire like a flattened cone.

HABITAT: Topsnails live on nearshore hard bottom and offshore reefs. Turbans and sundials live in sandy areas out to moderate depths.

DID YOU KNOW? Topsnails feed on algae, detritus, small bottom animals, and sponges. An extensive commercial harvest of large, Indo-Pacific turban shells fuels a high-end market for shell buttons. The snails are also the typical substitute "escargots" for the region's tourists. Our Southeastern turbans are too small for this enterprise, but are occasionally eaten locally. Most chestnut turbans feed on algae. Sundials spend their days buried spire-down in the sand and emerge at night to feed on sea pansies (p. 63).

Wentletraps

RELATIVES: Wentletraps are in the family Epitoniidae.

IDENTIFYING FEATURES:

Many-ribbed wentletraps *(Epitonium multistriatum)* are sharply pointed with about 19 crowded ribs on the body whorl, the last of 7–8 whorls.

Angulate wentletraps *(Epitonium angulatum),* have a rounded, thick-lipped aperture and distinct, widely spaced ribs. The body whorl has 9–10 thin ribs that are angled at the whorl shoulders.

Humphrey's wentletraps *(Epitonium humphreysii)* have 8–9 thick, rounded ribs on the body whorl.

Brown-band wentletraps *(Epitonium rupicola)* have rounded ribs of varying strengths and spiral bands of white, tan, and brown.

HABITAT: Wentletraps live in sandy areas to moderate depths. Wentletrap shells vacated by the mollusk are likely to be occupied by long-wristed hermit crabs (p. 149).

DID YOU KNOW? Angulate wentletraps get away with chewing chunks off living anemones by soothing them with a purple anesthetic. More than 20 wentletrap species are known from the southeastern US. "Wentletrap" comes from *wendeltreppe,* German for a winding staircase.

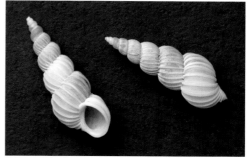

Many-ribbed wentletrap, max 0.5 in (1.3 cm)

Angulate wentletrap, max 1 in (2.5 cm)

Humphrey's wentletrap, max 1 in (2.5 cm)

Brown-band wentletrap, max 0.75 in (2 cm)

71

Marsh periwinkle, max 1 in (2.5 cm)

Zebra periwinkle, max 0.5 in (1.3 cm)

Live zebra periwinkles on a granite rock jetty

Periwinkles

RELATIVES: Periwinkles are in the family Littorinidae.

IDENTIFYING FEATURES:

Marsh periwinkles *(Littoraria irrorata)* have thick aperture lips and are patterned with dashed streaks on their spiral ridges.

Zebra periwinkles *(Echinolittorina placida,* or *Littorina ziczac)* have white and purple-brown wavy lines. Some have a dark middle band (**A**).

HABITAT: Periwinkles live at the high-tide line on firmly anchored substrates. Marsh periwinkles live almost exclusively on marsh grass, and zebra periwinkles live on rocks, especially jetties (p. 320), but also live on fallen boneyard-beach oaks (p. 14).

DID YOU KNOW? Periwinkles forage only at high tide and avoid both terrestrial and marine predators by splitting the difference between the two realms. Marsh periwinkles have a unique farming relationship with the fungi they eat. The snail chews wounds into live marsh grass, which becomes infected with fungi. Marsh periwinkles return frequently to graze in their fungus farm, moving up and down the grass stem with each tidal cycle. A century ago, zebra periwinkles were only on rare rocky beach outcroppings in the Gulf of Mexico. But following widespread installation of jetties (p. 317), the species hopscotched into the Atlantic as far north as North Carolina.

Ceriths and Eulimas

Dark Ceriths, Niso, and Melanella

Fly-speck Cerith

RELATIVES: Dark and fly-speck ceriths (family Cerithiidae) are distantly related to nisos and melanellas (eulimas in the family Eulimidae).

IDENTIFYING FEATURES: Ceriths are lumpy with distinct siphon canals opposite their pointed spires. Eulimas are glossy smooth cones.

Dark ceriths *(Cerithium atratum)* have 18–20 beaded ridges per whorl and occasional larger lumps. Beached shells vary from light to dark.

Fly-speck ceriths *(Cerithium muscarum)* have 9–11 ridges per whorl that are crossed by spiral lines. New shells are "fly-specked" with rows of dots.

Brown-line nisos *(Niso aeglees)* have an angled body whorl and a thin brown line on each whorl suture.

Intermediate melanellas *(Melanella intermedia)* are glossy white with a rounded body whorl.

HABITAT: Dark ceriths live in shell rubble. Fly-speck ceriths live in sea-grass. Eulimas live on sea cucumbers or other echinoderms within their varied habitats. All are in shallow waters less than 100 ft (30 m).

DID YOU KNOW? Ceriths feed on algae and detritus. Eulimas feed by chewing through the skin of sea cucumbers or urchins and sucking their blood.

Dark cerith, max 1.5 in (3.5 cm)

Fly-speck cerith, max 1 in (2.5 cm)

Brown-line niso, max 0.8 in (2.1 cm)

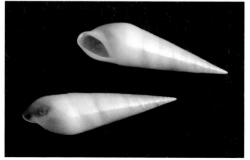
Intermediate melanella, max 0.5 in (1.3 cm)

73

Common purple sea snail, max 1.5 in (3.5 cm)

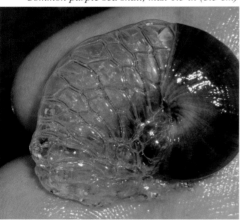

Common purple sea snail with bubble raft

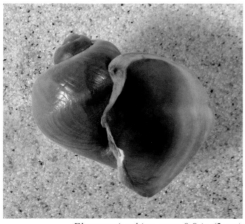

Elongate janthina, max 0.8 in (2 cm)

Janthina (Bubble-raft) Snails

RELATIVES: Janthina snails are in the family Janthinidae, distantly related to wentletraps.

IDENTIFYING FEATURES: These gastropods have fragile shells. Live snails have an elastic, translucent, bubble raft arcing from their aperture.

Common purple sea snails *(Janthina janthina)* have a low spire and D-shaped aperture. Their top whorls are pale and their base is violet.

Elongate janthina *(Janthina globosa)* are violet all over with rounded whorls, indented sutures, a distinct spire, and a pointed lower aperture.

HABITAT: Janthina snails live adrift on the open ocean. Unbroken snails are found in freshly beached wrack.

DID YOU KNOW? Two rarer species are known from Southeastern beaches. Pale janthina *(Janthina pallida)* are pale purple with a round aperture. Brown janthina *(Recluzia rollandiana)* are brown with a round aperture and sharp spire. The bubble raft of the brown janthina is also brown, to match the floating sargassum where it lives. Janthina snails cannot swim and will sink into oblivion if they lose their raft. They often sail along with, and prey upon, Portuguese men-o-war (p. 60) and by-the-wind sailors (p. 61). The snails' violet color blends with the color of the deep ocean and hides them from the birds and young sea turtles that eat them.

Conchs

Fighting Conch

Milk Conch

RELATIVES: These are true conchs (pronounced "konks") in the family Strombidae.

IDENTIFYING FEATURES:

Florida fighting conchs *(Strombus alatus)* are thick-shelled with blunt-knobbed whorls. Colors vary from pale yellow to chestnut-brown with occasional light spots and zigzags. The body whorl has fine spiral cords (ridges).

Milk conchs *(Strombus costatus)* are similar to Florida fighting conchs but have a more pointed spire and a more widely flaring aperture lip in adults. Their color is milky white.

HABITAT: Both of these conchs live offshore on reefs out to 120 ft (37 m) deep, especially the reefs south of Cape Lookout, NC.

DID YOU KNOW? Fighting conchs get their name from occasional bouts between rival males. They are spry for snails and can quickly flip themselves and walk using their pointed operculum. Both species feed on algae and detritus. Fighting conchs are being farmed experimentally as an edible alternative to the rarer and slower-maturing queen conch (*S. gigas*) of the Caribbean. Milk conchs are more common in the Bahamas and southern Florida. Although rare this far north, they occasionally wash in between Cape Fear and Cape Lookout following hurricanes.

Florida fighting conch, max 4 in (10 cm)

Juvenile Florida fighting conchs

Milk conch, max 8 in (23.3 cm)

75

Spotted slippersnail, max 1 in (2.5 cm)

Atlantic slippersnail, max 2.5 in (6.5 cm)

An arching stack of Atlantic slippersnails

Slippersnails *(Spotted and Atlantic)*

Spotted Slippersnail

Atlantic Slippersnail

RELATIVES: Slippersnails share the family Calyptraeidae with cup-and-saucer snails.

IDENTIFYING FEATURES: Slippersnails are arched with a conspicuous ventral shelf.

Spotted slippersnails *(Crepidula maculosa)* have a shelf with a straight edge angling away from the apex. Most have brown spots on white.

Atlantic slippersnails *(C. fornicata)* have a coiled apex bent to one side, a smooth exterior, and a shelf with an indented edge. Color varies widely.

HABITAT: Spotted slippersnails are most likely to be found on offshore reefs. Atlantic slippersnails live in shallow waters on rocks and on other shells.

DID YOU KNOW? Slippersnails grow where they settle as tiny "spat" and have shell shapes that conform to their location. Atlantic slippersnails are famous for growing in stacks. The bottom snail in a stack began life as a male and switched to female. The snail arriving to grow on the bottom female remained male until another snail settled on it. Each arriving young snail assumes a male's role until another snail arrives, a process that can continue to the height of ten or more slippersnails. The stacks do function in reproduction, but the snail's species name may innocently refer to its curved shape. *Fornix* is Latin for arch.

Slippersnails
(Eastern White, Convex, and Spiny)

White Slippersnail

Convex and Spiny Slippersnails

RELATIVES: Other slippersnails and cup-and-saucer snails. Each is within the family Calyptraeidae.

IDENTIFYING FEATURES:

Eastern white slippersnails *(Crepidula plana)* are white, thin, and flattened with a small, pointed apex.

Convex slippersnails *(C. convexa)* are small and deep shelled with an apex that curls. They are typically brown or purplish-brown with occasional dark spots or streaks. The deeply set shelf is white.

Spiny slippersnails *(C. aculeata)* differ in having roughened, sometimes spiny, radiating ridges. They are brownish with fine white rays.

HABITAT: These species live in shallow water where shell rubble is common. Eastern white slippersnails prefer to live inside vacated shells, especially pen shells and whelks.

DID YOU KNOW? All our slippersnails begin life as males and strategically switch sex based on environmental conditions. They make their living by filtering tiny food bits from the water. Slippersnails stay attached using the suction from their fleshy foot. One of their only travel opportunities is to have the old shell they live on hauled around by a hermit crab roommate, which is a common occurrence.

Eastern white slippersnail, max 1 in (2.5 cm)

Convex slippersnail, max 0.5 in (1.3 cm)

Spiny slippersnail, max 1 in (2.5 cm)

Striate cup-and-saucer, max 1.5 in (3.5 cm)

Brown baby ear, max 2 in (5 cm)

White baby ear, max 2 in (5 cm)

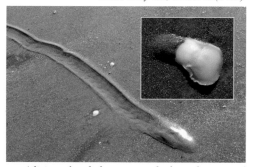

A living white baby ear tunnels through wet sand

Cup-and-Saucer Snail and **Baby Ears**

Cup-and-Saucer   Brown Baby Ear   White Baby Ear

RELATIVES: Cup-and-saucer snails are with slippersnails in the family Calyptraeidae. Baby ears share the family Naticidae with moonsnails.

IDENTIFYING FEATURES:

Striate cup-and-saucer snails *(Crucibulum striatum)* are shaped like a conical cap with a smaller cap attached within. Their apex is slightly turned and their exterior is lined with radiating ridges.

Brown baby ears *(Sinum maculatum)* have a large body whorl and gaping aperture but have a low spire like a flattened moonsnail. Their body whorl is sculptured with broad spiral grooves. Brown baby ears differ from white baby ears in having brown smudges and a higher, slightly pointed spire.

White baby ears *(Sinum perspectivum)* are similar to brown baby ears but have a more flattened spire. Shells are dull white or stained. Live animals have a white body enveloping their shell and look like a poached egg.

HABITAT: Brown baby ears live offshore. White baby ears are common within intertidal sands where their burrowing trails stand out at low tide.

DID YOU KNOW? Baby ear snails cannot withdraw their large foot into their shell. These species slide just beneath the surface of silty sands to prey on buried bivalves.

Moonsnails

Colorful and White Moonsnails — Northern Moonsnail — Miniature Moonsnail

RELATIVES: Moonsnails share the family Naticidae with baby ears and shark eyes.

IDENTIFYING FEATURES: All have a large, round body whorl, gaping aperture, and low, smooth spire.

Colorful moonsnails *(Naticarius canrena)* have a deep umbilicus half-filled with a traguslike pad (callus). They are creamy white with brown zigzags that are faded in old beach shells.

White moonsnails *(Polinices uberinus)* have no spiral cords over their glossy white exterior and have their umbilicus almost completely filled by a callus.

Northern moonsnails *(Euspira heros)* are large with a deep umbilicus. Their color is typically bluish-gray.

Miniature moonsnails *(Tectonatica pusilla)* are similar to white moonsnails but are smaller, rounder, and tan.

HABITAT: Northern moonsnails live in nearshore waters. The other moonsnail species live offshore.

DID YOU KNOW? These moonsnails prey on other mollusks by rasping drill holes into their victim's shells. They generally prowl along the bottom after dark and are able to "smell" the proteins given off by their prey. Living colorful moonsnails have a lovely patterned shell and an enormous brown-streaked foot spreading ten times their shell size.

Colorful moonsnail, max 2 in (5 cm)

White moonsnail, max 0.75 in (2 cm)

Northern moonsnail, max 4 in (10 cm)

Miniature moonsnail, max 0.25 in (6 mm)

Shark eye, max 3 in (7.5 cm)

The brown pad covering the umbilicus is the callus

Shark eye, size and color variation

Shark Eye

RELATIVES: Shark eyes (family Naticidae) are related to naticas, moonsnails, and baby ears.

IDENTIFYING FEATURES:

Shark eyes *(Neverita duplicata)*, or Atlantic moon snails, have a gaping aperture and a large body whorl that forms a smooth dome with a low spire. In many shells, an azure band on the lower whorls spirals inward to form a blue "eye." Color of the eye may also be purple, chestnut, or orange. The umbilicus is nearly covered by a brown, tragus-like pad (callus). Background shell color is tan, pinkish, brown-gray, blue-gray, or faded. The base of the shell is pale. The snail's thin operculum (aperture covering) is translucent amber. Shells in the northern end of our range tend to be browner with a more conical spire.

HABITAT: Offshore and in sandy shallows. Live shark eye snails are common in the swash zone during low tide off beaches with silty sands and protective shoals. The amber **opercula** from dead snails persist in the beach's wrack line.

DID YOU KNOW? Shark eyes plow through surf-zone sands in search of clams. Unlucky clams are enveloped by the snail's foot while an acidic secretion softens the clam's shell. A tooth-studded tongue (radula) then rasps a beveled hole (p. 133) at the softened spot. This hole allows a visit from the snail's proboscis, which injects enzymes to digest the clam's adductor muscles. With no muscles to hold it closed, the clam opens, allowing the shark eye to complete its meal of clam soup. The snail's favored diet includes surf clams (p. 118) and coquina clams (p. 121). Juvenile snails eat small clams, and larger adults eat large clams, each at a rate of almost a clam a day.

When plow-prowling for clams, shark eyes detect their prey like other moonsnails by "smelling" for telltale clam proteins. The clams are also able to detect the predatory snails and may flee to the sand's surface during a slow-motion attack. During a prowl, most of the snail's body is out of its shell and inflated with seawater. When picked up by a curious beachcomber, the snail must squirt out this water before it can withdraw into its shell and close its operculum.

Shark eyes breed in the surf zone by cementing their eggs with sand into a curled, gelatinous ribbon that cures into a rubbery **sand collar**. A circular opening atop the sand collar is where the snail's aperture was positioned as the collar formed. The collar is a study in hydrodynamics, being just the right shape to remain upright on shifting surf sands. To many, the shape suggests that the item was manufactured by humans and might be a discarded fragment of plastic. But a close examination reveals that the material of the collar is not uniformly molded and has thousands of transparent pockets. These pockets are the minute eggs, embedded within a single-layered matrix of sand grains cemented in gelatin. The collars disintegrate when eggs hatch, so whole collars found in the swash zone probably contain developing little snails.

A shark eye's amber operculum

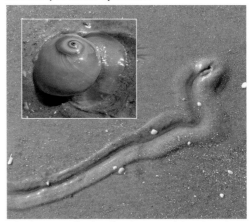

Shark eye tracks. Snail with exposed foot (inset)

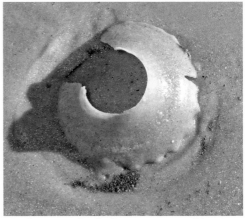

Shark eye "sand collar" eggs, max 4 in (10 cm)

81

Atlantic deer cowrie, max 5 in (13 cm)

Atlantic yellow cowrie, max 1.2 in (3 cm)

Coffeebean trivia, max 0.75 in (2 cm)

One-tooth simnia, max 0.75 in (2 cm)

Cowries, Trivia, and Simnia

Deer and Yellow Cowries and Trivia

One-tooth Simnia

RELATIVES: Cowries (family Cypraeidae) are distantly related to trivias (family Triviidae) and simnias (Ovulidae).

IDENTIFYING FEATURES:

Atlantic deer cowries *(Macrocypraea cervus)* have glossy, egg-shaped shells with a body-length, grinning aperture. Colors are chocolate with solid white spots or hazy brown with light bands.

Atlantic yellow cowries *(Erosaria acicularis)* are shaped like deer cowries but have a granular yellow pattern with marginal brown spots.

Coffeebean trivias *(Pusula pediculus)* are cowrie-shaped with riblets between a back groove and the aperture. They have three pairs of brown spots.

One-tooth simnias *(Simnialena uniplicata)* are spindle-shaped with an aperture stretching between each of its pointed ends. Colors vary from dark purple to yellow.

HABITAT: Cowries and trivias live on offshore reefs. Simnias live almost exclusively on sea whips (p. 66). All these shells are uncommon finds.

DID YOU KNOW? Cowries feed on algae and colonial invertebrates, and trivias feed on tunicates and soft corals. A one-tooth simnia matches the color of the sea whip it lives and feeds on. The Atlantic deer cowrie is the largest of the world's 190 cowrie species.

Giant Tun, Figsnail, and Triton

RELATIVES: Tun shells (family Tonnidae) are distantly related to figsnails (family Ficadae). Tritons are in the family Ranellidae.

IDENTIFYING FEATURES:

Giant tuns *(Tonna galea)* are almost spherical in shape with a wide aperture, prominent spiral ridges, and a plain cream or brown color. Most beach finds are in pieces.

Atlantic figsnails *(Ficus papyratia)* have delicately tapered shells with a low spire and are sculptured with fine spiral ridges. Colors range from cream to tan, sometimes with faint brown dots.

Giant hairy tritons *(Cymatium parthnopeum)* are recognized by their thick, wavy outer lip, which is mahogany inside with white teeth. Less beach-worn shells have a thick, brown periostracum (fuzz). The related Poulsen's triton *(C. cingulatum)* has a thin, white aperture and is less fuzzy.

HABITAT: Giant tuns, figsnails, and tritons live on offshore hard bottom.

DID YOU KNOW? Giant tuns feed on other mollusks, sea cucumbers, and fishes by engulfing their prey within a large expandable proboscis. Figsnails feed on sea urchins, and in life their shells are covered by a large, soft mantle. Tritons are rare finds on beaches; they live on offshore reefs where they are predators of varied invertebrates.

Giant tun shell, max 10 in (25 cm)

Atlantic figsnail, max 5 in (13 cm)

Giant hairy triton, max 3.5 in (9 cm)

83

Scotch bonnet, max 4 in (10 cm)

Clench helmet, max 12 in (30 cm)

Reticulate cowrie-helmet, max 3 in (7.6 cm)

Scotch Bonnet and Helmet Snails

RELATIVES: These gastropods are in the family Cassidae, distantly related to tun shells and figsnails.

IDENTIFYING FEATURES: All have a large body whorl with wide, toothy, grinning (or smirking) apertures.

Scotch bonnets *(Semicassis granulata)* have light shells with spiral grooves and a pointed spire. Colors range from white to cream with dark squares. The oldest beached shells are the most faded.

Clench (cameo) helmets *(Cassis madagascariensis)* have heavy shells with a low spire and a glossy, triangular aperture shield. Their whorl shoulders are studded with blunt knobs. Aperture teeth are light on chestnut.

Reticulate cowrie-helmets *(Cypraecassis testiculus)* have dense, egg-shaped shells with smooth spiral grooves and growth lines, and a rounded spire. They are chestnut to salmon with darker, blurry squares.

HABITAT: Offshore reefs. Shells are rarely beached except after storms.

DID YOU KNOW? North Carolina designated the scotch bonnet its state shell to honor its Scot forebears. The shell's color and shape almost resemble the plaid, woolen tam-o'-shanter cap worn by Scottish peasants. Scotch bonnets and helmet shells feed on sand dollars and sea urchins. Clench helmet populations are low and declining, perhaps due to trawling and habitat loss.

Nutmeg and Cantharus Snails

RELATIVES: Nutmegs (family Cancellariidae) and cantharus snails (family Buccinidae) are distantly related to auger snails.

IDENTIFYING FEATURES:

Common nutmegs *(Cancellaria reticulata)* have egg-shaped shells with a crosshatched texture and whorls indented at the sutures. The inner lip of the aperture has two white folds on the columella. Shell colors vary between cream white and tan with blurry brown streaks.

Common nutmeg, max 1.7 in (4.5 cm)

Tinted canthari *(Gemophos tinctus)* have a similar shape to nutmegs but without distinct whorl indentations. The outer lip is toothed and the columella is glossy. Background shell color is cream or bluish-gray. Most have streaks and smudges of brown.

Ribbed canthari *(Hesperisternia multangula)*, also called false drills, have large ridges that are sharply angled at the whorl shoulders.

Tinted cantharus, max 1.2 in (3 cm)

HABITAT: These snails live in sand, rubble, and seagrass to moderate depths.

DID YOU KNOW? Common nutmegs feed on soft-bodied animals buried in the sand. Canthari get their name from the cantharus, sacred cup of Bacchus, Roman god of wine. Cantharus snails prey on worms, barnacles, and other attached invertebrates.

Ribbed cantharus, max 1.2 in (3 cm)

Eastern auger, max 2.4 in (6 cm)

Concave auger, max 1 in (2.5 cm)

Sallé's auger, max 1.5 in (3.8 cm)

Sharp nassa, max 0.5 in (1.3 cm)

Augers and Sharp Nassa

Eastern Auger   *Concave Auger*   *Sallé's Auger*
           and Sharp Nassa

RELATIVES: Augers are allied in the family Terebridae. Sharp nassas share the family Nassariidae with mudsnails.

IDENTIFYING FEATURES: Augers have glossy, cone-shaped shells with short, distinct siphon canals.

Eastern augers *(Terebra dislocata)* are gray or orange-white with beaded spiral bands between whorls.

Concave augers *(T. concava)* resemble eastern augers except for the concave auger's namesake smooth, indented whorls. Color is white to yellow-gray.

Sallé's augers *(Hastula cinera)* are purple-gray with darkly streaked ribs below each whorl suture.

Sharp nassas *(Nassarius acutus)* have glossy, oval shells with conical spires. Their whorls have pointed beads connected by brown spiral lines.

HABITAT: Sandy shallows.

DID YOU KNOW? Augers feed on worms. Sallé's auger is an active hunter with a long stride and quick pace, nearly one "footstep" per second. It lunges when it finds a worm above the sand. Like other augers, Sallé's subdues its prey with a stab from a venomous, radular tooth. Their summer mating swarms are in the style portrayed by Burt Lancaster and Deborah Kerr in *From Here to Eternity,* with embracing pairs rolling in the swash zone.

Mudsnails

RELATIVES: Mudsnails and nassas are in the family Nassariidae.

IDENTIFYING FEATURES: These are small oval snails with conical spires.

Bruised nassa, max 0.75 in (2 cm)

Bruised nassas *(Nassarius vibex)* are light gray to dark with strong rounded axial ribs and a pointed spire. Their inner aperture lip is thickened by a wide glossy callus, which in darker shells bears a purple bruise.

Threeline mudsnails *(Nassarius trivittatus)* have yellowish-gray shells with shouldered (stepped) whorls and a woven, basketlike texture.

Threeline mudsnail, max 0.9 in (2.2 cm)

Eastern mudsnails *(Nassarius obsoletus = Ilyanassa obsoleta)* have solid brown shells with smooth, slanting, axial ribs. Their apex is typically worn. Live snails swarming over tidal flats are darkened by mud and algae.

HABITAT: Bruised nassas live in shallow seagrass and threeline mudsnails live on sandy bottom to moderate depths. Eastern mudsnails live over silty intertidal sands.

Eastern mudsnail, max 1.2 in (3 cm)

DID YOU KNOW? In Latin, *nassa* means wicker basket. Nassas and mudsnails eat algae, invertebrate eggs, carrion, and other easily outrun items. Eastern mudsnails swarm by the thousands where there is abundant food. They deposit their eggs in bristly capsules attached to hard surfaces, including other mollusk eggcases. Each 1-mm capsule contains several mudsnail eggs.

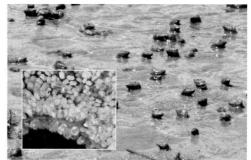

Eastern mudsnail swarm. Eggs, each 1 mm (inset)

Banded tulip, max 4 in (10 cm)

True tulip, max 5 in (13 cm)

Tulip snail egg capsules. Snails within (inset)

Tulip Snails

RELATIVES: Tulip snails (family Fasciolariidae) are related to spindle shells.

IDENTIFYING FEATURES: Tulip shells are shaped like pointed spindles with rounded curves and a stemlike siphon canal.

Banded tulips *(Fasciolaria lilium hunteria)* have cream to light gray shells with orange or gray splotches and fine spiral lines of reddish-brown. Their whorls are smooth.

True tulips *(Fasciolaria tulipa)* resemble banded tulips but have darker brown (or orange) splotches and interrupted, closer-set, spiral lines. Their whorls also differ in having fine ridges below each suture.

HABITAT: Banded and true tulips live on sand in water less than 100 ft (30 m).

DID YOU KNOW? True tulips prey on banded tulips, as well as on pear whelks and other mid-size gastropods. Tulip snails crawl into shallow waters during the winter to attach their clustered **egg capsules** to rocks, wood, and other bottom substrates. The egg capsules look like bouquets of smooth, flattened cones with frilly outer edges. Young tulip snails look like adults in miniature, and emerge from holes at the frilly end of each capsule. The capsules are formed of a tough, fingernail-like protein. If they rattle, the capsules are likely to contain tiny tulip shells. Several occupy each capsule.

Florida Horse Conch

RELATIVES: Horse conchs are spindle shells, which share the family Fasciolariidae with tulip snails.

IDENTIFYING FEATURES:

Florida horse conchs *(Pleuroploca gigantea)* are thick-shelled with knobbed whorls that form a pointed spire about half the total shell-length. Adults are unmistakably large with a whitish spire and are often covered with brown, flaky periostracum. Beach-worn adult shells are white with a glossy tan interior. Living horse conchs have an orange-red body and a thick operculum (aperture cover). A **juvenile horse conch** resembles the adult but is a lighter, more uniform, peach-gold. Dark fossil shells are common on some beaches.

HABITAT: Horse conchs prefer silty sand in waters as shallow as the low-tide line out to moderate depths. They may be most common near inshore oyster beds.

DID YOU KNOW? As the largest snail in North America, horse conchs are able to prey on big gastropods, including large whelks and other horse conchs. Their egg masses comprise dozens of flattened bugles clustered in a twisted clump. Unlike tulip snail capsules, each buglelike cone has multiple lateral ridges. Like tulip snail capsules, the young escape by dissolving plugs to open holes at the end of each capsule.

Adult Florida horse conch shell, max 19 in (48 cm)

Horse conch juveniles

Horse conch egg capsules. Snails within (inset)

89

Knobbed whelk, max 9 in (23 cm)

Kiener's whelk, a knobbed whelk variant

Knobbed whelks vary widely

Knobbed Whelk

RELATIVES: These snails share the family Melongenidae with other whelks.

IDENTIFYING FEATURES:

Knobbed whelks *(Busycon carica)* have large body whorls with distinct shoulders and a wide aperture tapering into their long siphon canal. Their shells are heavy and have several triangular knobs on the shoulder of the body whorl. Juveniles have brown stripes that fade as they become old adults, which often develop a glossy orange aperture. Background shell color is light gray to gray-brown. A variant form of knobbed whelk is the **Kiener's whelk**, which has a swelling at the lower body whorl and has shoulder spines that are extra large and recurved. Beach-worn knobbed whelk shells often remain intact although every edge is smoothed by surf-sanding.

HABITAT: Estuaries and nearshore waters out to depths of 150 ft (46 m). In estuaries, knobbed whelks can be common in oyster beds.

DID YOU KNOW? The knobbed whelk is the state shell of both Georgia and New Jersey, two states that are boundaries of the range where the species is most common.

These big snails feed on large bivalves like clams, oysters, and arks. The whelks use their sharp aperture lip to pry open the shell of their prey. During the sluggish attack, the whelk chips away at the tightly closed valves until an opening allows it to wedge its shell between the victim's valves and insert its foot. With a foot in the door, the whelk can eat. Many whelk shells show chipped apertures from this style of feeding.

Living knobbed whelks are most common in the intertidal zone during their two breeding seasons, which peak in late September and late April. Whelks larger than fist-size are mostly females, which are often pursued by one or more smaller males. Females grow faster than males, and reach maturity in about six years.

Like other whelks, knobbed whelks produce egg masses composed of dozens of disk-shaped capsules connected along a string. Disks at the earliest end of the string are small, contain no eggs, and serve as an anchor, often to a bit of shell rubble. The remainder of the disks each contain a dozen or more eggs. Egg-mass disk shape identifies the whelk species responsible. Knobbed whelk egg disks have simple, angled edges. Tiny hatchling whelks emerge from their egg capsules in about six weeks (Georgia) to six months (northern North Carolina). Egg-mass strings on beaches typically have holes indicating that the young snails have escaped, but some capsules rattle with the shells of those left behind.

A trawl fishery for knobbed whelks began in the nearshore waters of Georgia and South Carolina in the early 1980s. The meat was sold commercially for use in "conch" salads, chowders, fritters, and scungilli dishes. A peak in harvest occurred in the late 1980s, after-which the fishery collapsed. These states now have catch limits and hope to prevent overharvesting.

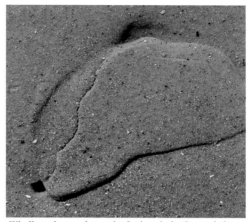

Whelk outline at low tide. Siphon hole (lower left)

A male knobbed whelk at low tide

Knobbed whelk egg mass string. Occupants (inset)

Lightning whelk, max 16 in (40 cm)

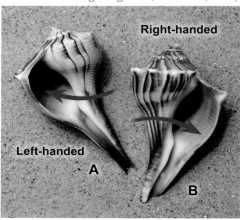

Right-handed

Left-handed

A

B

Lightning whelk (A), knobbed whelk (B)

Egg masses, with closeup of disks (inset)

Lightning Whelk

RELATIVES: These snails share the family Melongenidae with other whelks.

IDENTIFYING FEATURES:

Lightning whelks *(Busycon sinistrum)* have large body whorls with distinct shoulders bearing a dozen or more petite knobs. Like other whelks, they have a wide aperture tapering into their long siphon canal. The background color is cream or gray, with shells from younger whelks showing purple-brown axial streaks that look like lightning-bolts. Their shell is similar to the **knobbed whelk** (p. 90) except for being conspicuously left-handed, which puts the lightning whelk's body aperture (and body) on the left as it travels forward (spire in the rear). Most living lighting whelks have a charcoal-colored body, darker than knobbed whelks, which are cream.

HABITAT: Estuaries and nearshore sandy shallows.

DID YOU KNOW? The species name of the lighting whelk, *sinistrum,* describes the snail's left-handedness in Latin, not any malevolence. Nearly all other marine snails are right-handed. The same genes dictating left or right coiling in snails also govern our own asymmetry, such as the way our intestines coil. The **egg masses** strung together by lightning whelks have unique membranous edge projections that resemble plastic molding flash.

Channeled Whelk

RELATIVES: These snails share the family Melongenidae with other whelks.

IDENTIFYING FEATURES:

Channeled whelks *(Busycotypus canaliculatus)* have large body whorls and long apertures typical of whelks. Their angled whorl shoulders are edged by a lumpy spiral ridge, and a deep channel runs along the body-whorl suture well into the spire. Colors are gray to tan with only faint markings. The shell of a live channeled whelk is covered by a fuzzy, yellow-brown **periostracum,** which wears off in beached shells.

HABITAT: Channeled whelks live on intertidal sands and nearby shallows.

DID YOU KNOW? These snails scavenge and are often captured in baited traps. Whelks caught this way contribute to the scungilli served in Italian restaurants. The glossy white columella of this whelk was cut by Native Americans into beads that were strung into wampum belts, which were occasionally converted into colonial English currency. Whole shells were also used as drinking vessels. The whelk's sharp aperture edge, useful to the snail in prying open bivalve prey, provided a cutting tool for the earliest Americans. Channeled whelk egg masses are typical whelk "necklaces," but with individual disks having a unique, narrow, sharp-edged margin.

Channeled whelk, max 7.5 in (19 cm)

Live channeled whelk showing fuzzy periostracum

Channeled whelk egg disks. Young occupants (inset)

93

Pear whelk, max 5.5 in (14 cm)

Pear whelk egg disks. Young occupants (inset)

Pear (A) and channeled whelks (B) of similar size

Pear Whelk

RELATIVES: These snails share the family Melongenidae with other whelks.

IDENTIFYING FEATURES:

Pear (fig) whelks *(Busycotypus spiratus)* are similar in shape to the channeled whelk, but do not grow as large. The channel along the pear whelk's whorl suture is cut as with a "V" and disappears in earlier whorls near the spire's tip. The channel's cross section is U-shaped in the channeled whelk (p. 93). The pear whelk's angled shoulders are typically smooth. Colors are typically cream with brown, wavy, axial streaks. Live snails have a thin but fuzzy periostracum covering that wears off quickly after death.

HABITAT: Most common on muddy sand in shallow, quiet, bay waters.

DID YOU KNOW? Pear whelks feed on a variety of bivalves and would seem to compete for this food source directly with other whelks. But the large foot and rapid crawling speed of the pear whelk sets it apart in allowing capture of bivalves that flee (some bivalves just clam up to avoid predation). Pear whelks themselves commonly fall prey to stone crabs (p. 155). This whelk's golden egg masses are smaller than those of the other local whelks. Its individual egg disks have narrow projections that stem from weakly angled corners. As in other whelk egg chains, the tiny disks at one end contain no eggs and are used to anchor the egg mass in the sand.

Dovesnails

Greedy, Well-ribbed, Lunar, and Fat Dovesnails

West Indian Dovesnail

Greedy dovesnail, max 0.75 in (2 cm)

RELATIVES: Dovesnails are in the family Columbellidae.

IDENTIFYING FEATURES: Dovesnails are small with short siphon canals and toothed aperture lips.

Greedy dovesnails *(Costoanachis avara)* have 12 smooth ribs on their body whorl, each with a white splotch.

Well-ribbed dovesnails *(Costoanachis lafresnayi)* resemble greedy dove snails but have straight-sided whorls that telescope into the spire and have spiral ridges between prominent ribs.

Lunar dovesnails *(Astyris lunata)* are plump, smooth, and brown with dark wavy lines or pale spiral bands.

West Indian dovesnails *(Columbella mercatoria)* have thick shells with revolving grooves. The narrow aperture has a thick outer lip with many teeth.

Fat dovesnails *(Parvanachis obesa)* have plump shells with distinct vertical ribs and fine revolving lines. The outer lip has a few small teeth inside.

HABITAT: Lunar dovesnails live intertidally. Remaining species are found in seagrass, rubble, or bryozoan colonies out to moderate depths.

DID YOU KNOW? These dovesnails are carnivores or scavengers. Dovesnail eggs are laid within single capsules, and young emerge either swimming or crawling.

Well-ribbed dovesnail, max 0.5 in (1.3 cm)

Lunar dovesnail, max 0.2 in (5 mm)

West Indian dovesnail, max 0.6 in (1.5 cm)

Fat dovesnail, max 0.25 in (0.6 cm)

Giant eastern murex, max 7 in (18 cm)

Apple murex, max 4.5 in (12 cm)

A communal apple murex egg mass

Murices *(Giant Eastern and Apple)*

RELATIVES: Murices share the family Muricidae with drills and rocksnails.

IDENTIFYING FEATURES: Murex shells are highly sculptured with round apertures and tubular siphon canals.

Giant eastern murices *(Hexaplex fulvescens)* are turnip-shaped with a body whorl sculptured by about 8 axial ridges (varices), each bearing pronounced hollow spikes. Beached shells are white to gray and may have only worn knobs instead of spikes.

Apple murices *(Chicoreus pomum)* are cream with brown bands and have 3 lumpy varices per whorl. Their inner aperture lip has a thin, flared margin and a dark blotch opposite the siphon canal.

HABITAT: Giant eastern murices live on sand to about 325 ft (100 m). Apple murices inhabit nearshore waters as shallow as the intertidal zone.

DID YOU KNOW? These murices prey on bivalves by rasping holes in their shells. They prefer oysters. Both of these murex species take part in group spawning events where multiple females add their egg capsules to a communal mass. Females then remain nearby, do not feed, and presumably stand guard over the eggs. These egg masses can be dozens of times larger than an individual murex snail.

Pitted Murex
and Florida Rocksnail

Pitted Murex

Florida Rocksnail

RELATIVES: Murices and rocksnails are in the murex family, Muricidae.

IDENTIFYING FEATURES:

Pitted murices *(Favartia cellulosa)* have dull white shells with 5–7 lumpy varices per whorl and a narrow, upturned siphon canal.

Florida rocksnails *(Stramonita hae-mastoma)* have sculptured shells and wide apertures with a toothed outer lip. They are whitish to grayish and frequently show red-brown spots. Their shells are highly variable, but all have spiral cords and axial ridges that are most prominent at the shoulders, which may have knobs. The outer lip interior may have brown lines or fine white ribs.

HABITAT: Pitted murices live near oyster and mussel beds. Rocksnails are most common near jetties and nearshore hard bottom.

DID YOU KNOW? Rocksnails feed on bivalves, gastropods, and barnacles. Their eggs are contained in tan or purple-stained, vase-shaped capsules that are attached to rocks during communal gatherings of snails.

Pitted murex, max 1 in (2.5 cm)

Florida rocksnail, max 3 in (8 cm)

Florida rocksnail

97

Atlantic oyster drill, max 1.5 in (3.8 cm)

Thick-lip drill, max 1.3 in (4 cm)

Thick-lip drill egg capsules on an ark shell

Drills

RELATIVES: Drills are in the murex family, Muricidae.

IDENTIFYING FEATURES:

Atlantic oyster drills (*Urosalpinx cinerea*) have rounded shoulders and 9–12 rugged ribs per whorl. The aperture is oval with an open siphon canal. Colors range between yellow, orange, gray, and white, occasionally with brown streaks.

Thick-lip drills (*Eupleura caudata*) are pinkish with a long, thin siphon canal, an oval aperture, and a thick, toothed, outer lip opposite an equally thick ridge (varix) on the body whorl.

HABITAT: These drills live in estuaries within rocky, intertidal areas and oyster bars. Because of unintentional transport in ships' ballast water and in oyster seed beds, these drills now occur far outside their natural range, from England to the US Pacific.

DID YOU KNOW? Drills pierce young oysters by secreting acids onto their prey's shell and rasping the softened spot with a toothy radula. The resulting hole tapers to a small pinpoint, just wide enough for the drill to insert digestive enzymes and withdraw oyster soup. Female drills will attach dozens of flattened, leathery, urn-shaped **egg capsules** to a hard surface. Capsules are transparent and about half the length of the snail. Thick-lip drills lay capsules with a tiny side projection, and Atlantic oyster drill egg capsules are smooth.

Olive Shells and Marginella

Lettered Olive   *Dwarf Olive and Marginella*

RELATIVES: Olive shells are in the family Olividae, distantly related to marginellas, family Marginellidae.

IDENTIFYING FEATURES: All have glossy shells with elongate apertures.

Lettered olives *(Oliva sayana)* have a thick shell with a small pointed spire. Newer shells are covered with slightly blurry, brown zigzags.

Variable dwarf olives *(Olivella mutica)* are gray to brown, variably marked, and have a spire extending half their shell length. The aperture is triangular with an inner, ridged, parietal callus that extends beyond the aperture up to the next suture. Live snails leave conspicuous tracks on sandy, low-tide flats. It is commonest of several *Olivella* species.

Common Atlantic marginellas *(Prunum apicinum)* have a glossy, egg-shaped shell with a low spire and a thick, smooth, outer aperture lip margin extending up past the preceding whorl. Colors range from gray to tan.

HABITAT: Silty sand in waters as shallow as the low-tide mark.

DID YOU KNOW? These snails cover their shells with their sensitive mantle, which requires comfortably smooth, porcelain shell finish. Each species will scavenge, but lettered olives prey mostly on coquina clams in the surf zone. In 1984, South Carolina designated the lettered olive as its state shell.

Lettered olive, max 2.7 in (7 cm)

Variable dwarf olive, max 0.6 in (1.6 cm)

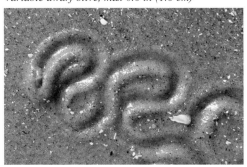

A live variable dwarf olive leaves a snaking trail

Common Atlantic marginella, max 0.5 in (1.3 cm)

Channeled barrel-bubble, max 0.25 in (6 mm)

Mottled sea hare, max 8 in (20 cm); arrow shows eye

Mottled sea hare, arrow shows rhinophores

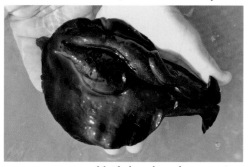

Mottled sea hare, brown variant

Bubble Shell
and Mottled Sea Hare

RELATIVES: Bubble shells (family Bullidae) and sea hares (Aplysiidae) are opisthobranchs (a group of gastropods containing sea slugs).

IDENTIFYING FEATURES:

Channeled barrel-bubbles *(Acteocina canaliculata)* have a fragile, smooth shell with an aperture open along two-thirds of the shell length and the earliest whorls submerged into the spire. Colors range from white to rusty. The similar Candé's barrel-bubble *(Acteocina candei)* has straight-sided whorls into a conelike spire.

Mottled sea hares *(Aplysia brasiliana)* when beached look like a slippery, writhing, elongate blob. Colors are mottled green to solid brown. In water, they reveal their blunt head with a rabbitlike face, fleshy moustache (oral tentacles), and beady eyes below two soft, rabbit-ear horns (rhinophores). They swim by undulating their winglike parapodia.

HABITAT: Both bubble shells and mottled sea hares live in bays and sounds.

DID YOU KNOW? Sea hares beach after population booms and when rough seas sweep them from the shallows. They are among few animals that feed on toxic cyanobacteria (blue-green algae). When stressed, seas hares release a harmless purple ink. They have both male and female working parts and perform as both in mating chains.

Sargassum Nudibranch, Blue Glaucus, and Pteropod

Arrows point out cryptic sargassum nudibranchs

RELATIVES: Sargassum nudibranchs and blue glaucus sea slugs are opisthobranchs (gastropods in the order Nudibranchia). Pteropods are distantly related gastropods in the order Thecosomata.

IDENTIFYING FEATURES:

Sargassum nudibranchs *(Scyllaea pelagica)*, 2.5 in (6.3 cm), are the color of fresh sargassum weed (p. 265) and have rhinophores shaped like the plant's leaves.

Beached blue glaucus, max 2 in (5 cm), on a fingertip

Blue glaucus sea slugs *(Glaucus atlanticus)* have tapered bodies and paired, handlike cerata. From above, they are deep blue on a silvery blue background. Below they are silver-gray.

Straight needle-pteropods *(Creseis acicula)* have glassy, needle-shaped shells that occasionally beach in massive numbers. This tiny, shelled sea slug has paired winglike flaps for swimming.

HABITAT: Sargassum nudibranchs live adrift on floating sargassum algae. Pteropods and blue glaucus sea slugs inhabit the surface of the open ocean.

A blue glaucus placed in water

DID YOU KNOW? Sargassum nudibranchs swallow sargassum floats to keep from sinking. The blue glaucus floats upside down (foot up) due to a swallowed air bubble in its stomach. Their cerata bear stinging cells taken in by feeding on Portuguese men-o-war (p. 60). Pteropods feed by trapping plankton in a mucous web.

Straight needle-pteropod, max 0.4 in (1 cm)

Blood ark, max 3 in (7.5 cm)

Transverse ark, max 1.4 in (3.6 cm)

Ponderous ark, max 2.8 in (7 cm)

White miniature ark, max 0.9 in. (2.2 cm)

Arks *(Blood, Transverse, Ponderous, and White Miniature)*

Blood, Transverse, and Ponderous Arks

White Miniature Ark

RELATIVES: Ark shells are allied within the family Arcidae.

IDENTIFYING FEATURES: Arks have thick shells with forward umbones and distinct ribs. In life, arks are coated with a brown, fuzzy periostracum.

Blood arks *(Lunarca ovalis)* have an oval shell with an arched hinge-line bearing about 7 teeth in front of the umbo and about 30 behind. Rear hinge teeth are largest and angled backward.

Transverse arks *(Anadara transversa)* have an elongate oval shell with a relatively straight hinge-line bearing mostly vertical teeth below a thin ligament scar the length of the hinge.

Ponderous arks *(Noetia ponderosa)* have a very thick, triangular shell with flat, divided ribs and an arched hinge-line below a broad moustachelike, grooved ligament area.

White miniature arks *(Acar domingensis)* have rear-pointed shells with heavy growth lines that give it a scaly look.

HABITAT: White miniature arks grow attached to offshore rubble. The other arks live in nearshore sands.

DID YOU KNOW? Robust shells make arks among the most common whole shells on high-energy beaches, where waves pulverize other mollusks. Blood arks have hemoglobin-red blood.

Arks *(Incongruous, Cut-ribbed, Mossy, and Turkey Wing)*

IDENTIFYING FEATURES:

Incongruous arks *(Scapharca brasiliana)* are thin-shelled for an ark. Their strong radial ribs have distinct beads like embossed dashes.

Cut-ribbed arks *(Anadara floridana)* have an elongate shell with a relatively straight hinge-line. The ribs are flattened, and each of the forward ribs (toward umbo) has a deep central "cut."

Mossy arks *(Arca imbricata)* have a straight hinge line almost the length of the shell. The ribs are beaded and the color is mostly chestnut brown.

Turkey wings (zebra arks) *(Arca zebra)* are similar to mossy arks but have less-beaded ribs and a longer hinge line. Turkey wings have nested, red-brown Vs or Ws at the umbo that turn into oblique lines or zigzags rearward.

HABITAT: Incongruous arks live within sandy shallows, and cut-ribbed arks live in offshore sands. Mossy and turkey wing arks grow attached to near-shore rubble.

DID YOU KNOW? The arched shell-gap opposite the umbo in mossy arks and turkey wings marks the opening where byssal threads anchor them to the bottom. The sand-dwelling arks use this attachment method only as juveniles. Arks feed like most bivalves, by inhaling water through a siphon and filtering out plankton with their gills.

Incongruous ark, max 3 in (7.5 cm)

Cut-ribbed ark, max 4.5 in (11.5 cm)

Mossy ark, max 2.5 in (6.3 cm)

Turkey wing, max 3.6 in (9 cm)

Giant bittersweet clam, max 4 in (10 cm)

Comb bittersweet clam, max 1.2 in (3 cm)

Asian green mussel, max 3.5 in (9 cm)

Bittersweet Clams
and **Asian Green Mussel**

Bittersweet Clams   *Green Mussel*

RELATIVES: Bittersweets (family Glycymerididae) may be distantly related to the arks. Mussels (family Mytilidae) are distantly related to penshells.

IDENTIFYING FEATURES: Bittersweet clams have heavy, rounded, circular shells with thick, arching hinge-lines bearing several prominent teeth on either side of the umbo.

Giant bittersweets *(Glycymeris americana)* have a small, rounded umbo and roughly 50 flattened ribs. They are glossy cream with concentric, blurry necklaces of tan or rust.

Comb bittersweets *(Tucetona pectinata)* have a relatively pointed umbo, and 20–30 raised ribs. They are slightly roughened by growth lines and are grayish-white with brown or purple spatters.

Asian green mussels *(Perna viridis)* have thin shells with a smooth, green and brown exterior. See other mussel features (p. 105).

HABITAT: These bittersweets live in sand out to moderate depths. Green mussels attach to shallow rubble and pilings.

DID YOU KNOW? Bittersweets taste as their name suggests. They live unattached and have light-sensitive eyespots along their mantle. Following accidental transport in ship-ballast water, green mussels have invaded our region from Asia and are pushing out native species.

Mussels *(Scorched and Ribbed)*

RELATIVES: Mussels (family Mytilidae) are distantly related to penshells.

IDENTIFYING FEATURES: Mussels have thin shells that fan out from their umbones and tend to retain their thin, shiny periostracum. Shell interiors are typically nacreous (lustrous, like pearls).

Scorched mussels *(Brachidontes exustus)* have shells with radiating ribs and 2–3 hinge teeth under the umbo.

Ribbed mussels *(Geukensia demissa)* have shells with radiating ribs and no hinge teeth. Shells without the brown periostracum are yellowed gray with occasional purple tinges.

HABITAT: These mussels grow attached to rocks, pilings, and rubble in waters as shallow as the intertidal zone. Live scorched mussels are abundant on rock jetties. Ribbed mussels are most common in saltmarsh.

DID YOU KNOW? Mussels form "beds" that are habitat for other animals. Scorched mussels are found in densities of nearly 5000 per square yard. Uncommonly for a bivalve, ribbed mussels spend considerable time above water at low tide and gape during this period in order to breathe. They have a close association with the roots of smooth cordgrass (p. 235) and gain an important fraction of their food from cellulose sloughed from the plant.

Scorched mussel, max 1.5 in (4 cm)

Mass of scorched mussels growing on a jetty

Ribbed mussel, max 5 in (13 cm)

Ribbed mussels in old marsh exposed on a beach

Hooked mussel, max 2 in (5 cm)

Blue mussel, max 2.5 in (6.5 cm)

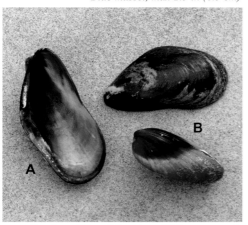

Southern (A) and American (B) horse mussels

Mussels *(Hooked, Blue, and Horse)*

Hooked and Horse Mussels

Blue Mussel

IDENTIFYING FEATURES:

Hooked mussels *(Ischadium recurvum)* have a curved, triangular shell with radial ribs that branch toward the end opposite the umbo.

Blue mussels *(Mytilus edulis)* have no ribs but have fine concentric growth lines. Outer colors range from violet to black, and inner color is shiny blue.

Horse mussels *(Modiolus* spp.) have inflated shells and an umbo just shy of their upper end. **Southern horse mussels** *(M. squamosus)* reach 2.5 in (6.5 cm), have less-inflated umbones, and are whitish or purple after beach wear. The similar **American horse mussel** *(M. americanus)* reaches 4 in (10 cm), has bulbous umbones, and is bright red through its golden periostracum.

HABITAT: These mussels grow attached to rocks or pilings in estuarine waters.

DID YOU KNOW? These mussels attach to their substrate by byssal threads made of an elastic protein ten times the strength of our own tendons. A gland makes the threads by secreting a fluid that solidifies upon contact with water. As juveniles, mussels also secrete an enzyme with their foot that dissolves the mussel's thread attachments. In making new attachments, the mussel can move over rocks like a mountain climber. Hooked mussels are the principal food eaten by many marsh duck species.

Penshells

RELATIVES: Penshells (family Pinnidae) are distantly related to mussels.

IDENTIFYING FEATURES: Penshells have thin, amber-brown, fanlike valves.

Sawtooth penshells *(Atrina serrata)* have about 30 radiating ribs bearing hundreds of short, hollow prickles.

Half-naked penshells *(Atrina seminuda)* have about 15 radiating ribs bearing a few to dozens of long tubular spines. Their posterior (fan end) muscle scar is completely within their pearly (or cloudy) nacreous area.

Stiff penshells *(Atrina rigida)* are darker and broader than half-naked penshells and have their posterior **muscle scar** outside the shiny nacre.

HABITAT: Sawtooth and half-naked penshells live in colonies with individuals buried in soft sediment out to 20 ft (6 m). Stiff penshells live in bays and sounds.

DID YOU KNOW? Penshells anchor themselves with golden byssal threads, which lead from their pointed (front) end to a small bit of rubble beneath the sand. Like most bivalves, they are filter feeders. Many living penshells have pale, soft-bodied shrimp or pea crabs (p. 151) living within their mantle cavity. Like pearl oysters, penshells occasionally produce pearls as a response to an irritant. These "pinna pearls" range from silvery to orange.

Sawtooth penshell, max 9 in (23 cm)

Half-naked penshell, max 9 in (23 cm)

Stiff penshell, max 11 in (28 cm). Arrow shows scar

107

Lion's-paw, max 6 in (15.2 cm)

Rough scallop, max 1.5 in (4 cm)

Atlantic sea scallop, max 6.5 in (16.5 cm)

Scallops *(Lion's-paw, Rough, and Atlantic Sea)*

Lion's Paw and
Rough Scallop

Sea Scallop

RELATIVES: Scallops are allied within the family Pectinidae.

IDENTIFYING FEATURES: Scallops have round or oval shells with winglike "ear" projections from the umbo.

Lion's-paws *(Nodipecten nodosus)* have thick, flattened shells with 7–8 large, roughly ridged ribs bearing occasional hollow knuckles. Their outer shell color is commonly orange or brick red, but may range from pale to dark purple.

Rough scallops *(Lindapecten muscosus)* have about 19 ribs that are roughened by tiny spoon-shaped prickles. Beach-worn shells are less prickly. Most rough scallops are solid-colored lemon, peach, or tangerine, but some are mottled with plum.

Atlantic sea scallops *(Placopecten magellanicus)* are smooth with fine concentric lines. Upper valves are purplish, sometimes rayed, and lower valves are mostly white.

HABITAT: These scallops live offshore in sandy rubble.

DID YOU KNOW? Sea scallops are rare on the beach, but are the target of a fishery that dredges them from the sea bottom offshore. The scallop's adductor muscles (meats) are dissected out and the rest discarded at sea. The harvest has grown to over 30,000 tons of scallop meats per year in the US Atlantic.

Scallops *(Calico and Bay)*

Calico Scallop

Bay Scallop

IDENTIFYING FEATURES:

Atlantic calico scallops *(Argopecten gibbus)* have shells with 19–21 rounded ribs. Shell colors vary through white, yellow, orange, red, purple, and gray, generally with splotches of dark on light. Their ears are typically worn.

Atlantic bay scallops *(Argopecten irradians)* have 17–18 ribs that are squared in comparison to calico scallops. Shell color is white, gray-brown, or orange.

HABITAT: Atlantic calico scallops live on sand bottom at depths to 1300 ft (400 m). Bay scallops live on muddy sands and seagrass in shallow waters.

DID YOU KNOW? Calico scallop fishing off North Carolina peaked in the 1980s, but diminished following a population crash from overharvest and habitat alteration. Pale scallop shells found on the beach are the right (lower) valves on which the scallop rests. To escape predators, a scallop can swim nine body-lengths per second by clapping its valves, which jets water out on either side of its hinge. In addition to people, scallops are eaten by gastropods, squid, octopodes, sea stars, and crabs. Bay scallops are also eaten by ring-billed and herring gulls, which pluck the scallops from the estuary at low tide, fly over a hard surface, and drop their catch to crack it open. This clever method carpets beach-side parking lots with broken shells.

Atlantic calico scallop, max 2.7 in (7 cm)

Atlantic bay scallop, max 4 in (10 cm)

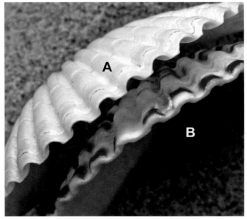

Bay scallop (A) and calico scallop (B)

109

Round-rib scallop, upper valve, max 2 in (5 cm)

Atlantic kittenpaw, max 1.2 in (3 cm)

Atlantic thorny oyster, max 5.1 in (13 cm)

Round-rib Scallop, Atlantic Kittenpaw, and Thorny Oyster

RELATIVES: Scallops are in the family Pectinidae. Kittenpaws (Plicatulidae) are distantly related to thorny oysters (family Spondylidae).

IDENTIFYING FEATURES:

Round-rib scallops *(Euvola raveneli)* have an upper valve that appears as if it were melted flat. This valve has round, separated ribs and varies from light gray to purple with rayed streaks. The lower valve is domed and white.

Atlantic kittenpaws *(Plicatula gibbosa)* have thick, tough, flattened shells with 6–10 curving, digitlike ribs. They are white to gray except for their tabby-orange ribs marked with numerous, thin, red-brown lines. The right (lower) valve (**A**) retains an impression of the hard surface on which it grew.

Atlantic thorny oysters *(Spondylus americanus)* have thick, circular, lumpy valves with occasional thorns (long in unworn shells). The hinge on the cup-shaped lower valve has two large cardinal teeth separated by a split, and the upper valve has two corresponding sockets. Colors are orange to brick red.

HABITAT: All live offshore in depths to 300 ft (91 m). Atlantic kittenpaws and thorny oysters live attached to rocks.

DID YOU KNOW? Left-valve kittenpaws are most common because the right valve often remains attached where the animal lived.

Common Jingle
and **Crested Oyster**

RELATIVES: Common jingles (family Anomiidae) are distantly related to crested oysters (family Ostreidae).

IDENTIFYING FEATURES:

Common jingles *(Anomia simplex)* have round, brittle, pearly-translucent shells with no obvious hinge. Their colors include silver-gray, white, yellow, and orange. Black shells have been stained by sulfurous sediments. Right (lower) valves have a hole and no umbo (top left in upper image).

Crested oysters *(Ostreola equestris)* have lumpy, oval shells that are ruffled along the top edge in older specimens. Hinges have pimplelike teeth and the muscle scar almost central.

HABITAT: Common jingles and crested oysters live in shallow water attached to rocks, wood, and other shells.

DID YOU KNOW? Most beached jingle shells are the unattached left valve. In life, the mollusk remains attached to a hard surface by calcified byssal threads that stem from the hole in their lower valve. Although brittle, jingle shells are strong for how thin they are. Like other nacreous shells, strength comes from microscopically thin hexagonal platelets that are laid in offset layers like bricks. This keeps crack lines from spreading. When crushed, the thin layers break into bits that refract and reflect light like glitter.

Common jingle, max 2 in (5 cm)

Common jingles crushed into shell glitter

Crested oyster, max 2 in (5 cm). Hinge (inset)

111

Eastern oyster, max 6 in. (15 cm)

Eastern oyster shells are abundant on many beaches

Oyster bed from former marsh, exposed in surf

Eastern Oyster

RELATIVES: Eastern oysters are allied with crested and frond oysters in the family Ostreidae and are distantly related to scallops, jingles, limas, and pearl oysters.

IDENTIFYING FEATURES:

Eastern oysters *(Crassostrea virginica)* have lumpy shells that vary from oval to clown-shoe shapes. They have no hinge teeth, and their inner surface is smooth with a purple muscle scar. The lower valve is flat and often remains cemented to the surface where the oyster lived.

HABITAT: Estuarine waters, typically less saline than where crested oysters live. Eastern oysters attach to rocks, debris, or other oysters, in vast beds.

DID YOU KNOW? Eastern oysters were formerly super-abundant and a staple food of native Americans in the region. In the late 19th century, industrial oyster harvest from the central Atlantic coast took 27 million bushels each year. By 2004, harvest had declined 99%. In addition to a vast overharvest, oyster beds also suffered from introduced diseases and loss of attachment habitat due to dredging. Although their importance to the menu of seafood raw bars is obvious, oysters also play a critical role in creating habitat for a variety of other animals. Their filter-feeding cleans estuarine waters, and they are sensitive to poor water quality, making oysters excellent environmental sentinels.

Oysters *(Frond, Pearl-, and Wing-)* and **Antillean Fileclam**

Frond Oyster and Fileclam

Pearl-oyster and Wing-oyster

RELATIVES: Frond oysters (Ostreidae), pearl and wing oysters (Pteriidae), and fileclams (Limidae) are distantly related.

IDENTIFYING FEATURES:

Frond oysters *(Dendostrea frons)* have yellow- or purple-colored oval shells with strong radial ridges ending in interlocking scalloped margins. Those attached by clasping, fingerlike shell projections to the branches of soft corals have the most elongate shell shape.

Atlantic pearl-oysters *(Pinctada imbricata)* have valves with a straight hinge with short, triangular front and rear wings. Unworn shells have a scaly, fringelike periostracum.

Atlantic wing-oysters *(Pteria colymbus)* look similar to pearl oysters but have longer wings that extend past the rest of the shell.

Antillean fileclams *(Limaria pellucida)* have thin white shells with fine riblets.

HABITAT: Frond, pearl, and wing oysters live attached to many objects, including sea whips (p. 66). Fileclams live in offshore crevices.

DID YOU KNOW? Both pearl and wing oysters occasionally produce tiny pearls. Fileclams live in a nest made of their own byssal threads and can swim away from predators by clapping their valves.

Frond oyster, max 1.5 in (4 cm)

Atlantic pearl-oyster, max 3.5 in (9 cm)

Atlantic wing-oyster, max 3.5 in (9 cm)

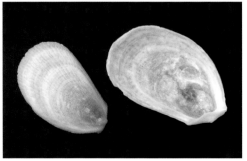

Antillean fileclam, max 1.1 in (2.8 cm)

113

Buttercup lucine, max 2.5 in (6.4 cm)

Cross-hatched lucine, max 1 in (2.5 cm)

Pennsylvania lucine, max 2 in (5 cm)

Lucines

| Buttercup | Cross-hatched | Pennsylvania |
| Lucine | Lucine | Lucine |

RELATIVES: Lucines are allied within the family Lucinidae.

IDENTIFYING FEATURES: Lucines have thick circular shells with forward-pointing umbones above a distinct, heart-shaped impression (the lunule) split by the valve opening.

Buttercup lucines *(Anodontia alba)* have a forward flare that forms a keel protruding more than the umbo. The outer shell is dull white with fine growth lines and the inner shell is butter-yellow or cream.

Cross-hatched lucines *(Divalinga quadrisulcata)* are moderately inflated with relatively thin valves sculptured by numerous, parallel lines that make the shell appear covered with fingerprints. Beached shells are glossy white or ivory.

Pennsylvania lucines *(Lucina pensylvanica)* have very thick, off-white valves with a deep furrow either side of the umbo. Thin, scaly, growth lines are separated by smooth bands.

HABITAT: All live in sandy shallows. Buttercup lucines and Pennsylvania lucines can live as deep as 300 ft. (90 m).

DID YOU KNOW? Lucines are named for Lucina, an aspect of the Roman goddess Juno who represented light and childbirth. These burrowing mollusks have a muscular foot that can extend six times their shell length.

Jewelboxes and Carditid

RELATIVES: Jewelboxes (family Chamidae) and carditids (family carditidae) are allied with clamlike bivalves.

IDENTIFYING FEATURES:

Florida spiny jewelboxes *(Arcinella cornuta)* are shaped like tubby commas bearing about 8 radiating ridges with hollow spines (or knobs, if beach-worn). They are white with a pinkish interior.

Leafy jewelboxes *(Chama macerophylla)* have thick, oval shells covered in numerous scaly ridges. Beach-worn shells are lumpy, but new shells may have long, hollow scales. They are generally yellow or chalky, but are often orange or lavender.

Corrugate jewelboxes *(Chama congregata)* have a corrugated exterior, fine ridges within the inner valve margins, and are reddish outside, purplish inside.

Three-tooth carditids *(Pleuromeris tridentata)* have small, thick triangular shells with beaded radial ribs. Colors are cream and rusty pink.

HABITAT: Jewelboxes live cemented to reefs and debris to moderate depths. Florida spiny jewelboxes detach when young to grow free within sandy rubble. Carditids live in shallow sands.

DID YOU KNOW? The spines and scales of jewelboxes are an important line of defense against being drilled by gastropod predators (p. 133).

Florida spiny jewelbox, max 2.5 in (6.3 cm)

Leafy jewelbox, max 3.1 in (8 cm)

Corrugate jewelbox, max 1 in (2.5 cm)

Three-tooth carditid, max 0.25 in (6 mm)

Atlantic strawberry-cockle, max 2 in (5.1 cm)

Atlantic giant cockle, max 5.2 in (13.2 cm)

Spiny papercockle, max 1.8 in (4.5 cm)

Florida pricklycockle, max 2.7 in (6.9 cm)

Cockles and Florida Pricklycockle

Strawberry-, Papercockle,
and Pricklycockle

Atlantic Giant Cockle

RELATIVES: Cockles are allied within the family Cardiidae.

IDENTIFYING FEATURES: Cockle shells are oval, inflated, and have a large umbo with one central tooth and socket.

Atlantic strawberry-cockles *(Americardia media)* are cream with red-brown specks and have flattened ribs that feel like sandpaper. An angled ridge runs across the longest part of the shell.

Atlantic giant cockles *(Dinocardium robustum)* are cream with brown or tan in segments along their ribs, which are rounded and bumpy along the shell's front, flattened and smooth in the rear.

Spiny papercockles *(Papyridea lata)* are compressed with rear ribs ending in protruding spines. They are mottled with pale pink, purple, orange, or red-brown. Similar *P. soleniformis* is more elongate and speckled brown on cream.

Florida pricklycockles *(Trachycardium egmontianum)* have about 30 ribs covered by strong scales (in unworn shells) and ending in a deeply serrated hind margin. External color is cream with tan or purple-brown splotches. Their valves inside are salmon and/or purple.

HABITAT: Sandy shallows off beaches.

DID YOU KNOW? Giant cockles are also called heart cockles because of the end-on profile that two valves make. Cockles are common in chowders.

Yellow Pricklycockle
and **Eggcockles**

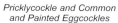

Pricklycockle and Common and Painted Eggcockles

Yellow Eggcockle

Yellow pricklycockle, max 2.5 in (6.4 cm)

RELATIVES: Pricklycockles and eggcockles are in the family Cardiidae.

IDENTIFYING FEATURES:

Yellow pricklycockles *(Trachycardium muricatum)* have about 35 ribs with small scales. They have tinges of yellow inside and out and may tend toward peach with occasional red-brown streaks.

Common eggcockles *(Laevicardium laevigatum)* have valves with an oblique oval shape and ridges along the inner margin. They are glossy white or yellow with occasional rosy tinges. Older beached shells are white and less glossy.

Painted eggcockles *(Laevicardium pictum)* have a compressed, skewed triangular shape. They are cream with blurry, orange or brown zigzags.

Yellow eggcockles *(Laevicardium mortoni)* are almost evenly rounded with a central umbo and are colored by relatively distinct rows of brown, purple, or orange zigzags.

HABITAT: Sandy shallows to offshore. Yellow eggcockles prefer shallow bays.

DID YOU KNOW? Prickles may help anchor pricklycockles in the sand. Eggcockles avoid predators differently—by leaping away using their muscular foot. This does not always allow yellow eggcockles to escape ducks, who have this bivalve on their favorite-foods list.

Common eggcockle, max 3 in (7.6 cm)

Painted eggcockle, max 1 in (2.5 cm)

Yellow eggcockle, max 1 in (2.5 cm)

117

Southern surfclam, max 5.1 in (13 cm)

Atlantic surfclam 8 in (20.3 cm)

Dwarf surfclam, max 0.75 in (2 cm)

Surfclams
(Southern, Atlantic, and Dwarf)

Southern Surfclam   Atlantic Surfclam   Dwarf Surfclam

RELATIVES: Surfclams share the family Mactridae with duckclams.

IDENTIFYING FEATURES: These clams have a spoon-shaped pit behind the central hinge teeth.

Southern surfclams *(Spisula raveneli)* have a central umbo and fine growth lines. Colors are white to dirty cream with rusty tones. Dark shells are stained.

Atlantic surfclams *(Spisula solidissima)* look similar to southern surfclams, but have thicker, more inflated shells with a more bulbous umbo.

Dwarf surfclams *(Mulinia lateralis)* have an umbo forward of center and a tapered hind end. Colors may be white, cream, gray, or purple-gray, with highlighted growth bands.

HABITAT: All live in sand from just off the beach out to moderate depths (165 ft or 50 m). Dwarf surfclams are also common in shallow lagoons.

DID YOU KNOW? Atlantic surfclams are commercially harvested for food between Virginia and New Jersey. The abundant dwarf surfclam feeds a host of estuarine animals including ducks and a hefty shell-crunching fish called the black drum *(Pogonias cromis)*. As their name suggests, these bivalves are most common just outside the surf zone.

Fragile Surfclam, Duckclams, and **Atlantic Rangia Clam**

Fragile Surfclam and
Duckclams

Atlantic Rangia Clam

Fragile surfclam, max 4 in (10.2 cm)

RELATIVES: These clams are allied with surfclams in the family Mactridae.

IDENTIFYING FEATURES: All have a spoon-shaped pit behind the central hinge teeth.

Fragile surfclams *(Mactrotoma fragilis)* are thin-shelled with a forward umbo. Shell color is cream with some remaining periostracum behind a ridgeline on the hind end.

Channeled duckclams *(Raeta plicatella)* have white, thin, ear-shaped shells with strong concentric growth ridges.

Channeled duckclam, max 3.2 in (8.1 cm)

Smooth duckclams *(Anatina anatina)* have thin, off-white, ear-shaped shells with smooth growth lines and a distinct ridge leading from the umbo.

Atlantic rangia clams *(Rangia cuneata)* have thick shells with an inflated umbo. Their front hinge tooth is large and rectangular and their rear tooth is a long, flat ridge. Beach shells are well worn.

Smooth duckclam, max 3 in (7.6 cm)

HABITAT: Fragile surfclams and channeled duckclams live in sand just outside the surf zone. Smooth duckclams live offshore. Atlantic rangia live in the muddy sands of brackish bays.

DID YOU KNOW? Each of these species lives buried with two united siphons that they extend just above the sand allowing the clam to filter-feed.

Atlantic rangia clam, max 2.7 in (7 cm)

Alternate tellin, max 2.7 in (6.9 cm)

Rainbow tellin, max .5 in (1.2 cm)

Texas tellin, max .5 in (1.2 cm)

Striate tellin, max 1 in (2.5 cm)

Tellins

RELATIVES: Tellins are allied with macomas in the family Tellinidae.

IDENTIFYING FEATURES: Like other tellins, each of these shells is less rounded in the rear where they bend right (outward in the right valve).

Alternate tellins *(Eurytellina alternata)* are shiny yellow-white with numerous concentric grooves between flattened concentric ridges. They may have yellow or pink radiating from the umbo.

Rainbow tellins *(Scissula iris)* have thin, translucent shells tinged with pink. The concentric growth lines are smooth.

Texas tellins *(Angulus texanus)* have opaque, white shells and are steeply sloped behind the hinge.

Striate tellins *(Merisca aequistriata)* have chalky shells with distinct growth lines and a strong radial ridge rearward.

HABITAT: Each of these tellins lives in sand off beaches out to moderate depths.

DID YOU KNOW? Tellins lie beneath the sand on their left valve so that their posterior curves upward. This accommodates their long intake siphon, which draws in surface morsels. They are deposit feeders rather than filter feeders. Their bladelike form and strong foot allow rapid burrowing should a predator approach. Like the arks, tellin bodies are red from the oxygen binding pigment, hemoglobin.

Coquina Clams

Living variable coquina clams, max 1 in (2.5 cm)

RELATIVES: Coquina clams (family Donacidae) are related to tellins.

IDENTIFYING FEATURES:

Variable coquina clams *(Donax variabilis)* have glossy, wedge-shaped shells with faint riblets. Grooved teeth line their inner margins. Patterns vary between solids, radial rays, and concentric bands, and may include any color.

Little coquina clams *(Donax fossor)* are similar to variable coquinas but have a rounder posterior end and umbo.

HABITAT: Variable coquinas live in the swash zone, and little coquinas are only slightly deeper.

DID YOU KNOW? Variable coquinas are one of the most abundant and ecologically important mollusks on our Southeastern beaches. Specialized for life in wave-washed sand, they filter-feed on algae and bacteria swept to shore and maximize their time in this zone by migrating back and forth with each tide. They are a critical food for shore birds and surf fishes, but would rather not be. Coquinas burrow rapidly to outrun predators. They also have a unique mutualistic relationship with a hydroid (p. 62) that grows attached to the clam's shell. Coquinas with hydroid colonies are less likely to be eaten by predatory moonsnails and fish. The hydroids also benefit; without the coquina, the colonies would have no attachment in the turbulent surf.

Coquina tracks at low tide. Extended siphon (inset)

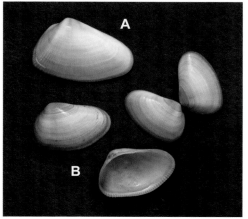

Variable (A), little coquina (B, max 0.7 in, 1.7 cm)

121

Purplish semele, max 1.3 in (3.4 cm)

Cancellate semele, max 0.75 in (1.9 cm)

Atlantic semele, max 1.5 in (3.8 cm)

Tellin semele, max 1 in (2.5 cm)

Semeles

| Purplish and Cancellate | Atlantic Semele | Tellin Semele |

RELATIVES: Semeles (family Semelidae) are related to tellins and coquinas.

IDENTIFYING FEATURES: Like tellins, a semele's hind end bends right. Their hinges have a diagonal depression angling back from the umbo.

Purplish semeles *(Semele purpurascens)* have smooth oval shells with an umbo toward the rear. They have smudge-streaks of blurry purple, brown, or orange.

Cancellate semeles *(Semele bellastriata)* are cream or gray with concentric ridges and radial riblets front and rear.

Atlantic semeles *(Semele proficua)* have a central umbo and are cream with occasional nervous purple lines.

Tellin semeles *(Cumingia tellinoides)* are dirty white and have a distinct point at the rear shell. At their hinge, a spoon-like depression beneath the umbo protrudes into the inner shell.

HABITAT: Purplish and cancellate semeles live in sand banks off beaches out to moderate depths. Atlantic and tellin semeles prefer inlet areas and shallow bays open to the sea.

DID YOU KNOW? A semele's hinge depression (chondrophore) bears a cushiony pad that springs the valves open when the animal's adductor muscles relax.

Tagelus (Short Razor) Clams

RELATIVES: Tagelus clams (family Solecurtidae) are related to semeles and tellins.

IDENTIFYING FEATURES: These clams have central umbones and elongate shells that gape at each end.

Stout tagelus clams *(Tagelus plebeius)* have thick, lumpy shells with smooth growth lines. They are white, ivory, light gray, or purplish. Freshly beached shells have a greenish periostracum.

Purplish tagelus clams *(Tagelus divisus)* have smooth, thin shells that are tinted purple inside and out. A darker purple ray from the umbo marks a slightly raised internal rib. Small shells may have a covering of brown periostracum.

HABITAT: These clams live in the sand or mud of shallow estuaries. Stout tagelus clams prefer closed lagoons and purplish tagelus clams prefer bays open to the sea.

DID YOU KNOW? Tagelus clams feed on suspended particles and live in deep burrows with only their siphons exposed. Old stout tagelus burrows are often conspicuous in the peat and mud from former marsh exposed on eroding beaches. In the living marsh, tagelus clams often compose more than 90% of the biomass on mud flats.

Stout tagelus, max 3.9 in (10 cm)

Stout tagelus burrows in former marsh mud

Purplish tagelus, max 1.6 in (4.0 cm)

123

Minor jackknife clam, max 5 in (13 cm)

Mass stranding of minor jackknife clams

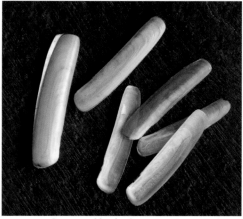

Green jackknife clam, max 1.5 in (3.8 cm)

Minor and Green Jackknife Clams

RELATIVES: Minor jackknife clams (family Cultellidae) are only distantly related to green jackknife clams (family Solenidae).

IDENTIFYING FEATURES:

Minor jackknife clams *(Ensis megistus)* have fragile shells with a curved straight-razor shape and are about nine times as long as they are wide. Shells are purplish inside and outside show a shell-length wedge of lavender growth bands against a whitish background.

Green jackknife clams *(Solen viridis)* have a straight upper-shell edge and are about four and a half times as long as they are wide.

HABITAT: Minor jackknife clams live burrowed into the sands of offshore shoals. Green jackknife clams live in the muddy sands of shallow sounds and bays.

DID YOU KNOW? Jackknife clams burrow vertically with astonishing speed and can dig to more than an arm-length's depth in the sand. To dig, they inflate their foot hydraulically, extend it down into the sand with the aid of squirting water, spread the foot into an anchor, and deflate the foot to pull the shell down. They can also swim. To do this, they fold their foot against the side of their shell and flick it backward. This action springs the clam forward. When rough seas erode offshore shoals, minor jackknife clams often strand on the beach in great numbers.

Venus Clams *(Quahogs)*

Southern Quahog

Northern Quahog

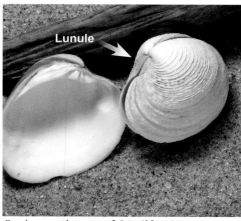

Southern quahog, max 5.9 in (15 cm)

RELATIVES: Quahogs are venus clams in the family Veneridae, distantly related to false angelwing clams.

IDENTIFYING FEATURES: All venus clams have three interlocking cardinal teeth atop each valve. A distinct lunule lies ahead of the umbo and is arrowhead-shaped when valves are together. Quahogs differ from false quahogs (p. 126) in having low, rounded teeth on their inside bottom edge.

Southern quahogs *(Mercenaria campechiensis)* have their mid-shell growth lines clearly visible, the largest of which are as wide as a pencil lead. They are gray outside with occasional purple zigzags and broad rays. Inside they are mostly white but may have hints of purple.

Northern quahogs *(Mercenaria mercenaria)* look similar to their southern cousins, but they differ in having finer growth lines that are smooth in the center of larger clams. Their inner margin tends to be deep purple.

Northern quahog, max 4.3 in (11 cm); and surf bits

HABITAT: These clams live in the muddy sands of shallow bays and lagoons.

DID YOU KNOW? Quahog is pronounced KO-hog. Its genus *Mercenaria* translates to "payment," a reference to the wampum (*wampumpeg*, Algonquin for valuable string of beads) made from the quahog's purple parts. Surf-smoothed bits of this purple shell (middle image) stand out in the shell hash (p. 18).

Young southern (A) and northern (B) quahogs

125

Lady-in-waiting venus clam, max 1.6 in (4.1 cm)

Cross-barred venus clam, max 1.3 in (3.3 cm)

False quahog, max 1.5 in (4 cm)

Gray pygmy-venus clam, max 0.4 in (1 cm)

Venus Clams *(Lady-in-waiting, Cross-barred, False Quahog, and Gray Pygmy-)*

Lady-in-waiting, Cross-barred, and Gray pygmy-

False Quahog

IDENTIFYING FEATURES: Venus clams have three interlocking cardinal teeth and a distinct lunule.

Lady-in-waiting venus clams (*Puberella intapurpurea*) have strong concentric ridges that are serrated on the lower hind end. Colors are cream, tan, or gray, often with brownish streaks.

Cross-barred venus clams *(Chione elevata)* have sharp, concentric ridges that cross radial riblets. Even beach-worn shells show a distinct cross-hatched look. Inside colors often include deep purple.

False quahogs *(Pitar morrhuanus)* look similar to quahogs (p. 125) but have thinner, rusty-gray shells, smooth concentric lines, no teeth on their lower edge, and are white inside.

Gray pygmy-venus clams *(Timoclea grus)* have ribs crossed by growth lines and are cream or gray, often with a purple-brown streak covering the hind end.

HABITAT: Nearshore sand and rubble.

DID YOU KNOW? Exposed clams risk predation. The rough shell sculpture of the cross-barred venus hinders its ability to dig into sediment, but keeps it in place once it is there. Because of this, it prefers quiet waters where severe wave erosion is minimal.

Venus Clams
(Calico, Sunray, and Imperial)

IDENTIFYING FEATURES:

Calico clams *(Macrocallista maculata)* have smooth, creamy shells with blurry brown rectangles and smudges.

Sunray venus clams *(Macrocallista nimbosa)* have smooth, elongate shells that are purplish-brown with darker, narrow rays streaking from the umbo. Beach-worn shells may be bone white.

Imperial venus clams *(Chione latili-rata)* have their shells thickened by 5–9 concentric, chunky rolls. They are whitish, light gray, or mottled tan with a few blurry rays.

HABITAT: Calico and imperial venus clams live in sand off beaches out to moderate depths. Sunray venus clams live in the muddy sands of shallow bays but may inhabit protected shoals within inlets and just offshore.

DID YOU KNOW? The sunray venus clam is popular with hungry oyster-catchers (p. 196), gulls (pp. 204–208), and other local chowder fans. The thickened shell rolls of the imperial venus add strength and may help this shallow burrowing clam avoid predation from shell-cracking predators. This clam is most common within the offshore beds of calico scallops.

Calico clam, max 3.5 in (8.9 cm)

Sunray venus clam, max 6 in (15.2 cm)

Imperial venus clam, max 1.4 in (3.6 cm)

127

Thin cyclinella, max 1 in (2.5 cm)

Disc dosinia, max 3 in (7.6 cm)

Elegant dosinia, max 3 in (7.6 cm)

Softshell clam max 6 in (15.2 cm)

Venus Clams *(Thin Cyclinella, Disc and Elegant Dosinias)* and Softshell Clam

Thin Cyclinella and Elegant and Disk Dosinias

Softshell Clam

RELATIVES: Venus clams are in the family Veneridae. Softshell clams (Myidae) are more closely related to angelwings and piddocks.

IDENTIFYING FEATURES:

Thin cyclinellas *(Cyclinella tenuis)* are flat white with fine but irregular growth lines. They are smaller and have thinner shells than the dosinias.

Disc dosinias *(Dosinia discus)* have ivory, circular shells with sharp forward-pointing umbones. They have fine concentric ridges too narrow for most folks to count without a hand lens.

Elegant dosinias *(Dosinia elegans)* look similar to disc dosinias, but their flattened concentric ridges are broad, easily seen, and readily felt.

Softshell clams *(Mya arenaria)* are chalky and lumpy with fine concentric lines and an interior spoon-shaped projection from the hinge area.

HABITAT: Each of these clams lives in sand or muddy sand from outside the surf zone out to moderate depths.

DID YOU KNOW? Dosinias have a hinge ligament strong enough to keep their valves attached long after their demise, surf tumble, and beaching. Softshell clams, also known as steamer clams, are the target of a major fishery in the northeast states.

False Angelwing, Mud-piddock, and **Geoduck**

False Angelwing and Mud-piddock *Geoduck*

RELATIVES: False angelwings (family Petricolidae) are closer kin to venus clams than to mud-piddocks (Pholadidae, the angelwing family) and geoducks (Hiatellidae), which are both distantly related to shipworms.

IDENTIFYING FEATURES:

False angelwings *(Petricolaria pholadiformis)* have winglike shells with a simple hinge margin bearing 3 (left valve) or 2 (right valve) cardinal teeth.

Atlantic mud-piddocks *(Barnea truncata)* are stubby, with pronounced shell gapes both front and rear. Freshly stranded shells have a long, delicate, spoon-shaped projection (apophysis) under the umbo.

Atlantic geoducks *(Panopea bitruncata)* are beached as large, off-white, lumpy, oblong shells that clearly did not close without large gapes at either end.

HABITAT: False angelwings and mud-piddocks bore into muddy clay, peat, or rotten wood on estuarine bottoms. Geoducks live in offshore burrows.

DID YOU KNOW? The siphons of an Atlantic mud-piddock extend 12 times its shell length. The Atlantic geoduck (pronounced GOO-ee-duk) lives in offshore burrows more than 5 ft (1.5 m) deep, which is why their beached shells are so uncommon.

False angelwing, max 2 in (5 cm)

Atlantic mud-piddock, max 2.8 in (7.1 cm)

Atlantic geoduck, max 9 in (23 cm)

129

Angelwing, max 6.7 in (17 cm)

Campeche angelwing, max 5 in (12.7 cm)

Campeche angelwing (L) and angelwing (R)

Angelwing
and Campeche Angelwing

Angelwing   *Campeche Angelwing*

RELATIVES: Angelwings (Pholadidae) are distantly related to shipworms.

IDENTIFYING FEATURES: Fragile, whitish, winglike shells with radial ribs. Freshly stranded shells have a long, delicate, spoon-shaped apophysis under the umbo.

Angelwings *(Cyrtopleura costata)* have a flared shell margin near the hinge that curves out at the umbo.

Campeche angelwings *(Pholas campechiensis)* have a flared margin in front of the hinge that curves out to cover the umbo. This membranous shell over the umbo is divided into several delicate compartments.

HABITAT: Angelwings bore into muddy clay, peat, or rotten wood on the bottoms of open bays. Campeche angelwings are most common in offshore clays. Abundant angelwings on the beach means that the beach has eroded into former estuary.

DID YOU KNOW? These angelwings live with much of their soft parts outside their shells, which are more important as a tool for burrowing than for protection. The shell's roughness abraids the sides of the angelwing's burrow allowing it to maintain a clear passage through which it moves quickly up and down. The angelwing's apophysis serves as an attachment site for its large foot muscles.

Piddocks and Shipworms

Wedge and Oyster Piddocks

Shipworms

RELATIVES: Wedge and oyster piddocks share the family Pholadidae with true angelwings and are distantly related to shipworms (Teredinidae), which are bivalves, not worms.

Wedge piddock, max 2 in (5 cm), in wood

IDENTIFYING FEATURES:

Wedge piddocks *(Martesia cuneiformis)* have wedge-shaped shells with rasplike concentric ridges and a groove from the umbo down. They burrow into wood.

Oyster piddocks *(Diplothyra smithii)* have weaker ridges than wedge piddocks and bore into thick shell and rock.

Oyster piddock, max 0.7 in (1.7 cm), in limestone

Shipworms (family Teredinidae) are evident as snaking **tunnels** through beached driftwood. The tunnels of these bivalves are lined with white, fragile, shell material. The animal is worm-shaped, having small, winglike, shell valves (generally deep in wood and not easily seen) in front and paddlelike "pallets" in the rear. *Teredo* shipworms have pallets hollowed like a vase, whereas *Bankia* has pallets of about 16 stacked funnels.

Shipworm tunnel shell, max 0.4 in (1 cm) diameter

HABITAT: Wedge piddocks and shipworms burrow in wood; oyster piddocks burrow in rock or shell.

DID YOU KNOW? Shipworms tunnel for protection and feed by filtering outside water taken in by siphon tubes. Their shell valves close like jaws to grind wood and their rear pallets plug their tunnel to prevent dehydration.

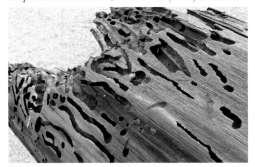

Shipworm tunnnels in driftwood

Circular Chinese-hat   Adam's Miniature Cerith

Amethyst gemclam   Contracted corbula

Pointed nutclam   Atlantic nutclam

Atlantic abra   Lunate crassinella

White strigilla   Many-line lucine

Miniature Mollusks

RELATIVES: Gastropods and bivalves

IDENTIFYING FEATURES: These shells are too small to be seen by folks on a casual stroll and are all less than about 0.25 inch (8 mm) as adults. The path into the amazing world of itty-bitty shells is traveled by those on their hands and knees. Peering into drift piles at the recent strand line will reveal many of this page's petite species in addition to miniature versions of the larger species shown on previous pages.

Dinky gastropods:

Circular Chinese-hat *(Calyptraea centralis),* family Calyptraeidae, rare north of Hatteras

Adam's miniature cerith *(Seila adamsii),* family Cerithiopsidae, shell rubble, all beaches

Itty-bitty bivalves:

Amethyst gemclam (*Gemma gemma*), family Veneridae, all beaches

Contracted corbula *(Caryocorbula contracta),* family Corbulidae, near inlets, all beaches

Pointed nutclam *(Nuculana acuta),* family Nuculidae, all beaches

Atlantic nutclam *(Nucula proxima),* family Nuculidae, all beaches

Atlantic abra *(Abra aequalis)*, family Semelidae, all beaches

Lunate crassinella *(Crassinella lunulata),* family Crassatellidae, all beaches

White strigilla *(Strigilla mirabilis),* family Tellinidae, rare north of Hatteras

Many-line lucine *(Parvilucina multilineata),* family Lucinidae, rare north of Hatteras

Shell Wars (Shell Bioerosion)

Beached mollusk shells often bear clues to how they met their demise and who made use of them after their death. This evidence includes boreholes, perforations, and grooves.

Shells with single, circular **boreholes** were likely eaten by a predatory gastropod. Atlantic oyster drills (p. 98) leave a straight hole, whereas thick-lipped drills leave a slightly beveled hole. Shark eye snails (pp. 80–81) leave a countersunk, circular borehole that has an outer diameter twice the inner diameter. Note in the top image that shark eyes can be cannibals. Two tactics used by hole-boring gastropods include edge drilling and umbo drilling. Drilling at the valve edge is the fastest because the shell there is thinner, but an edge-drilling snail risks a pinched proboscis from closing valves. Drilling the thick umbo is safer but takes time, during which a snail may have its prey stolen or become a meal itself. Drilling a thick shell can take a snail the better part of a day. Bivalve shells also may be penetrated by other bivalves like *Gastrochaena,* which leave oblong boreholes in either shell or rock. This bean-shaped clam lives out its life within the pit it forms.

Scattered **perforations** in a shell were likely made by boring sponges (p. 55). These sponges partially acid-digest living and dead shells and invade them as living space.

Other animals that use shells as living space include polychaete worms (bristle worms) like polydorids, which leave snaking **groove** marks. The worm makes these router-tool indentations by softening the shell with secreted acid and rasping with its bristled body.

Boreholes from gastropods (A) and bivalves (B)

Boring sponge perforations in a quahog

Polydorid polychaete worm grooves

Colorful incongruous arks from the same beach

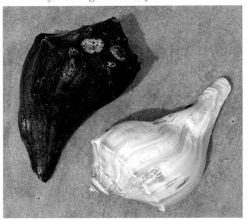

Stained and bleached knobbed whelks

The interior nacre of a penshell

Shell Color Variation

Although some shells are most colorful in life, other shells turn a variety of colors after their inhabitants die. These colors depend on the shell's afterlife experiences. Black shells were likely darkened by iron sulfide after burial in sulfurous muck. A beach speckled with numerous black shells shows that the surf zone was once a lagoon behind the barrier island. Pink, rust, or brown are the colors most shells turn after decades of exposure to the iron oxides in underwater beach sediments.

Shells out of water exposed to sunlight bleach pale gray or chalky white in just a few decades. Although glossy white shells are probably recent, bone-white shells may be fossils that have changed little over the millennia they've aged. Varied shell colors hint that most beaches in the Southeast have shells of mixed origin and age, but most shells on the upper beach are pretty old. There, the average shell is typically a few thousand years old.

The colors of recently living shells vary with what the mollusk ate and where it lived, in addition to what genes the animal inherited from its parents. Inherited color traits are dictated by use of four shell-color pigments—dark melanins, yellow carotenoids, green porphyrins, and indigoids that come in either blue or red. The iridescent sheen of **nacre** (mother of pearl) is not from pigment, but instead comes from the refraction of light by transparently thin layers of calcite. These rainbow colors are not seen while the mollusk is alive and do not contribute to its well-being. Nacre serves to smoothen the shell surface next to the mollusk's soft body.

Mollusk Bits and Pieces

For every whole shell found on a beach there are thousands of bits and pieces. Some surf-worn shards have the clear distinguishing features of the original shell. Do you recognize these?

A. Penshell (p. 107) inside nacre

B. Atlantic giant cockle (p. 116) ribs

C. Atlantic giant cockle (small) (p. 116) umbo and hinge area

D. Giant tun shell (p. 83) body whorl

E. Lettered olive (p. 99) body whorl

F. Northern quahog (p. 125) purple margin

G. Florida fighting conch (p. 75) body whorl

H. Clench helmet (p. 85) aperture teeth

I. Channeled whelk (p. 93) body whorl and spire

J. Shark eye (pp. 80–81) body whorl and spire

K. Campeche angelwing (p. 130) umbo end with apophysis

L. Lightning whelk (p. 92) left-handed columella

M. Knobbed whelk (p. 90) right-handed columella

N. Eastern oyster (p. 112) hinge scar

O. Channeled duckclam (p. 119) umbo and hinge

P. Atlantic figsnail (p. 83) siphon canal of body whorl

Q. Angelwing (p. 130) posterior margin

R. Scotch bonnet (p. 84) aperture shield and lip

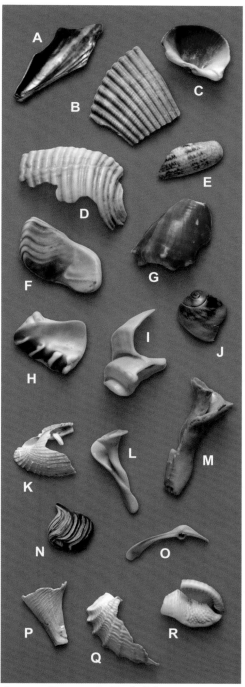

Some readily recognizable shell fragments

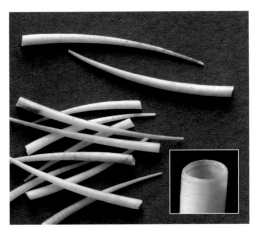

Ivory tuskshell, max 2 in (5 cm)

Ram's horn squid shell, max 1 in (2.5 cm)

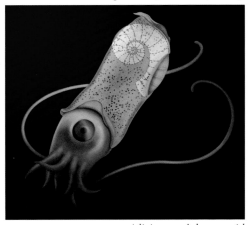

A living ram's horn squid

Tuskshell and Ram's Horn Squid

Ivory Tuskshell

Ram's Horn Squid

RELATIVES: Tuskshells are scaphopods (a separate class from the gastropods and bivalves) in the family Dentaliidae. The ram's horn squid is in a fourth class of mollusks, the cephalopods (including octopodes and nautili), family Spirulidae.

IDENTIFYING FEATURES:

Ivory tuskshells (*Graptacme eborea*) are white, delicate, curved and tapered tubes, open at each end. The foot and mouth of the living tuskshell were formerly located at the wide end, which is smooth and round. Several other tuskshell species occur in the region.

Ram's horn squid shells *(Spirula spirula)* are beached as white, chambered coils. In life, the coil is within the back end of the squid opposite its two large eyes and ten tentacles. The coil takes up almost half the squid, minus outstretched tentacles.

HABITAT: Ivory tuskshells live in sandy bottom offshore. Ram's horn squid live in the deep open ocean.

DID YOU KNOW? Tuskshells live with their wide (anterior) end in the seabottom where they use their oral tentacles to feed on forams (protozoa). Ram's horn squid use their buoyant, chambered coil to suspend themselves headdown in the water column. For protection, the squid can pucker up by withdrawing its head and tentacles into its body. They range worldwide.

136

Paper Nautilus and Octopus

Paper Nautilus *Common Octopus*

RELATIVES: These mollusks are cephalopods in the order Octopoda. Argonauts are in the family Argonautidae, and common octopodes are in the family Octopodidae.

IDENTIFYING FEATURES:

Paper nautili are the eggcases of the **greater argonaut** *(Argonauta argo)*, a species of open-ocean octopus. The female argonaut creates this paper-thin eggcase, which coils around the octopus similar to a wrinkled nautilus shell.

Common octopodes *(Octopus vulgaris)* are shell-less, reddish-brown cephalopods with eight arms that extend about three fourths of the animal's length. Arm suckers typically have dark rings.

HABITAT: Argonauts live in the deep open ocean. Common octopodes live on nearshore hard bottom.

DID YOU KNOW? Paper nautili eggcases are not true mollusk shells because they are not produced by the mantle. The case hardens from carbonates and proteins secreted by the webbing of the female's first pair of arms, and the case functions only in egg protection. The argonaut holds herself within the case, but is not attached to it. Sometimes, females strand on beaches along with the eggs they guard. Octopodes are smart. The common octopus is able to solve numerous laboratory puzzles, including unscrewing a jar to get a meal.

Paper nautilus, max 12 in (30 cm)

Living female argonaut stranded with her eggcase

Common octopus, max 20 in (50 cm)

137

Sargassum sea mat

Common bugula

Ambiguous bryozoan

Rubbery bryozoan, fingers to 0.2 in (5 mm) wide

Moss Animals (Bryozoans)

RELATIVES: Moss animals are in the phylum Bryozoa and are most closely related to annelid worms and mollusks.

IDENTIFYING FEATURES: All are colonies of individual animals (zooids).

Sargassum sea mat *(Membranipora tuberculata)* is a lacy crust covering sargassum algae and other drifters. Colonies may span 1 in (2.5 cm) and are composed of tiny rectangular compartments.

Common bugula *(Bugula neritina)* are palm-sized and brownish with tough branches. The zooids live in alternating positions on dual rows. Other *Bugula* species are white.

Ambiguous bryozoans *(Anguinella palmata)* are gray, limp, silty tufts.

Rubbery bryozoans *(Alcyonidium hauffi)* are branching, gray-brown rubbery fingers that are clear at the ends. They often envelop sea whips (p. 66).

HABITAT: Sargassum sea mat lives on things that float on the open ocean, Common bugula and rubbery bryozoans live attached to substrates in shallow waters. Ambiguous bryozoans are intertidal.

DID YOU KNOW? These bryozoans are some of the most common among more than a hundred species in the region. Bryozoan zooids filter-feed using a semicircle of mouth tentacles.

Tube Worms
(Soda Straw, Plumed, and Shingle)

RELATIVES: Segmented worms (phylum Annelida) in the class Polychaeta. Soda straw and plumed worms are in the family Onuphidae. Shingle worms (Oweniidae) are distantly related.

IDENTIFYING FEATURES: Unique tubes and fecal pellets.

Soda straw worms *(Kinbergonuphis jenneri)* live within 0.25-in (6-mm) wide sandy tubes that are tough and stretchy above sand and limp below. Those at low tide may accumulate oval **fecal pellets**. Eroding surf can fill the tide line with piles of **limp tubes**. Similar tubes from bamboo worms (*Clymenella torquata*, family Maldanidae) are fragile.

Plumed worms (*Diopatra cuprea*) live within shaggy straw-sized tubes that project from the sand near the low tide line. Messy glued shell bits and other debris thicken the end of each tube.

Shingle tube worms *(Owenia fusiformis)* live within a second skin of overlapping tiny shell shards. The tubes retract accordion-style for burrowing and are half the diameter of plumed worm tubes.

HABITAT: Intertidal and below within muddy sand on beaches with mild surf.

DID YOU KNOW? Plumed worms feed on small invertebrates that colonize their own shaggy tubes, and their neighbors' tubes as well.

Soda straw worm tube and fecal pellets (inset)

Limp soda straw worm tubes beached after a storm

Plumed worm tubes, 0.4 in (1 cm) diameter

Shingle (L, 5 mm wide) and plumed worm tubes (R)

139

Parchment tube worm tubes, worm at lower right

Sand-builder worm colony at low tide, and closeup

Fan worm tubes on a whelk shell

Tube Worms *(Parchment, Sand-builder, and Fan)*

Parchment Tube and
Sand-builder Worms

Fan Worm

RELATIVES: Parchment tube worms (family Chaetopteridae) are not closely related to sand-builder (Sabellariidae) and fan (Serpulidae) worms.

IDENTIFYING FEATURES:

Parchment tube worms *(Chaetopterus variopedatus)* live within pale, paper-like tubes up to 12 in (30 cm) long. Each tube was formerly U-shaped beneath the sand and was home to a worm with specialized segments employing paddle-like flaps, lobes, and cups. Storms erode the sands where these worms live and can fill the beach with their tubes.

Sand-builder worms *(Sabellaria vulgaris)* build tubes of cemented sand that intertwine to form reefs near the low tide line. The worm itself exposes only its pad of golden tentacles to feed.

Fan worms *(Hydroides* spp.) live in hard, whitish, calcareous tubes cemented to shells and other rubble. Diameter is typically less than 1.3 in (8 mm).

HABITAT: Parchment tube worms live near the surf zone. Sand builder worms encrust jetty rocks and other substrates. Fan worms live in estuarine and near-shore waters.

DID YOU KNOW? Although blind, parchment tube worms glow in the dark, emitting a luminous blue cloud of mucous when disturbed.

140

Palp, Rag-, and Blood Worms

Palp Worm and Ragworms   Blood Worm

RELATIVES: Palp worms are in the family Spionidae and are more closely related to sand-builder and serpulid worms than to ragworms (Nereididae) and blood worms (Glyceridae), which are together in the order Phyllodocida.

IDENTIFYING FEATURES:

Palp worms *(Scolelepis squamata)* live within inconspicuous subsurface tubes and have two long feeding palps.

Ragworms (clam worms) have multiple pairs of palps at their head-end, and have numerous, 2-lobed "feet" (parapodia). Most are predators and have a pharynx that can be everted to reveal strong jaws with teeth.

Blood worms *(Glycera* spp.) are sleek, pink worms that are tapered at either end. They have short body segments and numerous parapodia.

HABITAT: Palp worms live in the swash zone. Ragworms live in a variety of nearshore areas and are most common in estuaries. Bloodworms live within tidal mud flats, but are also common in the bait buckets of surf fishers.

DID YOU KNOW? Palp worms are the most common polychaete in the surf zone and may occur at densities greater than 200 per square meter. They are an important food for surf fishes and wading birds. Blood worms have a large eversible proboscis with four, mildly poisonous fangs. Yes, they bite.

The palp worm, Scolelepis, *max 1.4 in (3.5 cm)*

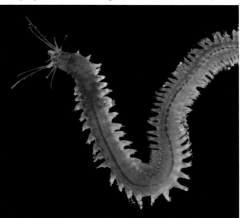

The ragworm, Platynereis dumerilii, *3 in (7.5 cm)*

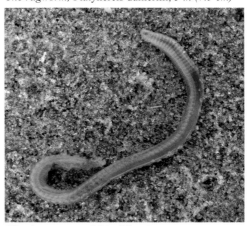

Blood worm, max 15 in (38 cm)

Fecal castings from lugworms seen at low tide

Lugworm egg mass

Ice cream cone worm tubes, 2 in (5 cm) long

Lugworm
and Ice Cream Cone Worm

RELATIVES: Both are polychaetes, although lugworms (family Arenicolidae) and ice cream cone worms (Pectinariidae) are not closely related.

IDENTIFYING FEATURES:

Lugworms *(Arenicola marina),* are easily recognized by their sandy fecal castings, which are in tight coils as if squeezed from a tube no bigger than 0.4 in (1 cm). Compare with the thicker feces of the acorn worm (p. 168). In Spring, lugworm egg masses are conspicuous as transparent amber or lavender gelatinous blobs up to a yard long. The living worms are up to 12 in (30 cm), and stout, with bushy red gills at mid body.

Ice cream cone worms *(Pectinaria gouldi),* build themselves a narrow cone-shaped tube out of a single layer of sand grains cemented with a protein glue. Typically, only vacant tubes are found. The head of the worm is at the larger end of the tube and has long ciliated feeding tentacles.

HABITAT: Both occur on muddy intertidal flats on protected beaches.

DID YOU KNOW? Regardless of sediment composition, an ice cream cone worm chooses consistent sand grain sizes to make its tube—fine grains for the narrow end and coarse grains at the wide end.

Barnacles Without Stalks
(Sea Whip, Fragile, Star, and Volcano)

| Sea Whip Barnacle | Fragile Barnacle | Star and Volcano Barnacles |

Sea whip barnacles, with (L) and without (R) sheath

RELATIVES: Barnacles (subclass Cirripedia) are crustaceans in the phylum Arthropoda. These barnacles without stalks are allied within the suborder Balanomorpha, acorn barnacles.

IDENTIFYING FEATURES:

Sea whip barnacles *(Conopea galeata),* 0.6 in (1.5 cm), are brown with a diamond-shape profile and are found on sea whip branches (p. 66). Living barnacles are covered by a sheath of sea whip polyps imbedded in tissue.

Fragile barnacles *(Chthamalus fragilis),* 0.4 in (1 cm), are flattened cones with six smooth plates.

Star barnacles *(Chthamalus stellatus),* 0.4 in (1 cm), are like fragile barnacles but have distinctly ribbed plates.

Volcano barnacles *(Tetraclita stalactifera),* 1.6 in (4 cm), have fused plates that form a rough-ribbed volcano shape with a small opening.

Fragile barnacles on a rock jetty

HABITAT: Sea whip barnacles live where sea whips do. Fragile, star, and volcano barnacles live on rocks and other hard substrates in the high intertidal zone.

DID YOU KNOW? Barnacles live attached for life, head down within their shells. They feed by gathering plankton with their feathery legs, which also act as their gills. At low tide their shells close to conserve water until the sea returns.

Star (small) and volcano (large) barnacles

Ivory acorn barnacles on driftwood

Striped acorn barnacle

Titan acorn barnacles on a jetty

Barnacles Without Stalks
(Ivory, Striped, and Titan Acorn)

Ivory Acorn Barnacle

Striped and Titan
Acorn Barnacles

RELATIVES: These are acorn barnacles in the family Balanidae.

IDENTIFYING FEATURES:

Ivory acorn barnacles *(Balanus eburneus),* 1.2 in (3 cm), are white and steep-sided with distinct plates and a wide opening.

Striped acorn barnacles (two similar species, *Balanus amphitrite* and *Balanus venustus),* 0.4 in (1 cm), are conical with purple stripes on their plates.

Titan acorn barnacles *(Megabalanus coccopoma)*, 2 in (5 cm), are pink with triangular plates that form an inflated cone with a circular opening. The similar *M. tintinnabulum* has straighter sides and a less rounded opening.

HABITAT: Striped and ivory acorn barnacles reach beaches by being attached to driftwood and flotsam. Ivory acorn barnacles are most common in estuaries. Titan acorn barnacles live on hard surfaces like jetties, groins, boats, and buoys.

DID YOU KNOW? The striped acorn barnacle is native to the southwestern Pacific and Indian oceans, but is now in every ocean. This cosmopolitan distribution was facilitated early on with the first ocean-spanning sailing ships, which served as mobile barnacle habitat. The titan acorn barnacle is a more recent (this decade) alien invader from the eastern Pacific.

144

Barnacles With Stalks

RELATIVES: Stalked barnacles are in the family Lepadidae, related to the other barnacles (subclass Cirripedia).

IDENTIFYING FEATURES: All have leaflike shells on fleshy stalks.

Goose barnacles *(Lepas hilli),* 1.5 in (3.8 cm), have a dark stalk and bluish-gray shell plates with distinct concentric growth lines.

Goose barnacles *(Lepas anserifera),* 1.5 in (3.8 cm), have white shells with radial grooves, and an orange stalk.

Duck barnacles *(Lepas pectinata),* 1 in (2.5 cm), have scaly, dark ridges and a spiny edge to their opening.

Pelagic goose barnacles *(Lepas anatifera),* 1 in (2.5 cm), have a purple-brown stalk and no radial grooves, but do show faint concentric growth lines on their smooth white shells.

HABITAT: Wood, seabeans, and other flotsam adrift on the open ocean. These barnacles reach the beach when their ride does. For some reason, the duck barnacle is the most common species growing on hard items such as floating pumice (p. 290) and the spiral of the ram's horn squid (p. 136).

DID YOU KNOW? These stalked barnacles feed on plankton and other tiny drifting food bits. They grow fast—from a swimming larva to adult size in a matter of weeks.

Freshly beached Lepas hilli *goose barnacle*

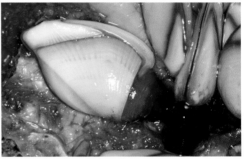

Lepas anserifera *showing its orange stalk*

Living duck barnacles on floating pumice

Pelagic goose barnacle

145

Beachhopper amphipods

Digger amphipod

Dock roach isopod

Marine roly-poly isopod

Amphipods and Isopods

RELATIVES: Amphipods (order Amphipoda) and isopods (Isopoda) are crustaceans in the phylum Arthropoda.

IDENTIFYING FEATURES: Amphipods have two kinds of legs and are generally hump-backed and laterally compressed. Isopods have one style of leg and have flatter backs.

Beachhopper amphipods *(Talorchestia* spp.), 0.8 in (2 cm), are the sand-colored, flealike critters that bounce frantically as moist beach wrack is disturbed.

Digger amphipods (family *Haustoridae)*, 0.4 in (1 cm), are abundant but seldom seen. Sieved from the sand, they curl into a pill, but actively dig in wet sand. We have many species.

Dock roaches *(Ligia exotica),* 1.5 in (3.8 cm), are charcoal-colored, swift-running, insectlike isopods.

Marine roly-polies (family *Sphaeromatidae)*, 0.4 in (1 cm), are brownish isopods with flattened tails (uropods). They curl into a ball when handled.

HABITAT: Beachhoppers live under seaweed piles. Digger amphipods are in intertidal sands. Dock roaches scurry on jetties and beach wrack. Marine roly-polies live amidst barnacles and other intertidal fouling organisms.

DID YOU KNOW? These crustaceans eat seaweed and detritus. Although beachhoppers look like fleas, they don't bite. They are an important food source for shore birds.

Ghost Shrimp

RELATIVES: Ghost shrimp are decapod crustaceans more closely related to mole and hermit crabs than to shrimps.

IDENTIFYING FEATURES:

Ghost shrimp burrow and pellets

Carolinian ghost shrimp *(Callichirus major)*, 3.2 in (8 cm), are best identified by their pencil-sized burrow openings, which are often surrounded by fecal pellets that look like chocolate ice-cream sprinkles. The animal itself is elongate, pale, and soft-bodied with one **claw** much larger than the other and bearing a curved finger. Old, exposed **burrows** on an eroded sand flat often show their dark, muddy, reinforced lining. The much smaller **Georgian ghost shrimp** *(Biffarius biformis)* 1.2 in (3 cm), has a burrow only half the diameter of its Carolinian cousin.

Exposed Carolinian ghost shrimp burrows

HABITAT: Ghost shrimp burrow in fine, intertidal sands on protected beaches.

DID YOU KNOW? Ghost shrimp burrow as deep as six feet (1.8 m). Their burrows house commensal animals such as pea crabs and copepods. An average Carolinian ghost shrimp produces about 500 fecal pellets a day, which feed hermit crabs and other intertidal critters. The digging from ghost shrimp circulates sand in an important ecological process called bioturbation This ecological engineering makes the sand and inhabiting fauna of a ghost shrimp colony different from a sand flat without these crustaceans.

Major claw of a Carolinian ghost shrimp

A Georgian ghost shrimp caught outside its burrow

147

Common grass shrimp

Peppermint shrimp

White shrimp on beached algae

Shrimps and Prawns

RELATIVES: Decapod crustaceans. Common grass shrimp and peppermint shrimp are caridean (true) shrimps and are more closely related to crabs and lobsters than to white shrimp, which are actually prawns (aka penaeoid shrimps).

IDENTIFYING FEATURES: Caridean shrimps have a double overlapping second abdominal segment that gives their "tail" an angular bend. Prawn tails flex into a gentle curve.

Common grass shrimp *(Palaemonetes vulgaris)*, 2 in (5 cm), are translucent except for their yellowish eyestalks.

Peppermint shrimp *(Lysmata wurdemanni)*, 2.8 in (7 cm), have candycane red stripes on a translucent body.

Atlantic white shrimp *(Litopenaeus setiferus)*, 7 in (18 cm), are white with pinkish sides, a green-edged tail, and reddish antennae almost three times their body length.

HABITAT: Common grass shrimp live in shallow estuaries. Peppermint shrimp live on reefs but also occur around jetties. Juvenile Atlantic white shrimp live in marshes and move offshore as adults.

DID YOU KNOW? Common grass shrimp eat algae and detritus and are an important food source for many estuarine fish and birds. Peppermint shrimp are cleaners that glean parasites and dead skin from a variety of fishes. Atlantic white shrimp have been fished commercially since the early 1700s.

Hermit Crabs

Long-wristed, Flat Claw, and Thinstripe Hermits

Giant Red Hermit

RELATIVES: Hermit crabs are crustaceans in the infraorder Anomura, shared with mole crabs. Long-wristed and flat claw hermits are in the right-handed family Paguridae. Thinstripe and giant red hermits are in the left-handed family Diogenidae.

IDENTIFYING FEATURES:

Long-wristed hermits *(Pagurus longicarpus),* 1 in (2.5 cm), have tan legs and an elongate right claw.

Flat claw hermits *(Pagurus pollicaris),* 1.2 in (3.2 cm), have white claws with the largest bearing wide, flat fingers.

Thinstripe hermits *(Clibanarius vittatus),* 1.2 in (3 cm), have brown-green legs with light stripes. Their claws are about equal in size.

Giant red hermits *(Petrochirus diogenes),* 7 in (18 cm), are red with heavy, knobby claws.

HABITAT: Giant red hermits live on reefs and may strand following storms. The other species live below low tide and are common in tide pools. Thinstripe hermits are tolerant of dehydration and can walk about on the low-tide flat.

DID YOU KNOW? Hermits eat detritus and carrion. Long-wristed hermits are known to gather sea foam with their waving arms and feed on its fats and protein. The flat claw hermit uses its flat claws as a door to the entrance of its shell.

Long-wristed hermit in a banded tulip shell

Flat claw hermit in a fixer-upper

A thinstripe hermit peers from a knobbed whelk

Giant red hermit at home in a shark eye shell

Atlantic sand crabs

As the wave recedes

Head

the mole crab digs

Atlantic sand crab swim-digging

Slender-eyed mole crab

Mole Crabs

RELATIVES: Mole crabs are anomuran decapod crustaceans related to hermit and porcelain crabs.

IDENTIFYING FEATURES:

Atlantic sand (mole) crabs *(Emerita talpoida),* 1.5 in (3 cm), also known as sand fleas, are teardrop-shaped little digging machines with short, fuzzy antennae. They are mottled green-gray on tan above and white below.

Slender-eyed mole crabs *(Albunea paretii),* 1 in (2.5 cm), have long antennae, slender eyestalks, and spiny projections across the carapace behind their head. They are an iridescent, pinkish-gray.

HABITAT: Atlantic sand crabs are locally abundant in the swash zone, even on beaches with big surf. Slender-eyed mole crabs burrow in fine sands at inlet areas and in deeper waters.

DID YOU KNOW? Both species feed on plankton and detritus driven into the surf by wind and waves. Atlantic sand crabs swim-dig backwards through flooded sands but are helpless if placed above the receding swash. They position themselves tail down and head seaward so their netlike antennae can inflate with the backwash from each spent wave. The crabs move with wave crashes so that they follow the tide up and down the beach. Surf fishers scoop mole crabs as preferred bait for pompano and other surf fish (pp. 172–173).

Porcelain Crabs and Pea Crab

Green Porcelain Crab *Olive Pit, Spotted Porcelain, and Squatter Pea Crabs*

RELATIVES: Porcelain crabs (family Porcellanidae) are not true crabs, but are anomuran decapods related to mole and hermit crabs. Pea crabs are true (brachyuran) crabs in the family Pinnotheridae.

IDENTIFYING FEATURES:

Green porcelain crabs *(Petrolisthes armatus)* have long antennae and are brown to speckled green with blue mouthparts.

Olive pit porcelain crabs *(Euceramus praelongus)* have a three-pointed rostrum and an indented rear carapace.

Spotted porcelain crabs *(Porcellana sayana)* are pink with blue-white spots.

Squatter (mussel) pea crabs *(Tumidotheres maculatus)*, are pale brown with weak legs and an oval carapace to about 0.5 in (1.2 cm) long.

HABITAT: Green, olive pit, and spotted porcelain crabs live in shallow-water rubble. Spotted porcelain crabs also share shells with hermit crabs. Squatter pea crabs squat inside living mussels, scallops, or pen shells. Other local pea crab species live similarly close to lugworms, ghost shrimp, or tube worms.

DID YOU KNOW? Green porcelain crabs are alien invaders from Brazil. Porcelain crabs get their name from their ability to lose appendages to escape predators. Pea crabs eat the particles of food filtered out by the various invertebrates they live with.

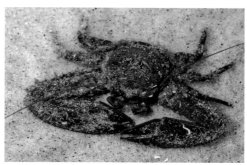

Green porcelain crab, 0.4 in (1 cm) body length

Olive pit porcelain crab, 1 in (2.5 cm) body length

Spotted porcelain crab, 0.5 in (1.3 cm) body length

Female squatter pea crab, in a penshell

151

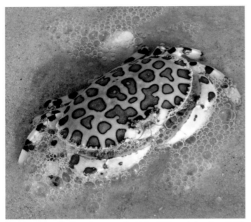

Calico box crab, 4 in (10 cm) body width

Mottled purse crab, 2.5 in (6 cm) body width

Longnose spider crab, 4 in (10 cm) body width

Crabs *(Box, Purse, and Spider)*

RELATIVES: These are true (brachyuran) crabs in the distantly related families Hepatidae (box crabs), Leucosiidae (purse crabs), and Pisidae (spider crabs).

IDENTIFYING FEATURES:

Calico box crabs *(Hepatus epheliticus)* have stout, smooth, variably speckled bodies, short legs, and wide claws that partially hide their faces.

Mottled purse crabs *(Persephona mediterranea)* have bumpy, rounded bodies, long legs, and narrow claws.

Spider crabs *(Libinia* spp.) look like their name and are often covered with sea-bottom growth. **Longnose spider crabs** *(L. dubia)* have six bumps on the carapace midline, whereas portly spider crabs *(L. emarginata)* have nine.

HABITAT: Calico box crabs and mottled purse crabs bury themselves in surf-zone sands on relatively calm beaches. Spider crabs are common in shallow waters and are swept onto beaches after rough weather.

DID YOU KNOW? Box crabs hide their faces to keep sand out of their gill chambers. Purse crabs may get their name from Persephone (winter-bringing Greek goddess) or their egg-protecting, purselike, under-curled abdomen. Juvenile longnose spider crabs ride and feed on cannonball jellies (see inset, left). Larger spider crabs move sluggishly on the bottom and decorate (camouflage) themselves with sponges and algae.

152

Swimming Crabs

Blue crab, 8 in (20 cm) body width

RELATIVES: Swimming crabs are true (brachyuran) crabs allied within the family Portunidae.

IDENTIFYING FEATURES: All have pointed projections on the sides of their carapace and swimming paddles on their hind legs.

Blue crabs *(Callinectes sapidus)* are greenish and blue. Females have orange highlights and clawtips, and are more commonly beached than males.

Speckled swimming crabs *(Arenaeus cribrarius)* are shaped like blue crabs but are grayish-tan with white spots.

Iridescent swimming crabs *(Portunus gibbesii)* have slender claws, purple legs, and iridescent patches above their toothed carapace margin.

Blotched swimming crabs *(Portunus spinimanus)* have a comparatively narrow carapace with small lateral projections, which are tipped in red-brown, as are the white-blotched claw fingers.

HABITAT: Blue crabs live in estuaries, and females occasionally beach as they migrate through inlets to spawn at sea. Speckled crabs bury themselves in swash-zone sands. Iridescent and blotched swimming crabs live on a variety of sea-bottom in inlets and offshore.

DID YOU KNOW? These crabs are swift predators that eat worms, mollusks, small fish, and other crabs.

Speckled crab, 5.5 in (14 cm) body width

Iridescent swimming crab, 3 in (7.6 cm) body width

Blotched swimming crab, 4.5 in (11 cm) body width

153

Lady crab 3.5 in (9 cm) body width

Squarebacked crab 1.1 in (2.8 cm) body width

Mottled shore crab 1.75 in (4.4 cm) body width

Tidal spray crab 1 in (2.5 cm) body width

Crabs *(Lady, Squarebacked, Mottled Shore, and Tidal Spray)*

Lady and Square-
backed Crabs

Mottled Shore
and Tidal Spray Crabs

RELATIVES: Lady crabs share the family Portunidae with other swimming crabs. Squarebacked (family Sesarmidae), mottled shore (Grapsidae), and tidal spray crabs (Plagusiidae) are related as grapsoid crabs.

IDENTIFYING FEATURES:

Lady crabs *(Ovalipes ocellatus)* have swimming paddles and a circular carapace with 5 spines on each side.

Squarebacked crabs *(Armases cinereum)* are speckled dark brown to olive. Their flat face has widely set eyes with no spine behind the eye socket.

Mottled shore crabs *(Pachygrapsus transversus)* are similar to squarebacked crabs but have larger claws, each with a spiny "biceps" joint (merus) and pinkish fingers. The carapace is mottled green with dark forward lines.

Tidal spray crabs *(Plagusia depressa)* have broad legs and a hexagonal carapace dotted with reddish bumps. The claws have purple stripes.

HABITAT: Lady crabs bury in sand below the tide. These three grapsoid crabs cling to rock jetties at the water line. Squarebacked crabs also favor dry intertidal areas with sand and rubble.

DID YOU KNOW? Tidal spray crabs are an alien invader from the tropical Indo-Pacific.

Crabs *(Stone, Hairy, and Mud)*

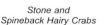

Stone and
Spineback Hairy Crabs

Harris and
Say Mud Crabs

RELATIVES: Stone crabs (family Menippidae), hairy crabs (Pilumnidae), and mud crabs (Panopeidae) are related as xanthoid crabs.

IDENTIFYING FEATURES: Stout-bodied crabs with unequal claws, each like Popeye's forearms.

Florida stone crabs *(Menippe mercenaria)* range from deep purple (juveniles) to olive with black spots (adults). Claw fingers are black.

Spineback hairy crabs *(Pilumnus sayi)* are covered with long hairs, which conceal prominent dark spines on the carapace sides and claws.

Harris mud crabs *(Rhithropanopeus harrisii)* have grayish fingers with lighter tips.

Say mud crabs *(Dyspanopeus sayi)* have claws that close like wire snips. Fingers are dark with light tips and have no large tooth on the movable finger. Similar species (not shown) have black fingers.

HABITAT: Stone crabs live in shallow rocky areas and offshore. Hairy crabs live on shelly bottom and fouled debris. Mud crabs prefer muddy bottom, with Harris mud crab mostly estuarine. All are most common near inlets.

DID YOU KNOW? These crabs eat barnacles and clams by crushing them with their strong claws. Mud crabs bury within polychaete worm colonies to avoid being eaten by blue crabs.

Stone crab, 5 in (13 cm) body width

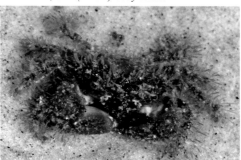

Spineback hairy crab 1.2 in (3 cm) body width

Harris mud crab 0.8 in (2.0 cm) body width

Say mud crab 1.2 in (3 cm) body width

Adult ghost crab, 2 in (5 cm) body width

Cryptic, juvenile ghost crab, feeding on crab larva

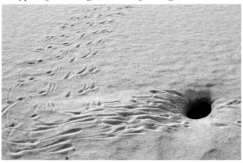

Ghost crab tracks and burrow

Atlantic sand fiddler, 1 in (2.5 cm) body width

Crabs *(Ghost and Fiddler)*

RELATIVES: These true crabs are related within the family Ocypodidae.

IDENTIFYING FEATURES: These crabs move about on land and have one claw (left or right) larger than the other.

Atlantic ghost crabs *(Ocypode quadrata)* are lightweight, swift-footed crabs with pale, square bodies and yellowish legs. **Juveniles** are a mottled, sand color. **Ghost crab tracks** appear as six rows of widely spaced commas. **Burrows** range from finger to wrist size.

Atlantic sand fiddlers *(Uca pugilator)* are purple-mottled crabs that live in colonies and seldom stray far from their burrow. Males have an oversized claw that they wave to impress females.

HABITAT: Both crabs live in burrows. Ghost crabs use the entire beach and dune. Sand fiddlers prefer the intertidal zone of protected beaches and inlets.

DID YOU KNOW? Ghost crab burrows are up to 4 ft (1.2 m) deep. At midday and over the winter, crabs retire in their burrows behind a plug of sand. Ghost crabs leave their burrows to feed before dusk and are active through dawn. Fiddlers feed at low tide by scraping up mud with their claws and pulling out algae, bacteria, and detritus with their mouth parts. They wait out high tide in their plugged burrows. Both crabs must wet their gills to breathe on land.

Horseshoe Crab

RELATIVES: These arthropods are not crustaceans, but are chelicerates (class Merostomata), more closely related to spiders than to crabs. Horseshoe crabs are likely the closest living relatives to the ancient trilobites.

A female horseshoe crab

IDENTIFYING FEATURES:

Horseshoe crabs *(Limulus polyphemus),* 2 ft (61 cm), have an unmistakable domed, U-shaped head (cephalothorax), a spine-edged abdomen, and a stiff, pointed, tail spine (telson). Live animals are chestnut brown or olive. **Molted exoskeletons** are lightweight, tan, complete versions of the animal that shed them.

Molts. Separated tail spines (inset)

HABITAT: Horseshoe crabs live in coastal lagoons and protected nearshore waters. Their habitats vary between sand, mud, rubble, and seagrass. Adults **mate** and nestle eggs into the upper swash zone of low-energy beaches. In winter, horseshoe crabs move into deeper waters.

DID YOU KNOW? Horseshoe crabs preceded the dinosaurs by millions of years. Although they look a little creepy, horseshoe crabs are gentle and safe to handle. Females take a decade or more to mature and live 20–40 years. The species is valuable in both pharmaceutical and biomedical research. Intense harvest for eel and whelk bait has caused severe population declines. This is bad news for the loggerhead sea turtles that eat them, and for the shore birds that feed on their eggs.

A male clings to a larger nesting female at low tide

A horseshoe crab making tracks to the sea

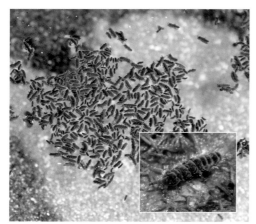

Seashore springtail aggregation. Closeup (inset)

Seaside dragonlet, male

Seaside dragonlet, female

Springtail and Seaside Dragonlet

Seashore Springtail

Seaside Dragonlet

RELATIVES: All share the arthropod subphylum Hexapoda. Springtails are primitive insectlike critters in the order Collembola. Dragonflies are true insects in the order Odonata.

IDENTIFYING FEATURES:

Seashore springtails *(Anurida maritima)*, 0.1 in (3 mm), are wingless, fuzzy, and slaty blue in color. Their water-shunning fuzz allows them to remain on the water's surface, where they often form dense aggregations. Unlike other springtails, they have no springy tail (furcula) and cannot leap.

Seaside dragonlets *(Erythrodiplax berenice)*, 1.4 in (3.5 cm), are clear-winged dragonflies with deep red eyes. Males are indigo and females are orange with black. Immature sexes have an indigo thorax and orange tail (abdomen).

HABITAT: Seashore springtails live in rocky intertidal areas with quiet pools. Seaside dragonlets live as nymphs in marshy estuaries and as adults are found in many coastal habitats.

DID YOU KNOW? Seashore springtails feed on carrion, slowly moving up and down the beach with the tide. If taken from the beach they will continue this rhythmic movement. Their aggregations may assist mating and are facilitated by pheromones. Seaside dragonlets hunt flying insects. As nymphs they tolerate higher salinities than almost any other insect.

Biting Flies

Mosquito, Biting Midge, and Stable Fly

Greenhead Fly

RELATIVES: Flies (order Diptera).

IDENTIFYING FEATURES: Flies have one set of wings. Biting flies have a taste for blood and will hurt you to get it.

Salt-marsh mosquitoes *(Ochlerotatus* spp.), 0.25 in (7 mm), have long, striped legs and are either golden-brown *(O. sollicitans)* or black *(O. taeniorhynchus)*. Both are active during dawn and dusk.

Biting midges *(Culicoides* spp.), 0.1 in (3 mm), also known as sandflies or no-see-ums, are gray-brown with black eyes. They are active during dawn and dusk.

Stable flies *(Stomoxys calcitrans)*, 0.25 in (7 mm), also called dog flies, look like a housefly with slightly lighter coloration. They are active during daylight.

Greenhead horse flies *(Tabanus nigrovittatus)*, 1 in (2.5 cm), have most of their head occupied by brilliant green eyes, occasionally crossed with reddish bands. They are active during daylight.

HABITAT: Salt-marsh mosquitoes lay eggs in wet soil and eggs hatch with rising water. Biting midges prefer to lay eggs in mud. Stable flies lay eggs in rotting grasses or livestock manure. Greenhead horse flies lay eggs on marsh grass.

DID YOU KNOW? These biting flies prefer people to other mammals and birds. Good news—folks bitten about a zillion times gain resistance to the injected saliva that causes itching.

Salt-marsh mosquito, Ochlerotatus sollicitans

Biting midge or no-see-um

Stable fly (dog fly)

Greenhead horse fly

159

Beach robber fly

Mating/feeding bearded robber flies

Seaweed fly on the carapace of a crab

Gulf fritillary, wingspan 3 in (7.5 cm)

Robber Flies, Seaweed Fly, and **Gulf Fritillary Butterfly**

RELATIVES: Robber flies (Asilidae) and seaweed flies (Anthomyiidae) are true flies (order Diptera). Butterflies are in the order Lepidoptera.

IDENTIFYING FEATURES:

Beach robber flies *(Laphystia litoralis)*, 0.5 in (1.3 cm), have a plump, banded abdomen and dark green eyes.

Bearded robber flies *(Efferia pogonias)*, 1 in (2.5 cm), have white segments near the end of their thin abdomen and legs of orange and black. In the image (left) a male (**A**) mates with a female (**B**) that has captured a white beach tiger beetle (**C**, p. 161).

Seaweed flies *(Fucellia* spp.*)* look like thin, small-eyed house flies.

Gulf fritillaries *(Agraulis vanillae)* are orange with black and silver highlights.

HABITAT: Robber flies prowl the upper beach. Seaweed flies are in the wrack line. Gulf fritillaries prefer to lay eggs on passion vines *(Passiflora* spp.*)*. Adults are widely distributed, but often migrate along beaches.

DID YOU KNOW? Robber flies capture insects many times their own size. Seaweed flies specialize in life on stranded seaweed. Both larvae and adults depend on this food source. These flies themselves are food for a variety of other insects and birds. The highest densities of gulf fritillaries occur in fall, when masses of the butterflies migrate south to overwinter in southern Florida.

Tiger Beetles

RELATIVES: Beetles are insects in the order Coleoptera. Tiger beetles are in the family Carabidae.

IDENTIFYING FEATURES: When not flying, beetles have their flight wings hidden by hard wing-covers called elytra. Each of these species is 0.5 in (1.3 cm) with long legs and large eyes. They make short, awkward flights and are among few beach insects active in daylight.

White beach tiger beetles *(Cicindela dorsalis)* are pearly colored with a scrawled pattern on the elytra.

Saltmarsh tiger beetles *(C. marginata)* have brownish elytra with a wavy tan pattern that connects along the margins.

Hairy-necked tiger beetles *(C. hirti-collis)* have brownish elytra with cream scrawls and have white hairy tufts on the sides of their thorax.

HABITAT: Adult tiger beetles hunt between the swash zone and dune and in areas of overwash. Their larvae ambush prey from tiny burrows on the upper beach and dune. White beach tiger beetles live only at the beach.

DID YOU KNOW? Glaring lights (which attract and kill adults) and foot/vehicle traffic (which destroys larval burrows) have eliminated tiger beetles from many beaches. Adults eat beach-hoppers, flies, and carrion. For their size, tiger beetles are believed to be the world's fastest running animal.

White beach tiger beetle

Mating pair of white beach tiger beetles

Saltmarsh tiger beetle

Hairy-necked tiger beetle

161

The tiny littoral rove beetle

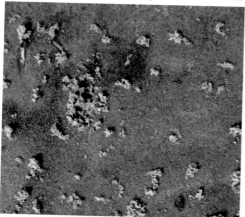

Surface trails from littoral rove beetles

Darkling beetles forage under moist wrack

Rove and Darkling Beetles

RELATIVES: Other beetles. Rove beetles are in the family Staphylinidae, and darkling beetles are Tenebrionidae.

IDENTIFYING FEATURES:

Littoral rove beetles *(Psamathobledius punctatissimus),* 0.1 in (3 mm), have short pearly elytra (wing covers) that cover only a third of their dark abdomen. Their abundant molelike surface trails are conspicuous on wet sand.

Darkling beetles *(Phaleria* spp.), 0.3 in (7 mm), are sluggish brown or black beetles with glossy, grooved elytra and tapered hind ends. At least three species occur locally; the most easily identified is *P. testacea* (bottom image, lighter beetles with darker markings on the rear).

HABITAT: Littoral rove beetles live in the upper intertidal zone. Darkling beetles forage under moist wrack on the upper beach.

DID YOU KNOW? Littoral rove beetles feed at night on single-celled algae (diatoms) in assemblages of over 2000 adults per square yard. The beetles remain buried in fine sands during high tide and breathe the air trapped between the sand grains. Mothers care for their larvae in special maternal burrows. These rove beetles are a critical food source for piping plovers (p. 193). Darkling beetles eat fungi and detritus under stranded seaweed and burrow into the sand when their wrack pile dries out.

Sea Stars

Lined and Common Sea Stars

Banded Sea Star

RELATIVES: Sea stars (class Asteroidea) are echinoderms (phylum Echinodermata), related to brittle stars, sea cucumbers, and sea urchins.

IDENTIFYING FEATURES:

Lined sea stars *(Luidia clathrata),* 6 in (15 cm), are grayish, brownish, or salmon with a dark stripe down each of their five arms.

Banded sea stars *(Luidia alternata),* 8 in (21 cm), are cream with bands of dark green, purple, or brown. Their underside has orange tube feet, and their arms are fringed with slender spines.

Common sea stars *(Asterias forbesi),* 6 in (15 cm), have stout arms and range from yellowish-orange to deep purple. They are roughly textured with pale spines and have a bright orange spot (madreporite) above one of their armpits.

HABITAT: All live in shallow nearshore waters. Common sea stars prefer rocky rubble.

DID YOU KNOW? A sea star's madreporite is a filter for its internal water-vascular system, which provides hydraulic pressure for their many tube feet. With these hydraulics, a common sea star can pull on the closed valves of a clam without fatigue, outlast the clam's muscles, and eventually poke its stomach into the open shell. Lined and banded sea stars swallow their prey whole.

Color variation in the lined sea star

Banded sea star

Common sea star. Juvenile (inset)

163

Small-spine sea star

Royal sea star. Purple form (inset)

Blood brittle star, arrow shows red tube feet

Sea Stars and Brittle Star

Small-spine Sea Star   *Royal Sea Star and Blood Brittle Star*

RELATIVES: Sea stars (class Asteroidea) are only distantly related to brittle stars (class Ophiuroidea).

IDENTIFYING FEATURES:

Small-spine sea stars *(Echinaster spinulosus)*, 6 in (15 cm), have light spines along gradually tapering arms with blunt tips. Colors are orange, red, or brown.

Royal sea stars *(Astropecten articulatus),* 6 in (15 cm), are purple-blue with tapered arms lined with marginal plates that are often bright orange. Edges are fringed with white spines.

Blood brittle stars *(Hemipholis elongata),* 4 in (10 cm), have five arms (others in the region have six) margined with small spines. Its tube feet are red.

HABITAT: Small-spine sea stars live on offshore reefs. Royal sea stars live buried in sandy shallows. Blood brittle stars burrow into subtidal sediments where plumed worms (p. 139) live.

DID YOU KNOW? Royal sea stars hunt sand-burrowers and are fond of variable dwarf olives (p. 99). The blood brittle star waves its arms to capture zooplankton with its long, sticky tube feet. Its red tube feet are colored by the hemoglobin in their vascular system, which helps them live beneath oxygen-poor sediments. Don't collect these sea stars thinking that they will keep their living colors; they won't.

Sea Cucumbers

RELATIVES: Sea cucumbers are in the class Holothuroidea. They share the phylum Echinodermata with sea stars and sea urchins.

IDENTIFYING FEATURES:

Hairy (brown) sea cucumbers *(Sclerodactyla briareus),* 4 in (10 cm), are soft, gray-brown lumps, elongate to almost spherical. The surf rubs away tube feet that cover their entire body in life.

Striped (green) sea cucumbers *(Thyonella gemmata),* 10 in (25 cm), are elongate, gray or green lumps with their tube feet in five relatively organized rows (stripes). They often retain the boomerang shape they had while in their burrows.

HABITAT: The sea cucumbers here live within burrows in shallow sandy areas and are swept onto beaches following rough weather.

DID YOU KNOW? Sea cucumbers gather plankton with a circle of ten, retractable, treelike tentacles. These animals are notorious for self-eviscerating. When sufficiently stressed, both hairy and striped sea cucumbers voluntarily expel their digestive, respiratory, circulatory, and reproductive organs. This drastic move may function to either fully occupy or disgust a predator trying to eat the sea cucumber. But the exercise also may be important in ejecting unwanted particulates and parasites. The organs grow back in several weeks.

A surf-tumbled hairy sea cucumber. Tentacles (inset)

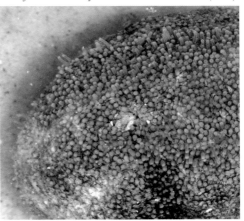

Fresh hairy sea cucumber with tube feet

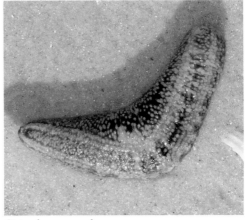

Striped sea cucumber

165

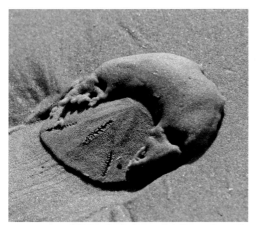

A living keyhole sand dollar at low tide

A green sea urchin adorned with shell bits

Purple-spined sea urchin

Sand Dollar and Sea Urchins

Keyhole Sand Dollar and
Purple-spined Urchin

Green Sea Urchin

RELATIVES: These echinoderms are related within the class Echinoidea.

IDENTIFYING FEATURES:

Keyhole sand dollars *(Mellita quin-quiesperforata),* 4 in (10 cm), in life are flat disks with a feltlike coating of fine, brown, moveable spines. They have five radiating slots and a central set of flow-erlike gills called petalloids.

Green (variegated) sea urchins *(Lyte-chinus variegatus),* 4 in (10 cm), are whitish, greenish, or mauve, with tubular spines that are lighter at their base and relatively blunt. They often hide under shell bits held by their tube feet.

Purple-spined sea urchins *(Arbacia punctulata),* 4 in (10 cm), have longer spines and smaller tests than the green urchin. They have sharp, purplish spines above and flattened paddles underneath.

HABITAT: Keyhole sand dollars live superficially buried in sandy shallows. On protected beaches near the low tide line, they are seen as sluggishly burrowing lumps with skidding trails. Green urchins graze on seagrass beds. Purple-spined urchins prefer turbulent rubble.

DID YOU KNOW? A sand dollar's slots provide a shortcut for food bits traveling from their topside to their mouth. They have a chewing apparatus made of five bird-shaped elements, collectively known as Aristotle's lantern.

Sand Dollar and Sea Urchin Tests

Heart Urchin

IDENTIFYING FEATURES:

Keyhole sand dollar tests *(Mellita quinquiesperforata)* tests (skeletons), 4 in (10 cm), are gray or bone white with five slots and a central set of petalloids.

Green sea urchin tests *(Lytechinus variegatus),* 3 in (7.5 cm), are greenish when fresh and bone-white when sun-bleached.

Purple-spined sea urchin tests *(Arbacia punctulata),* 1.5 in (3.8 cm), are whitish with purple highlights.

Heart (mud) urchin tests *(Moira atropos),* 2.5 in (6 cm), are egg-shaped with five radiating petal grooves. Most beached tests are bone white. In life, mud urchins are covered with short, delicate, tan spines.

HABITAT: See previous page. Heart urchins live in offshore muddy sediments.

DID YOU KNOW? It seems an immutable law that urchin tests can survive the pounding surf but are crushed into dust during transport in a beachcomber's pocket. These tests are made of 10 fused plates scattered with tiny holes for the urchin's tube feet. Each bump (tubercle) on the test is a former spine-attachment point. Heart urchins burrow and feed from the bottom of a muddy funnel open to the surface, where they stretch out specialized tube feet bearing tufts of fine hairs. The deep furrow of their test marks their front end, opposite a circular hole (periproct).

Keyhole sand dollar tests (lower surface top right)

Green urchin tests (lower surface right) and spines

Purple-spined sea urchin tests and spines

Heart urchin tests (lower surface right)

Acorn worm poop

Sea pork, a colony of tunicates

Sea liver tunicates

Acorn Worm and Tunicates

RELATIVES: Acorn worms (not really worms) are in the phylum Hemichordata, linked to both echinoderms and tunicates. Attached tunicates are in the class Ascidiacea, and share the phylum Chordata with fishes, birds, and us.

IDENTIFYING FEATURES:

Acorn worms (commonly *Balanoglossus aurantiacus)* are evident from their finger-width, sandy poops (fecal casts) that lie in coiled piles. The burrowing animals are wormlike with an acorn-shaped proboscis and reach 3 ft (1 m) in length. The area surrounding an acorn worm burrow smells like iodine.

Sea pork *(Aplidium stellatum),* 10 in (25 cm), is a colony of tunicate animals individually known as zooids. The colonies arrive at the beach as white, pink, yellow, green, red, or purple, rubbery lumps. They generally have a flattened side and may have several lobes. The zooids are imbedded within the collectively shared rubbery tunic.

Sea liver *(Eudistoma hepaticum),* 10 in (25 cm), is a colonial tunicate with a lumpy shape like sea pork but is softer, slimier, and dark purple when fresh.

Leathery (pleated) sea squirts *(Styela plicata),* 4 in (10 cm), are tunicates that look like wrinkled potatoes. They have a basal (formerly attached) end opposite a puckered end with 4 lobes around a siphon, which squirts when squeezed. They wash ashore in singles and in attached groups.

Sandy-skinned tunicates *(Molgula occidentalis)*, 2 in (5 cm), look like soft potatoes rolled in the sand. Their thin test is imbedded with mud, sand, and shell bits and they are often still attached to shells and rocks.

HABITAT: Acorn worms live in U-shaped burrows in the inter-tidal zone of low-energy beaches. Sea pork and sea liver colonies grow on rocks and other hard, shallow-water substrates. Leathery sea squirts and sandy-skinned tunicates live in shallow waters attached to rocks, docks, shells, and debris.

A mass of leathery sea squirts

DID YOU KNOW? Acorn worms swallow sand just below the surface creating a depression that accumulates bits of organic stuff coming in with the tide. The animal takes in this food along with a lot of sand. Their odor of iodine comes from a bromine compound that may be an antibiotic protecting the animal's soft, naked body from infections.

Although tunicates may be barely recognizable as a living animal, they have a lot in common with humans, including gill slits, a rigid notochord, and a hollow nerve cord (traits we each have during early development). Larval tunicates swim like tadpoles before settling into an attached existence. As adults, they are wrapped in tunics made of tough, fibrous cellulose.

A leathery sea squirt squirts when squeezed

All tunicates make a living by filtering particles from seawater. Even a plum-sized sea squirt can filter bathtubs of water each day, removing (and eating) about 95% of the suspended bacteria.

Sea pork resembles salt pork in appearance, but not in flavor. Tunicates are an acquired taste appreciated by tulip snails, stingrays, and sea turtles.

Sandy-skinned tunicates

A number of shark species hunt fish near the surf

Atlantic sharpnose shark

Bluntnose stingray (arrow indicates tail spine)

Atlantic stingray

Sharks and Rays

RELATIVES: These fishes are in the class Chondrichthys and are related to others with skeletons of cartilage.

IDENTIFYING FEATURES:

Sharks in the surf zone include: Bonnethead sharks *(Sphyrna tiburo)*, 3.2 ft (1 m), with a shovel-shaped head; **Atlantic sharpnose sharks** *(Rhizoprionodon terraenovae)*, 3.5 ft (1.1 m), with a relatively long snout; sand tiger sharks *(Carcharias taurus)*, 10 ft (3 m), with similar dorsal-fin sizes and thin snaggled teeth; and blacktip sharks *(Carcharhinus limbatus)*, 8 ft (2.4 m), with black fin-tips.

Bluntnose stingrays *(Dasyatis say)*, 3 ft (1 m) width, are disk shaped with a whiplike tail bearing a hardened spine at the base.

Atlantic stingrays *(Dasyatis sabina)*, 15 in (38 cm) width, resemble small bluntnose stingrays, but have a pointed snout longer than the distance between their eyes.

HABITAT: Sharks are most common in deeper waters but will enter the surf when small fish are plentiful. Bluntnose stingrays live in the surf and offshore. Atlantic stingrays live in estuaries.

DID YOU KNOW? Sharks bite Americans about 40 times per year. Dog bites send more than 330,000 annually to hospitals. Stingrays do not attack, but will thrust their spine if stepped on. The injury involves extreme pain. When wading, shuffle feet to flush buried rays.

Skate Eggcases

Clearnose Skate

Little Skate

RELATIVES: Skates are cartilaginous fishes, distantly related to sharks, that share the order Rajiformes with rays.

IDENTIFYING FEATURES:

Skate eggcases (mermaid's purses), 3.5 in (9 cm), are commonly from the **clearnose skate** *(Raja eglanteria)*, which breeds in the spring. The plasticlike eggcases are dark mahogany or black with four tendrils. Fresh ones without exit-slits may have a spherical yolk or wiggling **embryo.** The **little skate** *(Raja erinacea)* deposits eggcases with tendrils three-fourths their length, July through September.

HABITAT: Skates attach their eggcases, sometimes in clusters, to soft corals and other nearshore objects.

DID YOU KNOW? Clearnose skates reach 33 inches (84 cm) in length and little skates reach 21 inches (53 cm). These skates lay a pair of eggs every week or so during their breeding season. The clearnose skate may return to attach as many as 66 of these capsules to a single anchor spot. Eggs incubate about three months. As the embryo grows, a slit opens on the side of each horn, allowing seawater to enter. During this time, the skate embryo pumps water through its eggcase by beating its tail down one of the hollow tendrils. At hatching, the front of the eggcase ruptures and the skate emerges, unrolling its pectoral fins like a scroll.

Mermaid's purse bundle. Clearnose skate (inset)

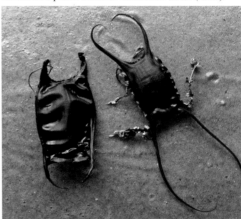
Clearnose skate (left) and little skate eggcases

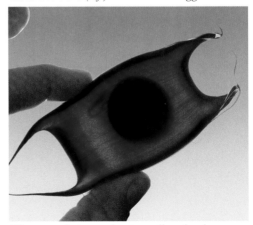
Clearnose skate egg showing yolk and embryo

171

Silver perch, max 11 in (30 cm)

Southern kingfish, max 20 in (50 cm)

Northern kingfish, max 18 in (46 cm)

Red drum, max 60 in (150 cm)

Atlantic croaker, max 21 in (53 cm)

Surf Catches *(Drums and Croakers)*

RELATIVES: These bony fishes (class Osteichthys, order Perciformes) share the family of drums and croakers (Sciaenidae).

IDENTIFYING FEATURES:

Silver perch *(Bairdiella chrysoura)* are silver with yellow fins. They have no chin barbel but do have a few spines on their preopercle (forward cheek) and a sharp anal fin spine.

Southern kingfish *(Menticirrhus americanus)* have a chin barbel and 7–8 dusky bands along their sides.

Northern kingfish *(Menticirrhus saxatilis)* resemble southern kingfish but with a dark V at the shoulder and a long spine extending from the first dorsal fin.

Red drum *(Sciaenops ocellatus)* are silver to bronze with one to several black spots on the upper tail base.

Atlantic croakers *(Micropogonias undulatus),* are grayish with brown spots forming wavy lines on their flanks. They have 3–5 chin barbels and a convex tail fin.

HABITAT: These are coastal and surf-zone fishes.

DID YOU KNOW? Members of this fish family are named for sounds they make, which the fish amplify using their air bladder as a resonating chamber. Kingfish are comparatively quiet.

Surf Catches *(Catfish, Bluefish, Jacks, and Flounder)*

Catfish   Bluefish and Jacks   Flounder

RELATIVES: Catfish (order Siluriformes) and flounder (order Pleuronectiformes) are only distantly related to bluefish and jacks, which share the order Perciformes with drums and croakers.

IDENTIFYING FEATURES:

Hardhead (sea) catfish *(Ariopsis felis)* have harpoonlike dorsal and pectoral spines, and distinct whiskers (barbels).

Bluefish *(Pomatomus saltatrix),* near shore, are blue-green above and light below with a large toothy mouth.

Florida pompano *(Trachinotus carolinus)* are silvery jacks with a yellowish anal fin and a low-slung jaw.

Jack crevalle *(Caranx hippos),* near shore, resemble pompano (same family) but have a larger eye and mouth.

Summer flounder *(Paralichthys dentatus)* have both eyes on their left side.

HABITAT: Coastal and surf zone.

DID YOU KNOW? Bluefish are separated by two distinct Southeastern populations: one that spawns in late summer between Cape Cod and Cape Hatteras, and one that spawns in early spring along the Gulf Stream between North Carolina and Florida. Pompano feed very close to the beach and specialize in sand-dwellers like coquina clams (p. 121) and mole crabs (p. 150).

Hardhead catfish, max 24 in (61 cm)

Bluefish, max 18 in (46 cm)

Pompano, max 17 in (43 cm)

Jack crevalle, max 18 in (46 cm)

Summer flounder, max 37 in (94 cm)

173

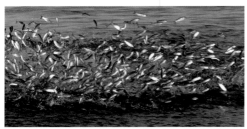

A leaping school of striped mullet, being chased

Striped killifish, male, max 6 in (15 cm)

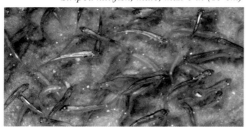

Atlantic silversides, max 4.5 in (11 cm)

Juvenile gulf kingcroaker, typically 4 in (10 cm)

Bay anchovy (A. mitchilli)*, max 4 in (10 cm)*

Other Fishes

RELATIVES: Mullets (order Mugiliformes), killifish (Cyprinodontiformes), silversides (Atheriniformes), croakers (Perciformes), and anchovies (Clupeiformes) are distantly related bony fishes.

IDENTIFYING FEATURES:

Striped mullet *(Mugil cephalus)* and white mullet *(Mugil curema)*, to 18 in (45 cm), have cylindrical bodies, widely separated dorsal fins and bulging eyes. They are similar in appearance and each can be seen in the surf as fingerlings being chased by predatory fish.

Striped killifish *(Fundulus majalis)* are silvery with an olive back and 15–20 black side bars (male) or dark longitudinal lines with bars near the tail (female).

Atlantic silversides *(Menidia menidia)* are slender with large scales and a mouth ending at the front of the eye. Colors are greenish above with a silver side band.

Gulf kingcroaker *(Menticirrhus littoralis)* juveniles are silvery with low-slung mouths and a single chin barbel.

Anchovies *(Anchoa* spp.) have a silvery body stripe and an enormous mouth for their size.

HABITAT: Coastal waters. These fishes are common in the surf and in runnels (beach lagoons, p. 29).

DID YOU KNOW? These fishes risk shallow waters and crashing surf to escape their many predators.

Alligator and Gopher Tortoise

Alligator

Gopher Tortoise

RELATIVES: Alligators (order Crocodilia) and turtles and tortoises (order Chelonia) are reptiles.

IDENTIFYING FEATURES:

American alligators *(Alligator mississippiensis),* max 14.5 ft (4.4 m) in males, 9.8 ft (3 m) in females, are unmistakable. Their tracks on beaches are alternating clawed footprints, with or without foot-drag swirls, aside a wavy tail-drag mark.

Gopher tortoises *(Gopherus polyphemus),* 14 in (36 cm) in shell length, are dark brown or grayish with shovel-like forelimbs and elephantine hind limbs.

HABITAT: American alligators live in brackish or fresh waters, including dune swales (p. 10), and nest in mats of old plant material. Gopher tortoises dig burrows in sandy scrub habitat including south Georgia's coastal dunes.

DID YOU KNOW? After unregulated hunting, alligators were close to extinction in the early 1960s. With a little over two decades of protection under the Endangered Species Act, populations recovered and the species was delisted in 1987. Gopher tortoises are considered Threatened in Georgia and Endangered in South Carolina. They occur on area beaches only on Cumberland Island, where they were introduced. The tortoises wander through dunes and feed on grasses and other plants.

A basking American alligator smiles in profile

American alligator tracks on a beach after a rain

Gopher tortoise, Georgia's state reptile

Beach tracks from a gopher tortoise

175

A female loggerhead scatters sand over her nest

A typical loggerhead nest the morning after

A late-emerging hatchling scurries to the surf

Loggerhead Sea Turtle

RELATIVES: Sea turtles are reptiles in the order Chelonia and share the family Cheloniidae with green turtles (p. 178).

IDENTIFYING FEATURES:

Loggerhead sea turtles *(Caretta caretta)* as adults average 37 in (95 cm) in shell length. They are orange-brown with a large head and a stout, tapered shell, which typically has scattered barnacles. **Nests** are circular or slightly elongate mounds with adjacent shallow pits. The **hatchling** has a lumpy, walnut-sized shell ranging from brown to gray.

HABITAT: Most loggerhead nests are between the wrack line and the dune. The majority of females nesting on Georgia and Carolina beaches have migrated from foraging areas between coastal Georgia and Delaware Bay. Some overwinter in Florida or in offshore Gulf Stream waters.

DID YOU KNOW? Loggerheads are federally protected as a Threatened species. Nests have 70–150 ping-pong-ball-sized eggs buried about 18 in (46 cm) beneath the sand. Each female loggerhead makes about five nests separated by two-week intervals during the May–August nesting season. Migrating hundreds of miles and laying hundreds of eggs is strenuous, which is why loggerheads typically take off 1–3 years between nesting trips. Hatchlings emerge from nests July–October, 45–60 days after eggs are laid. Nesting and the emergence of hatchlings occur mostly at night.

Signs of Sea Turtles

IDENTIFYING FEATURES:

Loggerhead tracks, 39 in (1 m) wide, have a wavy center straddled by alternating commalike swooshes from the turtle's rear flippers. Much less common on our local beaches, nesting green turtles *(Chelonia mydas)* crawl with a butterfly stroke and leave parallel flipper marks with slashes at the track margin. A thin tail mark is at the center.

Depredated nests are a hole in the beach with numerous scattered eggshells and animal footprints. Raccoons dig into nests from many angles and scatter eggs in all directions (p. 222). Foxes and dogs dig from one side only. Ghost crabs leave a burrow with eggshells near the entrance. Fish crows commonly feast on nests opened by other predators.

Hatchling emergence sign is typically a bowl-like depression with hatchling tracks fanning out seaward. Hatchlings leave their eggshells buried during a 1–5 day escape from the nest. The tracks of loggerhead hatchlings are 2–3 fingers wide and like miniature versions of the adult tracks.

DID YOU KNOW? In the southeast US, raccoons eat more sea turtle eggs than any other predator. Ghost crabs are a distant second. Hatchlings emerge at night and orient toward the brightest horizon. Because of this, the glow of some developed beaches lures hatchlings landward where few survive. Should a female hatchling beat the odds and survive to adulthood, she will return to nest on the beach where she hatched. This faithfulness to their natal beaches makes loggerheads nesting on Georgia and Carolina beaches genetically distinct from those nesting in Florida.

Tracks from a loggerhead sea turtle

Eggshells excavated by a ghost crab

Flipper tracks from dozens of emerged hatchlings

177

Dead loggerhead, marked with paint

A stranded juvenile green turtle

Diamondback terrapin

Sea Turtle Strandings and Terrapin

Strandings

Terrapin

IDENTIFYING FEATURES:

Strandings occur when turtles in nearby waters succumb to boat strikes, hooking or entanglement by fishing gear, drowning in trawls, or disease. **Stranded loggerhead sea turtles** *(Caretta caretta)* are subadults or adults, 20–37 in (50–95 cm) shell length, and have a large head with 4–6 scales between their eyes. **Stranded green turtles** *(Chelonia mydas)* are typically juveniles, 12–24 in (30–60 cm) shell length. They have smooth brown shells and two large scales between their eyes. Dead sea turtles recorded by biologists are marked with paint.

Diamondback terrapins *(Malaclemys terrapin,* family Emydidae) have a brownish carapace with deep growth rings. Most of their skin is gray with a peppering of black spots. Females reach 9 in (23 cm); males grow to half this size.

HABITAT: Loggerheads and green turtles live in coastal waters. Diamondback terrapins live in saltmarsh and bays and nest on the back sides sof barrier islands.

DID YOU KNOW? Stranded sea turtles represent important information, and live turtles can be rescued and released. Report strandings to state wildlife agencies. These turtles have different diets. Loggerheads eat whelks, horseshoe crabs, and other hard-shelled invertebrates. Green turtles eat seagrass and algae. Terrapins feed on small snails, clams, worms, and crustaceans.

Lizards and Snakes

Green Anole　　*Racerunner*　　*Black Racer*

RELATIVES: Lizards are reptiles that share the order Squamata with snakes.

IDENTIFYING FEATURES:

Green anoles *(Anolis carolinensis),* 7 in (18 cm), have a long tapered head and change their colors between an earthy brown and spring-leaf green. Males have a bright pink throat fan (dewlap).

Six-lined racerunners *(Cnemidophorus sexlineatus),* 9 in (23 cm), are brownish-gray whiptail lizards with six light lines down their back. They are fidgety and occasionally sprint at blazing speeds.

Black racers *(Coluber constrictor),* 5 ft (1.5 m), are indeed black and racy. They are nervous, sleek-bodied snakes with shiny scales and a white chin and belly. Juveniles to 12 in (30 cm) are tan with gray-brown blotches. Other snakes near beaches include eastern indigo snakes *(Drymarchon corais)* and eastern coach-whips *(Masticophis flagellum).* **Snake tracks** are either sinusoidal, wavy slithers, or straight caterpillar crawls.

HABITAT: Green anoles are slinky climbers and prefer leafy canopies. Racerunners are found on the ground in open dune areas. Black racers occupy all of these habitats.

DID YOU KNOW? These lizards feed on small insects. Each of these snakes is harmless. The venomous eastern diamondback rattlesnake is a rare beach visitor. Leave rattling snakes alone.

A male green anole displays his dewlap

Six-lined racerunner

Black racer with tracks inset

179

Adult common loon, winter

Red-breasted mergansers often "snorkel"

Adult red-breasted merganser, winter

Common Loon and Mergansers

RELATIVES: Loons (Gaviiformes) belong to a different order of birds from mergansers (Anseriformes), which are related to ducks and other waterfowl.

IDENTIFYING FEATURES:

Common loons *(Gavia immer),* 24 in (61 cm), are diving birds the size of a large duck and have a straight, pointed bill. Their winter plumage is a drab charcoal pattern with a whitish throat and breast. Loons sit low in the water.

Red-breasted mergansers *(Mergus serrator),* 16 in (41 cm), are diving ducks with a thin reddish bill and shaggy head-crest. They have a cinnamon head and gray back, except males November to May, who show a dark green head. Common mergansers *(Mergus merganser)* are not common in salt water and have lighter bodies with a white chin.

HABITAT: Loons and mergansers are occasionally found diving for fish in the surf but are more common in estuaries.

DID YOU KNOW? Loons from the northern US and Canada winter in the Southeast. They are often stressed by the long migration and end up stranding on our beaches (p. 220). On land, even healthy loons can't walk. Their feet are behind them, like an outboard motor, and can only make swimming movements. Mergansers work in groups to herd fish and often "snorkel" with their heads under water.

Northern Gannet

RELATIVES: Gannets (family Sulidae) are in the order Pelecaniformes, which includes pelicans and cormorants.

IDENTIFYING FEATURES:

Northern gannets *(Morus bassanus),* 31 in (79 cm), are big, sleek seabirds with thick bills. Their tapered wings span six feet (1.8 m). Adults are white with black wing tips and have a wash of pastel yellow covering the head. Immature birds are brown with white flecks.

HABITAT: Gannets are oceanic birds that are sighted off beaches when the fishing is good. They are recognizable at a distance due to their steep, forceful, folded-wing dives into offshore waters. Sick and injured gannets often strand on the beach during the winter. Summer breeding for northern gannets occurs on steep cliffs and rocky islands around Newfoundland. The birds nest in dense colonies and reuse their nest site annually, creating prominent piles of feathers and fish remains.

DID YOU KNOW? Gannets are supreme divers: their eyes aim forward for binocular fish-spotting, they have no nostril holes, and their bills seal water-tight even under high water-impact. Their smack into the water is cushioned by a system of air cells beneath their skin. Dives begin as high as 100 ft (30 m) and end as deep as 50 ft (15 m) below the water's surface.

Juvenile in flight

A juvenile's flecks expand into solid, adult white

Adult

181

Adult brown pelican in flight

Immature brown pelican diving

Adults in winter. Left bird is molting

Brown Pelican

RELATIVES: Pelicans share the order Pelecaniformes with gannets, cormorants, and frigatebirds.

IDENTIFYING FEATURES:

Brown pelicans *(Pelecanus occidentalis),* 41 in (104 cm), are bulky birds with a long, pouched bill and stubby legs. They are one of our largest birds and have a wingspan to 7 ft (2.1 m). Winter adults have grayish bodies, a white neck, and a pale yellow cap. During summer breeding, the back of the bird's long neck turns chestnut brown in both sexes. Immature birds are brown above and light below. Pelicans fly with their head resting back on their shoulders. White pelicans *(Pelecanus erythrorhynchos)* are mostly white with yellow bills and are rare at the beach.

HABITAT: Brown pelicans dive for fish off the beach, float just outside the surf, and use the beach for resting. They are equally common in coastal lagoons. Their colonial nesting sites are mostly in mangroves on small coastal islands.

DID YOU KNOW? Yes, "his bill will hold more than his belican": about three gallons of fish and water, twice the capacity of his stomach. But before a pelican swallows its catch, it drains its bill from the corners of its mouth. Fish are carried in its gullet, never in its bill pouch. So the Dixon Merritt limerick, "he can take in his beak, enough food for a week," is not completely accurate.

Double-crested Cormorant

RELATIVES: Cormorants (family Phalacrocoracidae) are distantly related to pelicans and gannets.

IDENTIFYING FEATURES:

Double-crested cormorants *(Phalacrocorax auritus),* 27 in (69 cm), are snake-necked waterbirds with a hooked bill. They fly with rapid wingbeats, as ducks do. Adults are blackish with a naked, orange throat pouch and turquoise eyes. Immature birds are lighter, especially on the throat and breast, and have brown eyes. Cormorants fly with a distinctive crook in their neck.

HABITAT: Cormorants surface-dive for fish outside the surf but are most common in bays and marshes. They nest in trees on coastal islands. During migration, they are seen flying in large V-shaped flocks and on the water in dense **rafts**.

DID YOU KNOW? With poor oil glands, cormorants must hang their wings out to dry before flying. But their lack of feather sealant makes them less buoyant and allows them to swim deeper. Their nests were formerly fashioned of sticks and seaweed, but now include "recycled" materials such as rope, fishing nets, and shredded plastic. Chicks occupy these open nests during the heat of summer. To prevent overheating and dehydration, adults shade their young and bring them water, poured from the adult's mouth to that of the begging chick.

Double-crested cormorant in flight

Double-crested cormorant drying its wings

A raft of cormorants

Black vulture soaring

Adult black vulture

Turkey vulture soaring

Adult turkey vulture

Vultures

Black Vulture

Turkey Vulture

RELATIVES: Our vultures (family Cathartidae) are newly thought to be more closely related to falcons (order Falconiformes) than to the vultures of Asia and Africa.

IDENTIFYING FEATURES: Vultures are dark, broad-winged, soaring birds.

Black vultures *(Coragyps atratus),* 22 in (56 cm), are black with whitish wingtips and a stubby, squared tail. Adults have a gray, wrinkled face, and juvenile faces have a less-wrinkled, youthful look. Black vultures soar with straight wings and give quick flaps between glides.

Turkey vultures *(Cathartes aura),* 25 in (64 cm), are blackish-brown with pale flight feathers and have a long, rounded tail. They have a bare head (red in adults, dark in juveniles) with large nostrils. These vultures soar with wings held up in a V, rocking erratically as if trying to maintain a drunken balance.

HABITAT: Both vultures catch dune updrafts and use the beach as a travel corridor. Vultures on the beach are there because of dead fish and other stranded delicacies. Eggs are laid on the ground in spring, often in thick brush.

DID YOU KNOW? Turkey vultures find carrion by smell and are often first to arrive. Black vultures find carrion by sight, and in groups they are tougher competitors at a carcass.

Great Egret

RELATIVES: Egrets share the family Ardeidae with other herons and are distantly related to storks, sharing with them the order Ciconiiformes.

IDENTIFYING FEATURES:

Great egrets *(Ardea alba),* 32 in (81 cm), are tall, white wading birds with a long slender neck, yellow, spearlike bill, and long, dark legs. In breeding adults, the bill is more orange, the skin in front of the eyes (the lores) is lime green, and long, wispy plumes extend from the back beyond the tail (both sexes). Great egrets fly with their neck folded into an S-shape.

HABITAT: Great egrets stalk the surf and other coastal waters for fish but are more common inland. They nest in trees May–August and share island colonies with other herons and with ibises.

DID YOU KNOW? Egrets specialize in skewering fish with their sharp-pointed bill. By the late 1800s, plume hunting had reduced numbers of egrets in the southeast US to near extinction. The newly formed National Audubon Society began a mission to protect these birds from hunting, which has resulted in the recovery of great egrets and in the selection of this bird as the symbol of the Society. Key accomplishments in conserving these and other wading birds have included protections under state laws, the Migratory Bird Treaty of 1916, and the establishment of our national wildlife refuges.

In flight, an egret's neck is held in an S-shape

Great egret with mullet

Breeding plumage shows long plumes past the tail

185

Snowy egret in flight

Juvenile with yellow leg-stripes. Adult foot (inset)

Adult with a surf-caught Atlantic thread herring

Snowy Egret

RELATIVES: Egrets share the family Ardeidae with other herons.

IDENTIFYING FEATURES:

Snowy egrets *(Egretta thula),* 20 in (51 cm), are delicate, medium-sized wading birds with a shaggy head and all-white plumage. They have a thin neck and a black bill with yellow skin in front of their eyes. Their legs are black with yellow toes. Adults in breeding plumage have especially long, lacy plumes, and the skin on their face develops a tinge of red or orange. Juveniles look similar to adults except for a paler bill and a yellow stripe up the back of each leg.

HABITAT: Snowy egrets stalk calm shallows in the swash zone, in runnels, and near inlets. They also occur in freshwater systems. Their nests are made February through August in trees, often hanging over water.

DID YOU KNOW? Snowy egrets were decimated by plume hunters during the late 1800s but recovered dramatically following a ban on plume hunting. In the last couple of decades, snowy egrets have resumed their decline, losing almost three-fourths of their numbers due to loss of coastal wetlands. These egrets use a foot-stirring method to rake up small fish and shrimp from the bottom in shallow waters. Their golden toes may help achieve success by either spooking or luring their potential prey.

Reddish Egret
and **Tricolored Heron**

Reddish Egret

Tricolored Heron

Adult reddish egret in flight

RELATIVES: Egrets and herons are in the family Ardeidae.

IDENTIFYING FEATURES:

Reddish egrets *(Egretta rufescens),* 25 in (64 cm), are mid-sized wading birds with dark legs and a long neck. Their two color forms, dark and white, are not related to age. Dark-form adults are gray with a rusty head and neck, and dark juveniles are pale gray. White-form birds (least common) are all white with a pinkish, dark-tipped bill. Breeding adults get shaggy neck plumes.

Tricolored herons *(Egretta tricolor),* 21 in (53 cm), are slender with a dark, slate-blue neck and back, white and rust throat stripe, light ponytail plumes, and a white belly. The bill is blue with a dark tip. Juveniles are rusty reddish on their neck and sides.

A frenetically fishing reddish egret juvenile

HABITAT: Reddish egrets chase fish in the swash zone. Tricolored herons stalk calm lagoons and marshy shorelines.

DID YOU KNOW? Reddish egrets have a more energetic fishing style than other wading birds. They often work to concentrate schools of small fish by running in circles around their prey and flailing their wings. They may also use their wings to shade the water, reducing the surface glare that would hide a small stationary fish.

Adult tricolored heron in spring

187

A great blue heron, just taking flight

Adult great blue heron

The spearlike bill is suited for large fish

Great Blue Heron

RELATIVES: Herons are allied with egrets in the family Ardeidae.

IDENTIFYING FEATURES:

Great blue herons *(Ardea herodias),* 38 in (97 cm), are tall, grayish wading birds with a long neck and a thick, pointed bill. Adults have a shaggy foreneck, rusty nape, and a white face. Breeding adults have a white crown stripe and stylish black head streaks that trail thin, ponytail plumes. Bands of three colors at the shoulders and down the legs share the pattern of Neapolitan ice cream. Immature birds have a subdued cast to the adult colors and have no plumes. The all-white form of the great blue heron is rare in Georgia and the Carolinas.

HABITAT: These herons stalk the swash zone, giving a scrutinizing sideways scan to each spent wave. Most nesting is in early spring atop tall trees near water.

DID YOU KNOW? These are America's largest herons. They specialize in fish but also eat frogs, snakes, birds, and rodents. Those claiming surf fishermen as territory will give intimidating displays to interlopers. Conscientious fishermen never feed fish carcasses to lurking herons. The herons can choke to death trying to eat a filleted fish that is too large to swallow.

White Ibis

RELATIVES: Ibises are in the family Threskiornithidae and are distantly related to herons and storks.

IDENTIFYING FEATURES:

White ibises *(Eudocimus albus),* 22 in (56 cm), are medium-sized wading birds with a long neck and long, down-curved bill. Adults are white with black wing tips. In breeding, their pinkish legs and faces turn scarlet, and their normally pink bill becomes black toward the tip. Juveniles are brown with a white belly and have a dusky orange bill and grayish legs. As juveniles mature, white patches grow to replace their brown plumage.

A group of adults probing for mole crabs

HABITAT: White ibis groups stroll along the swash zone using their bills to probe the wet sand. Their long legs and bills allow them to capture buried mole crabs as waves surge around them. They also feed in marshes, swamps, mud flats, and occasionally, on lawns and golf courses. During late spring, they make their nests in trees near water.

Juvenile in the swash

DID YOU KNOW? These are social birds. Feeding flocks may contain dozens, and separate flying V-formations may comprise hundreds. Colonies formerly included thousands of pairs, but this bird has suffered severe declines of 90% since the 1940s due to loss of wetlands. Parents feeding chicks need access to food from fresh water. Although adults enjoy coastal crustaceans, chicks cannot tolerate such a salty diet.

Adults have red faces and blue eyes

189

Maturing wood stork with contrasting wing pattern

Adult

Adult showing scaly, featherless head

Wood Stork

RELATIVES: Wood storks are in the family Ciconiidae.

IDENTIFYING FEATURES:

Wood storks *(Mycteria americana),* 35 in (89 cm), are large wading birds with a dark, bald head and a thick, down-curved bill. Adults have a naked, wrinkled neck, and white body plumage with black feathers bordering the trailing edges of their wings. The sexes look alike, although males are slightly larger. Immature birds have a grayish, feathered neck. Flying wood storks extend their necks and trail their long legs.

HABITAT: Coastal wood storks are most common near inlets. Nesting occurs in late winter and early spring in tall wetland trees.

DID YOU KNOW? Wood storks hunt in shallow waters using a method called "grope feeding" to catch fish and other small animals. Aquatic critters touching a stork's submerged, open bill get snapped up in one of the fastest reflex moves known for any vertebrate. Unfortunately, many wood storks occupy beaches because they are fed fish carcasses, which are not good for them (see page 220). These birds have declined in number by about 75% in the last several decades and are federally listed as Endangered.

Osprey

RELATIVES: Ospreys are allied with hawks, eagles, and kites within the family Accipitridae, order Accipitriformes.

IDENTIFYING FEATURES:

Ospreys *(Pandion haliaetus),* 22 in (56 cm), are large raptors with long, narrow wings. Their upperparts are dark brown, and their breast, belly, and leg feathers are mostly white. Ospreys have a white head and a dark stripe behind each eye. In flight, an osprey holds its wings with a characteristic bend at the wrist (mid-wing). Females are slightly larger than males and have a more streaked breast. Immature birds look like adults but have streaked breasts and lighter backs.

HABITAT: Ospreys live and breed near open water. They are most likely to nest in dead trees, normally the tallest in the area. But where tall trees have been removed, ospreys nest atop towers, electrical poles, and channel markers.

DID YOU KNOW? Ospreys hover over water to target fish, then plunge feet-first to grab their prey. In addition to oversized, curved talons, an osprey's feet have spiked pads for gripping slippery fish. In flight, fish are held aerodynamically head-forward, as if they were a bomb ready to be dropped. This fore-and-aft grip is possible due to the osprey's reversible outer toes.

Hovering over a target fish precedes a plunge

A feet-first catch

Fish are carried as aerodynamic cargo

191

Winter plumage showing white rump

Adult male before spring migration

Adult in winter. Note the tiny hind toe

Black-bellied Plover

RELATIVES: Plovers are in the family Charadriidae and are allied within the order Charadriiformes, which includes other shorebirds, gulls, and terns.

IDENTIFYING FEATURES: Plovers of all stripes have a habit of running in straight lines and stopping abruptly in a still, head-up posture.

Black-bellied plovers *(Pluvialis squatarola),* 9.5 in (24 cm) tail to bill tip, are medium-sized, stocky shorebirds that have gray legs and a dark, thick bill. Most beach birds have a pale, mottled back and breast with white underparts and a white rump. In spring and late summer, many show either the beginnings or vestiges of breeding plumage, which is black from face to belly, with a thick white border around the face and throat. Sexes appear similar although the female breeding plumage is less vibrant than the male. Immature birds look like winter adults but have a streaked breast and more contrast to their spotted upperparts.

HABITAT: These plovers breed in Arctic tundra. Southeast beaches are one of many wintering locations. They feed on worms and mole crabs in the swash zone.

DID YOU KNOW? Black-bellied plovers are sensitive to disturbance and end up being sentinels for other shorebird species. They are the only American plover to have a hind toe (albeit tiny) on its foot.

Piping Plover

RELATIVES: Piping plovers share the family Charadriidae with other plovers.

IDENTIFYING FEATURES:

Piping plovers *(Charadrius melodus),* 5.5 in (14 cm) tail to bill tip, have a white collar and orange legs. During summer breeding, mature birds sport a black forehead, dark breastband, and a dark orange bill with a black tip. Immature birds and winter adults lack the dark markings on the head and breast.

HABITAT: These plovers are found in coastal areas and require barren dry sand for their nesting. Important nesting habitat includes overwash areas (p. 12) or inlet flats with unvegetated access to the estuary. In winter, they rest on the upper beach and forage for insects and worms in the wrack, swash zone, and nearby mudflats. Piping plovers nest April–August from North Carolina to Canada.

DID YOU KNOW? Piping plovers are disappearing, and are federally listed as Threatened. An important threat to these birds has been the loss of undisturbed areas for breeding, feeding, and resting. North Carolina's Outer Banks provide the southernmost nesting beaches for this bird, with about 50 pairs nesting there in recent years. The plovers arrive at potential breeding areas in mid-March. If undisturbed, pairs will look after 2–4 sand-colored eggs in a scrape nest and remain in the vicinity 3–4 months until chicks are fledged.

Adult piping plover in winter

Immature piping plover

Adult with chick

193

Immature Wilson's plover with a mole crab (p. 150)

Female on eggs within a "scrape" nest

Precocious days-old chicks stay close to parents

Wilson's Plover

RELATIVES: Other plovers, family Charadriidae.

IDENTIFYING FEATURES:

Wilson's plovers *(Charadrius wilsonia)*, 6.25 in (16 cm) tail to bill tip, are small shorebirds with grayish-brown upperparts and white underparts. They have a white collar, and a white patch between their eyes. The stout black bill and tan legs of Wilson's plover distinguish it from other small plovers. During spring breeding, the male has a black breast-band, and the female's band is brown. Immature birds look like winter adults but with scaly-patterned upperparts and an incomplete breastband.

HABITAT: Wilson's plovers nest mid-March through June near the dune on sparsely vegetated overwash flats and sand spits (p. 50). They feed on fiddler crabs, mole crabs, and other invertebrates on beaches and tidal mudflats.

DID YOU KNOW? Like other plovers, Wilson's uses "distraction displays" to lure predators away from its nest. These include false brooding, in which the parent moves from the nest and crouches, pretending to sit on a nest. Parents also feign a broken wing by walking away from the nest with one wing dragging on the ground. Each display is meant to lure away potential predators and should be a clue to savvy beachcombers that they are causing a dangerous disturbance (p. 220).

Semipalmated Plover

RELATIVES: Other plovers, family Charadriidae.

IDENTIFYING FEATURES:

Semipalmated plovers *(Charadrius semipalmatus),* 6 in (15 cm) from tail to bill tip, are the most common plover on most Southeastern beaches. They have brown upperparts with a white collar and white underparts. Their bill is short and thin and their legs are yellow-orange. In flight, white stripes are visible on the wings and the dark tail has a fringe of white. In breeding plumage, semipalmated plovers have a thick, black, breastband and an orange base to their bill. The sexes look similar although the female is larger and duller in color. Immature birds resemble adults but have yellower legs and pale, scaly upperparts.

HABITAT: These active little plovers breed during summer in open areas near the Arctic Circle south to Nova Scotia. They forage on small invertebrates found in the wrack and swash zone of varied beaches. They are also common in saltmarsh and on tidal mudflats.

DID YOU KNOW? In their northern breeding areas, semipalmated plover parents swim with their chicks across water channels to forage on islands and land spits. They are aided by a partial webbing between their toes, which is how the semipalmated plover got its name.

Semipalmated plover showing wingstripes

Adult before spring migration

Adult in winter

Landing adult showing black head and white belly

Adult sexes look alike, summer and winter

Adults have an orange ring around a yellow eye

American Oystercatcher

RELATIVES: Oystercatchers are alone in the family Haematopodidae and are distantly related to plovers, sandpipers, gulls, and terns.

IDENTIFYING FEATURES:

American oystercatchers *(Haematopus palliatus),* 16 in (41 cm), are large, boldly colored, long-billed shorebirds. Their back is a deep brown, their neck and head are black, and their belly is stark white. They have an unmistakable red-orange bill, orange rings encircling their yellow eyes, and robust, pinkish legs. Breeding and winter plumage are almost identical and the sexes look similar. In comparison to adults, juveniles have a darker end to their bill, a darker eye with a less conspicuous eye ring, and lighter upperparts. American oystercatchers are usually seen on beaches in pairs or in small groups.

HABITAT: These skittish shorebirds forage for oysters, clams, crabs, sea urchins, marine worms, and mole crabs along estuarine shores and ocean beaches. They nest on undisturbed beaches and on exposed shell/sand bars between March and July.

DID YOU KNOW? Oystercatchers overwinter throughout the Southeast, but the most important nesting area is near Cape Romain, SC. As their name suggests, oystercatchers use their chisel-like bills to open oysters and other bivalves.

Willet

RELATIVES: Willets are allied with other sandpipers in the family Scolopacidae and are distantly related to plovers, gulls, and terns.

IDENTIFYING FEATURES:

Willets *(Tringa semipalmata),* 14 in (35 cm), are long-legged, long-billed, somewhat drab-looking shorebirds. Most birds are gray-brown above and white below with a gray chest. Their long, straight bill is dark and their legs are bluish-gray. In flight, willets show a striking wing pattern with a deeply contrasting white band. In breeding plumage, willets are mottled on the upper wings, back, neck and head. The sexes look alike with the female being slightly larger. Juveniles resemble adults but are browner with scaled, white-edged back feathers. Wintering willets are from a western race with a longer, thinner bill.

HABITAT: Eastern willets breed along our coast April through mid-June. Most birds seen at other times are from a western race that breeds on the prairies of the northern US and southern Canada. Our eastern willets nest in grassy dunes and saltmarsh. They forage in coastal waters and are common on beaches in the swash zone, where they probe for coquina clams and mole crabs.

DID YOU KNOW? The willet gets its name from the alarming and repetitious *pill-will-willet* call it produces while aggressively defending its nesting area.

Adult in winter showing contrasting wing pattern

Western willet in winter

Eastern willet adult in spring

Ruddy turnstones reveal bold patterns in flight

Winter adult. Juvenile (inset)

Spring adult male on a migration stopover

Ruddy Turnstone

RELATIVES: Ruddy turnstones are sandpipers in the family Scolopacidae.

IDENTIFYING FEATURES:

Ruddy turnstones *(Arenaria interpres),* 7 in (18 cm) tail to bill tip, are stocky shorebirds with orange legs and a dark, wedge-shaped bill. In flight, all ages show a bold set of white wing stripes and a white rump. Juveniles and winter adults are white below with a brownish head, bib, and back, but juveniles have a paler face. Breeding turnstones before and after their spring migration have a black and white head, white belly, black bib, and a rusty-red back and wings. Breeding males have a whiter head with less streaking than the female.

HABITAT: Turnstones forage on both the lower and upper beach but favor the wrack line. They are also common near other coastal waters and on fishing piers. These birds migrate to nest on islands in the Canadian Arctic and return to winter on Southeastern beaches.

DID YOU KNOW? Ruddy turnstones earn their name by flicking aside beach wrack that may hide amphipods, insects, and other tasty invertebrates. These birds often allow close observation by cautious beachcombers and are a joy to watch. On their Arctic breeding grounds, male turnstones make nestlike scrapes in the ground as part of their courtship ritual, but the female constructs the actual nest.

Red Knot

RELATIVES: Red knots are sandpipers in the family Scolopacidae.

IDENTIFYING FEATURES:

Red knots *(Calidris canutus),* 10 in (25 cm) tail to bill tip, are stout, robin-sized sandpipers with greenish legs and a straight black bill. Red knots in flight show a pale, mottled-gray rump as their key identifier. Southeastern birds are generally pale gray above and light below. Some area red knots may show hints of breeding plumage during the spring and late summer, when the bird's head and breast turns brick red, and the back turns gray with rusty spots.

HABITAT: Red knots prefer the lower beach for foraging and roost on upper beaches that are broad and undisturbed. They migrate to nest on the high, open tundra of the central Canadian Arctic.

DID YOU KNOW? Recoveries of banded birds show that red knots wintering in southern South America fly over 20,000 miles (32,000 km) each circuit. Keep this in mind when you see a flock on the upper beach being "lazy." Chances are, the birds are taking some critical downtime between connecting flights. Many red knots on Southeastern beaches during spring and fall are just passing through. Some of their most important staging areas for spring migration lie north in Delaware Bay where formerly massive flocks fed on eggs from spawning horseshoe crabs (p. 157).

Red knots have mottled rumps

Winter adult, with colored leg bands

Red knots on a Georgia beach, passing through

199

All sanderlings show a white wing stripe

Adult in spring

Adults probing for mole crabs, winter

Sanderling

RELATIVES: Sanderlings are sandpipers in the family Scolopacidae.

IDENTIFYING FEATURES:

Sanderlings *(Calidris alba),* 7 in (18 cm) tail to bill tip, are frantic, wave-chasing little sandpipers with black legs and a straight, black bill. In winter, adult and immature plumage is pale gray above and white below. Summer immatures are checkered black and white above and white below. Spring adults are rusty on the back, head, and breast. All plumages show bold white wing stripes and a white rump divided by a broad line.

HABITAT: Sanderlings probe for mole crabs like tiny sewing machines in the wet sand briefly exposed between swash and backwash. They migrate in spring to nest on the Arctic tundra.

DID YOU KNOW? Females occasionally lay eggs in two nests, each belonging to a different male, although most sanderlings are monogamous. At the opposite extreme, some birds not ready to nest will remain in winter foraging areas while most other birds migrate. Sanderlings dodge waves to catch mole crabs (p. 150) and other small invertebrates that burrow within swash-zone sands. They may either swash-run in groups, or go it alone. Lone birds may be defending a patch of beach with an abundance of mole crabs. These territorial birds can be seen to chase other sanderlings away in a hunched-over run.

Least, Semipalmated, and Western Sandpipers

Least and Western Sandpipers

Semipalmated Sandpiper

RELATIVES: Other sandpipers, family Scolopacidae.

IDENTIFYING FEATURES:

Least sandpipers *(Calidris minutilla)*, 5.5 in (14 cm), are our smallest sandpiper. They look much like the other "peeps" on this page but have yellow-green legs and a thin, droopy, black bill.

Semipalmated sandpipers *(Calidris pusilla),* 6 in (15 cm), have a bill that is short, stout, and straight. Like the western sandpiper, adults in winter are gray-brown above and in late summer are rufous above with dark mottling and a streaked breast. Semipalmated sandpipers taking flight give out a *cherk* call.

Western sandpipers *(Calidris mauri),* 6 in (15 cm), have a bill that is moderately long with a slight droop. Otherwise, they look similar to semipalmated sandpipers and are most reliably distinguished by their flight call, which is a high-pitched *cheep*.

HABITAT: All are most common on tidal flats and low-energy beaches. They breed in the Arctic tundra. Semipalms do not winter here and are just passing through during spring and late-summer migrations, en route to South America.

DID YOU KNOW? Semipalmated sandpipers are named for their webbed feet. This trait is rare in sandpipers, but western sandpipers have it too.

Least sandpiper in winter

Semipalmated sandpiper, late summer

Western sandpiper, late summer

201

Dunlins in flight, winter

Adult dunlin in winter

Purple sandpiper on a rock jetty in summer

Dunlin and Purple Sandpiper

Dunlin

Purple Sandpiper

RELATIVES: Other sandpipers, family Scolopacidae.

IDENTIFYING FEATURES:

Dunlins *(Calidris alpina),* 7.5 in (19 cm) tail to bill tip, are medium-sized sandpipers with dark legs and a slightly droopy, long, black bill. Flying dunlins show their white rump with a dark central line. Adults with rusty-red backs and black belly patches are seen near Southeastern beaches before and after their summer breeding migrations. The sexes look similar, although the female is slightly larger.

Purple sandpipers *(Calidris maritima),* 8.5 (22 cm), are dark and plump with a long, curved bill and stout legs. The base of the bill is yellow-orange, as are the legs. Despite the name, this bird is mottled gray in breeding plumage and slate-gray in winter, perhaps with a faint tinge of purple.

HABITAT: Dunlins prefer to probe for invertebrates on low-wave-energy tidal flats, and purple sandpipers are seldom far from beach rocks. Each migrates to nest on the Arctic tundra, May–July.

DID YOU KNOW? Dunlin bill length differs 30 percent or more between individuals, which may reflect connections between the world's dunlin populations. Some American dunlins overlap their breeding areas with birds that winter in Asia. Purple sandpipers winter farther north than any of our other sandpipers.

Marbled Godwit and Short-billed Dowitcher

Marbled Godwit

Short-billed Dowitcher

RELATIVES: Other sandpipers, family Scolopacidae.

IDENTIFYING FEATURES:

Marbled godwits *(Limosa fedoa),* 20 in (50 cm), are large shorebirds with a long, slightly upturned bill, which has a pink base and a dark tip. Plumage is marbled buff-brown with cinnamon wing linings. Breeding birds have chest barring; nonbreeding and immature birds have a plain breast.

Short-billed dowitchers *(Limnodromus griseus),* 10 in (25 cm), are medium-sized shorebirds with a plump body, greenish-yellow legs, and a long, straight, dark bill. Winter birds are grayish, and birds ready to breed become flecked with cinnamon and black. Adult sexes look similar.

HABITAT: Both prefer to probe deeply for invertebrates within tidal flats. Marbled godwits breed on islands over the Canadian Arctic, and short-billed dowitchers nest near water in central Canada.

DID YOU KNOW? Marbled godwit nests are well hidden. A parent's tactic is to remain still when a predator intrudes, to the extent that a biologist can pick a bird up off its nest. More than other sandpipers, dowitchers have a flexible bill tip that allows them to grasp deeply buried prey (and do the Elvis lip-curl).

Marbled godwit showing cinnamon wing linings

A trio of marbled godwits, late spring

A short-billed dowitcher in winter

203

Adult (L). Yawning gull (R) is in its first summer

Breeding adult in flight

Juvenile before its first winter

Laughing Gull

RELATIVES: Gulls are allied with terns and skimmers in the family Laridae and are distantly related to plovers and sandpipers.

IDENTIFYING FEATURES:

Laughing gulls *(Larus atricilla)*, 16 in (40 cm), are slender, long-winged gulls. Adults have a smooth gray back and dark legs. Juveniles are brownish with a scaly back. Like most gulls, their bill tip droops. In breeding plumage, laughing gulls have a black head and a deep red bill and legs.

HABITAT: These gulls are common on beaches and throughout other coastal areas. They nest May–June on partially bare islands within bays and sounds along the Atlantic coast.

DID YOU KNOW? Laughing gulls are the beach bird most likely to steal food from your hand, and their call will make you think that they've thoroughly enjoyed the prank: *ha-ha-ha-hah-haah-haah*. Their forward nature is promoted by beachgoers who keep these birds addicted to high-test junk food. Their natural forage is opportunity seafood, including relatively fresh wrack-line treats (sea carrion). Breeding males and females build their nest together, but if a male has no mate, he may begin his own nest platform and use it to attract a single female.

Ring-billed Gull

RELATIVES: Gulls share the family Laridae with terns and skimmers.

IDENTIFYING FEATURES:

Ring-billed gulls *(Larus delawarensis),* 18 in (45 cm), are medium-sized, large-headed gulls with pale gray backs. Their light bill has a distinct black ring at its tip. Juveniles have brownish scalloping above, a black band on their grayish tail, pink legs, and a wide ring at the end of their pinkish bill. Adults are lighter, have a yellow bill with a narrow band, and sport yellowish legs. Sexes look alike, although the male is slightly larger.

HABITAT: Ring-billed gulls loaf and search for food at beaches, bays, lagoons, lakes, and urban areas. They migrate to breed in southeastern Canada and bordering New England states.

DID YOU KNOW? This gull is a resourceful scavenger with the reputation of being the "fast food gull." This comes from their habit of hanging out at beach-side burger joints where they will gladly ensure that dropped french fries don't go to waste. The healthier part of their diet comes from fish dipped on-the-fly from surface waters and from treats gleaned from wrack lines and mudflats. These birds show orientation to the Earth's magnetic field as youngsters, and adults return to nest sites within a few paces of the previous year's location.

Adult in late winter

A juvenile's first winter plumage

Adult winter plumage

205

Adult in flight showing black trailing wing edge

First-year plumage

Bonaparte's gulls often paddle along the surf

Bonaparte's Gull

RELATIVES: Gulls share the family Laridae with terns and skimmers.

IDENTIFYING FEATURES:

Bonaparte's gulls *(Larus philadelphia),* 11 in (28 cm), are dainty, ternlike gulls with a gray back, gray wings with a black trailing edge, and a light head with a dark spot behind the eye. Its legs are pinkish-orange and its bill is thin and black. Juveniles are brown above with dark markings on the head and paler legs. First-year birds look similar to juveniles but have gray, dark-patterned upperparts. Breeding adults (not seen in the Southeast) have a jet-black head with white crescents above and below the eyes. Sexes appear similar.

HABITAT: Bonaparte's gulls are winter visitors to Southeastern beaches, where they loaf near quiet tidepools or pluck small fish from the water, either on-the-fly or while paddling the surf. They breed during summer in middle Canada where they nest in fir and spruce trees.

DID YOU KNOW? This gull is named for Charles Lucien Bonaparte (a nephew of Napoleon), who made important contributions to ornithology in America. Bonaparte's is the only gull that commonly nests in trees. During the summer breeding season, most of their diet consists of insects.

Black-backed Gulls

Great Black-backed Gull   *Lesser Black-backed Gull*

RELATIVES: Gulls share the family Laridae with terns and skimmers.

IDENTIFYING FEATURES:

Great black-backed gulls *(Larus marinus),* 28 in (71 cm), are extra-large gulls with a thick bill and pink legs. Juvenile birds have brownish plumage with a checkerboard back and a dark bill. Over three winters, maturing gulls gradually assume adult plumage: white underparts and a sooty-black back. Breeding adults have a yellow bill with a red spot on the lower tip.

Lesser black-backed gulls *(Larus fuscus),* 20 in (52 cm), are similar in appearance to great black-backed gulls but are much smaller. Other differences are that adult lesser black-backed gulls have a dark gray (not black) back, more head-streaking in winter, and yellow legs.

HABITAT: Both gulls are seen loafing on beaches either alone or in small groups. Lesser black-backs nest on the Icelandic tundra. Great black-backs breed on small islands and beaches of the northeastern US and eastern Canada, and in winter may feed far out at sea.

DID YOU KNOW? The great black-backed gull is the largest gull species. It was hit hard by the feather trade prior to the 1900s. Lesser black-backs are much more common in Europe.

Immature great black-backed gull. Adult (inset)

1st (L) and 2nd (R) winter great black-backed gulls

Juvenile lesser black-backed gull. Winter adult (inset)

207

Adult in spring

Adult in winter

First-year plumage

Herring Gull

RELATIVES: Gulls share the family Laridae with terns and skimmers.

IDENTIFYING FEATURES:

Herring gulls *(Larus argentatus),* 23 in (59 cm), are our most commonly seen large gull. Juveniles and first-year birds are brownish and have a dark bill with a pale base. Second-year birds become paler with a hint of gray and have a pinkish, black-tipped bill. Adults have a light gray back, pink legs, and a yellow bill with a red spot on the lower tip. Although the adult's head is streaked in winter, breeding birds have a head that is an immaculate white. The sexes look alike with the male being slightly larger.

HABITAT: Our herring gulls breed in summer on islands across the northern US and Canada. They feed most commonly near water but also frequent garbage dumps. They loaf on open beaches as well as beach-side parking lots.

DID YOU KNOW? Herring gulls are moving south. Some of their northernmost breeding areas have been taken by great black-backed gulls and their southern shift has displaced some laughing gulls. Most herring gulls seen on Southeastern beaches are immature birds and non-breeders. Breeding birds often stay near nesting areas. These birds inspired Richard Bach's novel *Jonathan Livingston Seagull.* Despite the title there are no "seagulls." These seabirds are most correctly described as "gulls."

Gull-billed Tern and Black Tern

Gull-billed Tern   *Black Tern*

RELATIVES: Terns share the family Laridae with gulls and skimmers, and are distantly related to plovers, oyster-catchers, and sandpipers.

IDENTIFYING FEATURES:

Gull-billed terns *(Sterna nilotica),* 14 in (35 cm), are stocky, mid-sized terns with wide wings, a stout black bill, and black legs. Breeding adults have a black cap, and in winter, the head is white with a dark smudge behind the eyes. Wings are pale with black tips. Immature birds resemble winter adults.

Black terns *(Chlidonias niger),* 10 in (25 cm), are small, dark terns with a thin black bill. Breeding adults have a dark head and chest and gray wings. Winter birds are white in front with a dusky crown and nape. Immature birds look like winter adults but have scaly-patterned backs.

HABITAT: Gull-billed terns nest on barrier island beaches near estuarine marsh. Black tern colonies occur within inland freshwater marshes. Both terns winter on the northern coast of South America.

DID YOU KNOW? Gull-billed terns have an unusually broad diet that includes insects, small crabs, and chicks of other tern species. Black terns seen feeding near Southeastern beaches, mostly in August, are on a prolonged southerly migration.

Breeding adult gull-billed tern

Immature black tern at sea in summer

Adult black tern in summer, on flotsam

Adult in fall

Adult in spring

Adult in winter

Caspian Tern

RELATIVES: This tern shares the family Laridae with gulls and skimmers.

IDENTIFYING FEATURES:

Caspian terns *(Sterna caspia),* 20 in (49 cm), have black legs, a black cap, and a thick, pointed, reddish bill with a dark tip. They are our largest terns. Immature birds have black edging to their back feathers but adults are silvery gray and white. In winter, their cap fades into speckles, beginning on their forehead. The sexes look alike.

HABITAT: These terns loaf on beaches and sandbars as singles or in small groups where they are often outnumbered by royal terns. They feed on fish by plunge-diving into coastal waters. Caspian terns nest in summer near water around the Great Lakes, in eastern Newfoundland, some artificial islands on Florida's gulf coast, and on Little Egg Island, Georgia (p. 47). Except for a few Southeastern breeding islands, most of these birds seen August–October are on their way to southern Florida and the Caribbean.

DID YOU KNOW? Caspian terns share nesting colonies with other terns and black skimmers. These birds can live a long life. One wild Caspian tern was re-sighted over a 26-year period. Like most seabirds, these terns drink salt water and are able to excrete excess salt through their nasal glands.

Royal Tern

RELATIVES: This tern shares the family Laridae with gulls and skimmers.

IDENTIFYING FEATURES:

Royal terns *(Sterna maxima)*, 18 in (45 cm), are large terns with a dark cap and a relatively slender orange bill. In comparison to Caspian terns, royal terns are smaller with a lighter bill. In winter, the royal tern's cap trails shaggy feathers in the style of wind-blown male-pattern baldness. Immature birds look similar to winter adults, and the sexes look alike.

HABITAT: Royal terns feed on fish from coastal waters. Most nesting is in large colonies on coastal islands, April–July. Important colonies occur in Virginia, North Carolina, and Little Egg Island, Georgia. Royal terns make a scrape-nest on shelly sands. The mated pair surrounds their egg (often only one) with a circular nest rim that is cemented with their own guano. Wintering royal terns fish near shore near many Southeastern beaches.

DID YOU KNOW? Royal tern chicks from many nests hang out together in a group known as a crèche, which may eventually accept every chick in the colony. Parents find their own chick among hundreds by recognizing its call. Juveniles are fed by parents for months, even after migrating away from the breeding colony. Although parents seem pestered by these begging kids, the meals may greatly enhance growth and survival.

Immature royal tern, winter

A first-year bird (right) begs a parent for food

Breeding adult (L) and immature (R)

Winter adult in flight

Adult (L) and begging first-year bird (R)

Adult with mustard-colored bill tip

Sandwich Tern

RELATIVES: This tern shares the family Laridae with gulls and skimmers.

IDENTIFYING FEATURES:

Sandwich terns *(Sterna sandvicensis)*, 16 in (40 cm), are medium-sized terns with a black cap, black legs, and a long, thin, black bill. Adults have a pale yellow tip to their bill. Their black cap is complete during summer breeding and shows a male-pattern baldness style during winter. Immature birds look like winter adults, and the sexes look alike.

HABITAT: These terns plunge-dive for fish in the surf and other shallow coastal waters. They nest May–July on coastal islands from Virginia to Florida. Most nesting occurs with royal terns. These two species often share crèches in which chicks are communally looked after.

DID YOU KNOW? You can remember this bird by its mustard-tipped bill, as in sandwich mustard. The tern is named for the Sandwich Islands (as Captain James Cook named them), now known as the Hawaiian Islands. Both the islands and the sandwich were named for the Earl of Sandwich (one of Cook's financial backers and a fan of meals between bread slices). Ponder that full circle as you eat your picnic lunch and watch the terns dive for theirs.

Forster's Tern

RELATIVES: Terns share the family Laridae with gulls and skimmers.

IDENTIFYING FEATURES:

Forster's terns *(Sterna forsteri)*, 13 in (33 cm), are medium-small terns with a long, forked tail and orange legs. Winter birds have a black eye mask, which turns into a cap by the spring breeding season. The bill is dark with an orange base. Immatures resemble winter adults, and the sexes look alike.

HABITAT: These terns feed on small fish in shallow coastal waters and commonly loaf on Southeastern beaches in winter. Forster's terns nest on floating mats of grass in marshes scattered from the western Gulf to the Great Lakes and New York State. They nest singly or in loose colonies and feed on insects while at inland breeding sites.

DID YOU KNOW? Although the range of a Forster's tern can span the US from north to south, this bird actually has one of the smallest ranges of our tern species. They breed in the same areas as black terns (p. 209), where some cross-species feeding of chicks apparently occurs. Their nests are often atop old muskrat dens or abandoned waterbird nests. This bird is named for Johann Reinhold Forster, a pastor and naturalist who made many ornithological discoveries with Captain Cook on his world voyage in 1772.

Adult in flight showing deeply forked tail

Beach-resting adult in late summer

In winter, masks fade to eye spots

213

Adult hovering above the surf before a plunge

A male courts a female with a gift anchovy

A female succumbs to her fisherman's charm

A least tern chick tries to look like the beach

Least Tern

RELATIVES: Terns share the family Laridae with gulls and skimmers.

IDENTIFYING FEATURES:

Least terns *(Sternula antillarum),* 9 in (23 cm), are tiny terns with short yellow legs and a yellow bill with a black tip. During spring and summer breeding, adults have a black cap with starkly contrasting white forehead. Winter adults have a black eyestripe, a white cap, and a dark bill. Immature birds resemble winter adults, and the sexes look alike.

HABITAT: These terns feed on small fish in coastal waters. Least terns breeding in the southeastern US winter in South America from Venezuela to Brazil. Their nesting here was mostly on beaches, but due to human disturbance most colonies have retreated to gravel rooftops of large buildings built near water. Breeding takes place from late April to early August.

DID YOU KNOW? Breeding least terns are sensitive to disturbance and will dive-bomb nest-colony intruders. With undisturbed beaches rare, and their second-choice of gravel rooftops being replaced with more modern roofing, the future of our littlest tern is uncertain. Southeastern states have designated this species as Threatened, Endangered, or a species of concern, because of nesting habitat loss. A few remote beaches remain where careful human visitors can enjoy the bird's aerial feats and family life from a distance.

214

Common Tern

RELATIVES: Terns share the family Laridae with gulls and skimmers.

IDENTIFYING FEATURES:

Common terns *(Sterna hirundo),* 15 in (38 cm), are mid-sized terns similar in appearance to Forster's terns (p. 213). Common terns differ in having much darker wingtips and a dark outer edge to the tail. Adults in spring and summer have a black cap, red legs, and a red bill with a black tip. Winter adults and immature birds have a black nape and dark bill.

Common tern in flight showing dark wing tips

HABITAT: Common terns breeding between the Carolinas and New England nest April–June on bare, isolated islands in saltmarsh and sounds. They often roost on wide beaches and delta islands (p. 50), and feed in loose groups on small fish they catch a few miles offshore. Early spring and fall migrants along the Atlantic coast may also be birds that breed near the Great Lakes and across central Canada. The common tern winters along the northern coast of South America.

Adult showing dark tail edges, red legs and bill

DID YOU KNOW? Male and female common terns have distinct parental roles. Males "courtship feed" females before and during egg-laying. Both sexes attend the nest, but females sit on the eggs more. Once the chicks hatch, females stay at the nest while males forage. About 75 percent of a chick's food comes from the male.

Immature bird in late summer

A black skimmer skimming

Black skimmers nest in colonies

Skimmers loafing on the lower beach

A knife-thin lower bill allows skim-fishing

Black Skimmer

RELATIVES: Skimmers are in the family Laridae with gulls and terns.

IDENTIFYING FEATURES:

Black skimmers *(Rynchops niger),* 16 in (41 cm), are medium-sized, short-legged seabirds decked out in Halloween colors. They have a long, unmistakable, scissorlike bill with a red-orange base and dark tip. Their lower bill is knife-thin and much longer than the upper bill. Adults have a black cap and upperparts, and immatures are darkly mottled above. Sexes look alike, although males are slightly larger and have a longer bill.

HABITAT: Skimmers fly so that their lower bill can skim through surface waters where small fish are caught unaware. They nest May–August on beaches, exposed sand bars, and gravel rooftops, often with various tern species. Most of our skimmers winter along the coast from southern North Carolina through Central America.

DID YOU KNOW? Skimmers are able to fish by feel during dawn, dusk, and at night. Birds resting during the day have probably returned from a very early morning of fishing. They appreciate each other's company and typically cluster in dense groups. If disturbed, these birds will yip like a pack of excited Chihuahuas. Southeastern states consider this seabird to be Threatened, Endangered, or a species of concern, because of nesting habitat loss.

Swallows and Fish Crow

Tree and Barn Swallows

Fish Crow

RELATIVES: Swallows (family Hirundinidae) and crows (family Corvidae) are in the order Passeriformes with many other "perching" birds.

IDENTIFYING FEATURES:

Tree swallows *(Tachycineta bicolor)*, 6 in (15 cm), have a darting, erratic flight pattern and are shaped like stubby fighter jets. They are white below, shiny blue-green on top, and have a short bill. Similar **barn swallows** *(Hirundo rustica)* have a longer, forked tail and are rusty-orange below.

Fish crows *(Corvus ossifragus)*, 16 in (41 cm), are robust, dark, broad-winged perching birds. They are similar to the inland American crow *(C. brachyrhynchos)* but are slightly smaller and have a different call. Fish crows express a two-toned, nasal-sounding *UH-uh*, like the negative indication children give when they don't want to do something.

HABITAT: Both swallow species migrate and feed in flight along the dune line, late summer and spring. Fish crows haunt many coastal habitats, and on beaches they frequent the wrack line. They nest high in trees, usually near water, April–May.

DID YOU KNOW? Tree swallows often form dense flocks that swirl in flight like a bird tornado. Crows are clever, with smarts to rival chimpanzees. These birds use stick tools and can count.

Tree (upper) and barn (lower) swallows in flight

A fish crow searches the beach for opportunities

In sun, a crow's black plumage appears iridescent

217

A juvenile common grackle feeds on seaoats

An adult common grackle catches a mole crab

Red-winged blackbirds. Males show epaulets

A female red-winged blackbird plucking seaoats

Blackbirds

RELATIVES: Blackbirds are passerines in the family Icteridae.

IDENTIFYING FEATURES:

Common grackles *(Quiscalus quiscula),* 13 in (32 cm), are long-legged blackbirds with a tapered, down-curved bill. Juveniles are brown with dark wings and dark eyes. Adults are dark from a distance, but iridescent indigo in the sun. An adult's eyes are bright and golden.

Red-winged blackbirds *(Agelaius phoeniceus),* 8 in (20 cm), are stocky blackbirds with a thin, conical bill. Females are dark brown with light streaks and a white eyebrow. Males are glossy black with distinct shoulder patches (epaulets) of red and yellow.

HABITAT: Common grackles feed in a wide array of open areas and nest in inland treetops. Red-winged blackbirds feed in open space near water and nest in marsh reeds.

DID YOU KNOW? Both of these gregarious blackbird species feed on seaoats in the dune, but are most common inland. The most popular red-winged blackbird males may have up to 15 mates. These males fiercely defend their breeding territories, spending about a quarter of their daylight hours chasing others away. Interlopers drawing ire include other males, potential nest predators, and even big animals, including horses.

Bird Migrations

Southeastern beaches are a guiding line along the Atlantic flyway—the route taken by hundreds of species of birds in eastern North America during their spring and fall migrations. Many of these birds use beaches temporarily for roosting or feeding, but others are only seen high above as their flocks pass by in V-formations. Birds that are likely to stop in for a beach visit include large flocks of **sandpipers** (p. 197–203), **purple finches** *(Carpodacus purpureus)*, and **yellow palm warblers** *(Dendroica palmarum)*. Other birds passing through in high-altitude flocks include ducks, geese, and swans. Some birds that are seldom seen in groups, like the great blue heron (p. 188), can be seen migrating in formation along this well-flown aerial highway.

A mixed-species flock of migrating sandpipers

Birds of prey typically pass though as individuals. Of these, peregrine falcons *(Falco peregrinus)* may swoop in over the dune in attempts to catch unwary shorebirds. To avoid both predation and heat stress, many songbirds are nocturnal migrants, warbling to each other to keep the flock together as they navigate using the stars to maintain their course.

A purple finch snacks on northern sea rocket fruit

Migrations are difficult for birds. Long-distance migrants like red knots (p. 199) can lose more than half their body weight during their 4300-mile (6900-km) nonstop flights, losing not just fat but mass of muscle and internal organs as well. The benefits driving arduous fall trips are prospects for better food availability and weather. In the spring, migrations are directed northward where similar benefits favor raising the next generation of birds.

A migrating yellow palm warbler in the dune

"Loafing" shorebirds aren't lazy, they're exhausted

A stranded common loon

A royal tern hooked and entangled by fishing line

For the Birds

Birds are beautiful but vulnerable. As much as we appreciate them, they are among the first elements lost from a living beach. Keeping birds part of the beach experience requires accommodating some of their needs and offering occasional assistance.

LEAVE SOME SPACE: In part, birds hang out on beaches to relax (sound familiar?). Birds that seem to be "loafing" are probably desperate to get a little rest after an exhausting flight, swim, or run. Give resting birds a wide berth, enjoy them from a distance (get close with binoculars), and never allow dogs or children to scatter a flock. Breeding birds (April–August) need extra room. When intruders approach, agitated tern parents take flight and plovers feign wing injury to distract predatory attention. These are clues that you are too close. Their nests are mere scrapes, eggs are cryptically beach-colored, and chicks resemble fluffy, mottled cotton balls with legs that virtually disappear when still. Both eggs and chicks are easily stepped on or run over, and continual harassment forces parents to leave their young to die.

LEND A HAND: Don't feed bony fish carcasses to begging birds (exposed spines can pierce their insides), don't fish where birds will go after your bait, and never miss the opportunity to pick up discarded fishing line. If you hook a bird, never just cut the line. Reel the bird in and toss a shirt or towel over it (to calm the bird and control its bill). To complete the rescue of hooked, entangled, or otherwise troubled birds, phone 411 and ask for your local wildlife hospital.

Armadillo and Eastern Mole

Armadillo

Eastern Mole

RELATIVES: Armadillos (family Dasypodidae) are distantly related to anteaters. Moles are insectivores in the family Talpidae.

IDENTIFYING FEATURES:

Nine-banded armadillos *(Dasypus novemcinctus),* 28 in (71 cm), are hump-backed, armor-plated, troll-like critters with stubby legs, a long, tapered tail, and cupped ears. This squinty-eyed Mister Magoo of the animal world is likely to be found with its sensitive nose (and most of its head) probing the ground in a seemingly oblivious search for small subsurface animals and eggs.

Eastern moles *(Scalopus aquaticus),* 7 in (17 cm), have gray fur, a naked snout, spadelike forelimbs, and tiny eyes covered by skin and fur. They are always underground and are best recognized by their ridge tunnels.

HABITAT: Armadillos prefer woody, moist areas and are active on beaches only at night. Eastern moles search for earthworms and insects hiding beneath grassy fields with sandy soils.

DID YOU KNOW? Armadillos invaded the US from Mexico about 150 years ago. Moles dig deep nest-burrows with an array of tunnels that form the hub for shallow ridge tunnels, which are used only for gathering groceries. Moles on the beach are either brave explorers or desperately lost.

Armadillos are armored mammals

Armadillos leave tracks with a tail-drag mark

Temporary tunnels (ridges) made by an eastern mole

221

A raccoon bandit raiding a sea turtle nest

Raccoons are nervous in open daylight

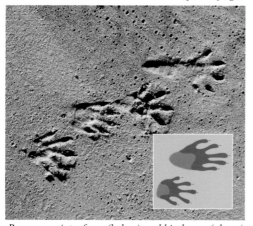
Raccoon prints, fore- (below) and hindpaws (above)

Northern Raccoon

RELATIVES: Raccoons share the family Procyonidae with coatis and kinkajous, and are distantly related to bears.

IDENTIFYING FEATURES:
Northern raccoons *(Procyon lotor),* 35 in (89 cm), are lumbering, heavy-bodied critters with a dark mask and a thick, ringed tail. Their coat color varies with habitat but most are grayish-red or buff. Raccoons have dexterous forepaws and a reputation for troublesome handiwork. Like most mammals, they are mostly nocturnal, but their activity on beaches leaves conspicuous handlike **tracks**.

HABITAT: Adaptation to suburban life has made the raccoon one of the most common wild mammals found in human-populated areas. It is likely that fresh water from mosquito impoundments and lawn irrigation, and food subsidies from garbage cans and fishing discards, have allowed raccoons to densely populate some beach areas.

DID YOU KNOW? The northern raccoon is one of seven raccoon species from North America and the Caribbean islands. Suburban raccoons are clever and coordinated enough to lift trashcan lids, climb bird feeders, and open simple latches. Purposefully feeding raccoons encourages all sorts of delinquent behavior. This crafty mammal is responsible for the vast majority of depredated sea turtle nests on Southeastern beaches.

Red Fox and Mink

Red Fox

American Mink

RELATIVES: Foxes share the family Canidae with dogs and coyotes. Minks are weasels that share the family Mustelidae with otters and skunks.

IDENTIFYING FEATURES:

Red foxes *(Vulpes vulpes)*, 39 in (100 cm), look like dainty dogs with a narrow muzzle and bushy, white-tipped tail. **Tracks** are like a small dog with extra fur between the paw-pads. Gray foxes (*Urocyon cinereoargenteus*) have a black tail tip and are rarer on beaches.

American mink *(Neovison vison)*, 24 in (61 cm), have a sleek body with short legs. Their fur is a glossy, chocolate-brown with a milk-white chin patch.

HABITAT: Because red foxes prefer open areas, they are the most common fox seen on beaches. Expecting parents dig dens out of old burrows and protect their litter of kits there until they can hunt on their own. American mink are semi-aquatic predators of crabs and fish in the saltmarsh behind many barrier island beaches. They den within rock jetties on saltmarsh-backed beaches. Both species are mostly nocturnal.

DID YOU KNOW? The red fox has the widest distribution of any member of the canine family, occupying most of the land in the northern hemisphere. American mink have declined drastically in the Southeast, and are being reintroduced to some South Carolina coastal saltmarshes.

Red fox

Sea turtle nest dug by a fox. Tracks (inset)

An American mink pops up in a rock jetty

223

Bobcats are seen mostly at dawn and dusk

Bobcat tracks   *Dog tracks*

Eastern cottontail, hop-and-stop tracks, droppings

Bobcat and Rabbit

Bobcat   *Eastern Cottontail*

RELATIVES: Bobcats (family Felidae) are distantly related to mink, dogs, and others in the order Carnivora. Cottontails (Leporidae) are with rabbits and hares in the order Lagomorpha.

IDENTIFYING FEATURES:

Bobcats *(Lynx rufus),* 35 in (89 cm), resemble super-sized house cats with ear tufts and stubby tails. Their spotted coats are tawny-gray in winter and reddish-brown in summer. **Tracks** are as from a middleweight dog but without claw marks.

Eastern cottontail rabbits *(Sylvilagus floridanus),* 17 in (43 cm), are reddish-brown rabbits with a white belly and their namesake cotton tail. Their pea-sized fibrous **droppings** are in piles, often near their conspicuous **tracks**.

HABITAT: Bobcats are nocturnal and prefer to hunt small mammals and birds where dense growth meets open space. Eastern cottontails are most active dawn and dusk. They are rare on the beach but regular foragers just behind the dune.

DID YOU KNOW? About 12 bobcat subspecies roam North America. They are solitary, territorial, and require hundreds of acres of living space. The rabbit droppings you find have probably been digested twice. Because rabbits cannot digest plant fiber, and the microbes in their intestine can, re-ingesting pea-sized feces is the only way to gain complete nutrition.

Feral Horses and Wild Boar

Feral Horse   *Wild Boar*

RELATIVES: Horses are odd-toed ungulates in the family Equidae. Wild boars are even-toed ungulates in the pig family, Suidae.

IDENTIFYING FEATURES:

Feral domestic horses *(Equus ferus)*, 60 in (152 cm) at the withers, have a familiar long face and a single-hooved track. Two breeds have developed on Southeastern barrier islands—the Cumberland Island horse of the Georgia island by the same name, and the Banker horse of North Carolina's Shackleford Banks, Ocracoke Island, and Currituck Banks.

Wild boars *(Sus scrofa)*, 24 in (60 cm), are dark, coarse-haired, scruffy wild-types of the familiar domestic pig. Their dual-toed **tracks** differ from deer in having rounded hoof tips.

HABITAT: Bands of feral horses range throughout the barrier islands they inhabit and graze in dunes and salt-marsh. Wild boar occupy nearly all terrestrial island habitats.

DID YOU KNOW? Each species has a lineage tracing back to intentional or accidental releases by Spanish explorers in the 1500s. Non-lethal horse population control is used to minimize destruction of native plants and bird nests. Wild boar are highly destructive to native wildlife and are dealt with more severely.

A horse grazes on seaoats, Cumberland Island, GA

Part of a feral band on Shackleford Banks, NC

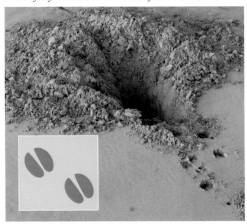

Beach rooting by a wild boar. Tracks (inset)

225

Bottlenose dolphins playing just off the beach

North Atlantic right whales have a V-shaped blow

The tail fluke of a North Atlantic right whale

Dolphin and Whale

Bottlenose Dolphin   North Atlantic Right Whale

RELATIVES: Cetaceans are divided between the toothed whales (Odontoceti, like dolphins) and baleen whales (Mysticeti, like the right whale).

IDENTIFYING FEATURES:

Bottlenose dolphins *(Tursiops truncatus),* 8.5 ft (2.6 m), are small, sleek, toothed whales that are gray above and white below. Their dorsal fin is rounded back and their head is melonlike with a distinct snout.

North Atlantic right whales *(Eubalaena glacialis),* 56 ft (17 m), are large black whales with no dorsal fin and a large head bearing pale, wartlike growths called callosities. They commonly swim in shallow water right off the beach. Right whales have two widely separated blowholes that create a V-shaped blow.

HABITAT: Bottlenose dolphins inhabit coastal and inshore waters and often swim, feed, and play off beaches. North Atlantic right whales feed on plankton in subpolar waters and migrate to nearshore waters off Georgia and northeastern Florida to bear their calves January through March.

DID YOU KNOW? North Atlantic right whales are Endangered; only about 350 remain. Vessel strikes are their leading threat. To protect whales and people, it is illegal for boats to approach right whales within 500 yards. Report whale sightings to the US Coast Guard.

Marine Mammal Strandings

A "strand" is a coastal area, and to be stranded means to helplessly run aground. Stranded marine mammals are often called **strandings**, as are the events involving these animals. Strandings commonly involve dolphins and other toothed whales, but also include large baleen whales and seals. Marine mammals that reach the shore are often unable to escape the surf because they are ill, injured, weak, or disoriented. Seals, however, are known to "haul out" on beaches to rest and bask.

Marine mammals are protected species, and their strandings are important events. A coordinated network of varied groups responds to these occurrences in the southeastern US. To contact this network, call 411 and ask for your state's "Marine Mammal Stranding Hotline." Live animals can be helped. Responders are trained to make humane decisions about euthanasia and transport for rehabilitation. Beach-stranded animals should not be pushed into the surf. While waiting for help for live animals, drape a wet cloth over the animal and keep the blowhole clear.

Dead stranded marine mammals can provide valuable conservation information. Biologists take measurements and samples that help resource managers understand marine mammal population changes and why strandings occur. In many cases, stranded animals show identifiable disease, or negative interactions with humans such as vessel strikes, ingestion of plastics, and entanglement in fishing gear. In other cases, the cause of the stranding is a mystery.

A right whale injured by a boat propeller

Bottlenose dolphins are common strandings

A stranded pygmy sperm whale (Kogia breviceps)

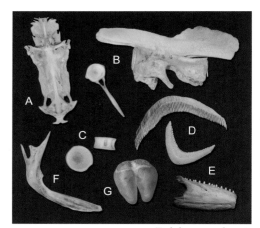

Fish bones and parts

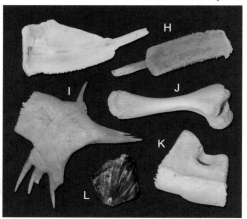

Sea turtle bones and scute

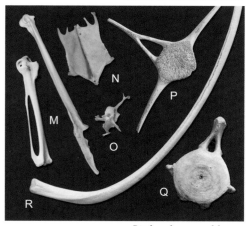

Bird and mammal bones

Verte-bits

Vertebrates are animals with backbones. These critters commonly leave bits of their bony skeletons on beaches.

Fish skulls contain many small bones that come apart, although a catfish cranium (**A**) is easily recognized by its spadelike shape and underlying crucifix. Vertebrae (backbone segments) from bony fishes (**B**) and sharks (**C**) are deeply cupped at each end. Eagle ray teeth (**D**) and toothy bluefish jaws (**E**) have odd shapes, and the shoulder girdle bones supporting bony fish fins are curved and thin (**F**). Dried fish swim bladders (**G**) look like inflated pants.

Sea turtles have large scales and dense bones with strange shapes. Their ribs are fused with upper-shell bone (**H**); flat, spiked plastron (lower-shell) bones (**I**); stout limb bones (**J**); marginal shell-bones (**K**); and carapace (upper-shell) scales or scutes (**L**) are often found where strandings (p. 178) have occurred.

Birds have bones so light that some can float in water. Easily recognized bird bits include long, thin wing bones (**M**) and the breastbone or sternum (**N**), which have keels and other processes to anchor the bird's large flight muscles. Bird neck vertebrae (**O**) often have delicate projections.

Marine mammals have large, dense bones. Dolphin vertebrae have long, flat processes (**P, Q**) and their ribs are gently curved (**R**). Whale ear bones are very persistent; there are fossilized examples of these in the *Beach Minerals* section.

BEACH PLANTS

What are Beach Plants?

Plants use sunshine to turn carbon dioxide and water into sugar, starch, fiber, and wood. But pulling this off at the beach can be difficult. Sure, the beach has sunshine, but it also has toxic salt, desiccating sands, and earth-altering sea-storms to reckon with. These tough conditions cull the list of dune plants that can thrive at the beach, and the hardy few making the list share some exquisitely adaptive characteristics.

As you'll see, not all beach plants have their roots anchored in sand. Some of the plants commonly found on the beach live elsewhere, such as marine plants—algae and seagrasses. These are what most folks would call "seaweed." At sea, these plants are fundamental pillars of marine food chains, and on the beach they are essential elements of the wrack (p. 17). The energy they gather out at sea is put to good use within the beach community. Many beach plants and animals are dependent upon the regular arrival of this gift from the sea.

Some of the most intriguing beach plants are those we never see except for their ocean-drifting pieces and parts. These plants may live many hundreds of miles away in places far from a sandy beach. But because their parts persist and float, they are able to travel the globe and announce their presence on our beaches. The seeds, nuts, fruits, and pods that make these journeys are collectively known as seabeans. Other drifting plant parts include stems, corky bark, and entire tree trunks—the sea-borne stuff generically categorized as driftwood. Note that despite its woody origin, lumber is placed in the section called *Hand of Man.*

The delicate blossom of the otherwise tough, waxy, water-stingy, prickly-pear cactus (p. 253)

Seaoats

RELATIVES: All of the following dune plants are angiosperms, which are flowering plants. Seaoats are a grass in the family Poaceae.

IDENTIFYING FEATURES:

Seaoats *(Uniola paniculata)*, leaves 2 ft (60 cm) high, dominate most Southeastern dune faces. It is a perennial grass with curl-edged blades growing from clumps that spread by underground stems (rhizomes). The gracefully flagging clusters (panicles) of golden oatlike seeds mature in summer and reach 6 ft (1.8 m).

HABITAT: These grasses grow on the dune and out onto the open, upper beach. They are among the most important dune-creating and dune-stabilizing plants.

DID YOU KNOW? Seaoats flower in July and are fertilized by wind-blown pollen. By late summer, winds also disperse the oatlike seeds throughout the dunes. Seeds remain dormant through the winter and germinate with spring rains. This grass lives in partnership with nitrogen-fixing bacteria and water-absorbing fungi that help the plants live in barren beach sands. Wild seaoats are protected from collection due to their critical role in maintaining dunes. Many native nurseries sell seaoats.

An immature clump of seaoats

Mature, midsummer seaoats blanketing a dune

Seaoat panicles, August

231

An immature clump of bitter panicgrass

Mature bitter panicgrass in summer

Bitter panicgrass panicles

Bitter Panicgrass

RELATIVES: Other grasses in the family Poaceae.

IDENTIFYING FEATURES:

Bitter panicgrass, or beach panicum *(Panicum amarum),* 2 ft (60 cm) high, is a perennial grass with waxy, bluish-green, broad blades. This grass grows in clumps spread by rhizomes. Its pale panicles with small seeds mature in late summer and reach 6 ft (1.8 m) tall.

HABITAT: Scattered clumps grow in the dune and on the open, upper beach. The dense clumps hold tenaciously to dune sands.

DID YOU KNOW? This plant's name belies its courage in facing frightening coastal growing conditions. The panic in its name actually refers to its seed-bearing panicles. Like seaoats, bitter panicgrass has a symbiotic relationship with nitrogen-fixing bacteria and water-absorbing fungi. The root-held fungi (mycorrhizae) send out microscopic tendrils (mycelia), much thinner than the tiniest rootlet, that vastly increase the cooperative surface area for absorbing water and nutrients. These mycorrhizae are chemically adept at taking in certain important nutrients. Such a plant-fungus partnership is essential for plant growth in barren soil, which means that it is critical for dune development.

232

Coastal Sandbur, Common Reed, and **Seashore Paspalum**

Sandbur   *Common Reed*   *Paspalum*

RELATIVES: Other grasses in the family Poaceae.

IDENTIFYING FEATURES:

Coastal sandbur *(Cenchrus spinifex)*, 6 in (15 cm) high and sprawling, is a perennial grass most conspicuous when its stickers penetrate tender feet. Winter through July, the plants may be without burs and look like lawn grass species.

Common reed *(Phragmites australis)*, 13 ft (4 m) high, is a large perennial grass with stiff, vertical stems and flat, straplike, tapering leaf blades that alternate along the top half of the stem. The plumelike flowers are silvery tan.

Seashore paspalum *(Paspalum vaginatum)*, 30 in (76 cm), is a prostrate, perennial grass with forked pairs of spikelets on long stems.

HABITAT: Sandburs grow throughout the dune and have the endearing habit of sprawling into foot-trails. Common reed grows in marshy back dune areas occasionally flooded by brackish waters. Seashore paspalum grows on the dune and within mowed turf near the beach.

DID YOU KNOW? To unstick sandburs, spit on the fingers you use to pull them out and don't squeeze. This keeps the micro-barbs on the bur-spines from clinging anew. Seashore paspalum is used as a hardy, salt-tolerant turfgrass on coastal golf courses.

Coastal sandbur, with seeds (burs, stickers)

Common reed, with seeds

Seashore paspalum, with forked spikelets

233

Seashore dropseed

Partially buried seashore dropseed, upper beach

American beachgrass

Seed spikes of American beachgrass

Seashore Dropseed
and American Beachgrass

Seashore Dropseed *American Beachgrass*

RELATIVES: Other grasses in the family Poaceae.

IDENTIFYING FEATURES:

Seashore dropseed *(Sporobolus virginicus),* 18 in (46 cm) high, is a perennial grass with long runners above or below the sand. On the beach, this grass grows upright with long blades. In the dune it may spread densely and have shorter, spiky blades. The seed head is a single spike evident in summer and fall. The similar seashore saltgrass *(Distichlis spicata)* has a seed head with several spikelets.

American beachgrass *(Ammophila breviligulata),* 30 in (76 cm) high, is a perennial grass that grows in erect, wiry clumps surrounding a single flowering spike or seed head.

HABITAT: Both species inhabit the dune but may also spread out onto the open beach.

DID YOU KNOW? Before irrigation, seashore dropseed was an important forage grass for grazing cattle in dry coastal areas. Although beachgrass can dominate dunes, it does poorly away from the coast. This may be due to its susceptibility to soil pathogens, which cannot survive the repeated erosion of sands near beaches. This beachgrass may actually require tough conditions that would torture other plants to death.

234

Smooth Cordgrass
and Saltmeadow Cordgrass

RELATIVES: Other grasses in the family Poaceae.

IDENTIFYING FEATURES:

Smooth cordgrass *(Spartina alterniflora),* 42 in (107 cm), has tough 1/4-in-wide (6-mm-wide) blades that are ribbed above and smooth below. Flower spikes appear in spring. Although the grass is a perennial, its stems die back in late fall.

Saltmeadow cordgrass *(Spartina patens),* 39 in (1 m) high, is a perennial grass with wiry (inrolled) blades in dense bunches. The grass flowers in late summer. Multiple, dark spikelets diverging from each stem mature with light brown seeds in the fall.

HABITAT: Smooth cordgrass grows in intertidal saltmarsh (p. 15). Where beach sand has washed into this habitat following overwash events (p. 12), smooth cordgrass may colonize the barren area from the marsh while saltmeadow cordgrass invades from the dunes. Saltmeadow cordgrass is less tolerant of being covered by sand than seaoats (p. 231) or American beachgrass (p. 234).

DID YOU KNOW? Smooth cordgrass dominates the intertidal zone of our coastal saltmarsh, an ecosystem that is among the most productive on Earth. Saltmeadow cordgrass has been used as a coastal source of hay for livestock.

Smooth cordgrass. Flower spike (inset)

Saltmeadow cordgrass in winter

Multiple spikelets identify saltmeadow cordgrass

235

Purple sandgrass. Flowers (inset)

Little bluestem

Pink muhly grass in late-summer bloom

236

Purple Sandgrass, Shore Little Bluestem, and Pink Muhly Grass

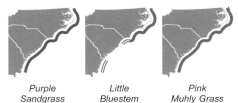

| Purple Sandgrass | Little Bluestem | Pink Muhly Grass |

RELATIVES: These are grasses in the family Poaceae.

IDENTIFYING FEATURES:

Purple sandgrass *(Triplasis purpurea),* 39 in (1 m) high, is a thinly clumped, sprawling annual grass with tiny purple flower clusters (August and September). Leaf blades are short, stiff, and alternate on stems that arc upward.

Shore little bluestem *(Schizachyrium littorale),* 36 in (91 cm), is a perennial grass that grows in erect clumps with light green or light blue leaf blades that curl outward. The grass turns tan to wine-red during the fall and winter.

Pink (hairawn) muhly grass *(Muhlenbergia capillaris),* 36 in (91 cm) high, grows in dense, wiry clumps without runners. August through October, wispy, purplish-pink flower heads appear.

HABITAT: These grasses grow in low dunes and dune slacks (p. 10).

DID YOU KNOW? Purple sandgrass hedges bets on the next generation by producing large seeds on low spikelets, and smaller seeds at upper levels. Large, low seeds sprout best if sands bury the plant and its neighbors. Otherwise, small upper seeds blow free of local competitors. Shore little bluestem is the host plant for the rare Loammi skipper butterfly *(Atrytonopsis loammi).*

Yellow Nutsedge and **Marsh Fimbry**

RELATIVES: Nutsedges and fimbries are sedges, family Cyperaceae.

IDENTIFYING FEATURES: Sedges have edges (3-angled central stems).

Yellow Nutsedge *(Cyperus esculentus)*, 8.5 in (21 cm), is a perennial sedge with an erect central stem, mostly covered by sheaths of the leaves. Light green leaf blades congregate at the base. The stem ends in clusters of yellowish floral spikelets, which appear July through September.

Yellow nutsedge

Marsh Fimbry *(Fimbristylis castanea)*, 39 in (1 m) high, is a densely clumped, perennial, grasslike sedge with narrow, inrolled, dark green leaf blades. The chestnut-brown stems end in cone-shaped terminal spikelets covered with brown scales.

HABITAT: Yellow nutsedge grows in scattered areas of the dune and landward. Marsh fimbry grows in salty, overwashed dune swales (p. 10).

Marsh fimbry in late summer

DID YOU KNOW? Yellow nutsedge grows from an edible tuber that has a sweet, nutty flavor. Its species name, *esculentus,* is Latin for succulent and delicious. Because nutsedge is a tough plant that grows with turf grass, and because its tubers persist after the plant is yanked, this native sedge has not made friends with connoisseurs of perfect lawns.

Conelike spikelets of the marsh fimbry

237

Adam's needle

Spanish bayonet

Mound-lily yucca. Flower stalk (inset)

Adam's Needle, Spanish Bayonet, and **Mound-lily Yucca**

Adam's Needle　　*Spanish Bayonet and Mound-lily Yucca*

RELATIVES: These plants are allied with other agaves and yuccas in the family Agavaceae. They are distantly related to lilies and asparagus.

IDENTIFYING FEATURES: Yuccas have swordlike leaves. In spring bloom, a panicle of creamy-white flowers extends upward on a tall stalk.

Adam's Needle *(Yucca filamentosa),* 2.5 ft (76 cm) high, has curled filaments along the edges of limp, blue-green leaves.

Spanish bayonet *(Yucca aloifolia),* 10 ft (3 m) high, has deep-green leaves with finely serrated edges and sharp, stiff tips. Browned leaves are commonly retained on the tall stem.

Mound-lily yucca *(Yucca gloriosa),* 6.5 ft (2 m) high, has bluish-green leaves with smooth margins and gently pointed tips.

HABITAT: All grow on the dune crest and landward.

DID YOU KNOW? Spanish bayonet grows for decades to a precarious height, falls over, and keeps growing. The flowers of many yucca species are edible either raw or cooked. Adam's needle flower petals enhance salads with a taste similar to Belgian endive.

Cabbage Palm and Saw Palmetto

Cabbage Palm

Saw Palmetto

RELATIVES: These palms are together in the family Arecaceae.

IDENTIFYING FEATURES: These palms have fan-shaped leaves (fronds).

Cabbage (sabal) palm *(Sabal palmetto),* 50 ft (15 m) high, has a vertical trunk and fronds with an arcing midrib. It flowers and fruits in summer.

Saw palmetto *(Serenoa repens),* 10 ft (3 m) high, has a sprawling, branching trunk. Its fronds have a serrated leafstalk and no obvious midrib. Most Atlantic-coast palmettos are silver-green. The palms flower and bear fruit spring through summer.

HABITAT: Both palms grow on the dune crest and landward; saw palmetto is the most tolerant of salt spray.

DID YOU KNOW? The cabbage palm is South Carolina's state tree. "Cabbage" comes from the taste of its edible bud or "heart," the harvest of which kills the tree. "Palmetto" comes from the Spanish word *palmito,* meaning little palm. Saw palmetto berries have become popular with maturing male baby-boomers, who benefit from an extract that treats prostate swelling. These may be some of the oldest plants in the Southeast; the largest specimens may be up to 700 years old.

Cabbage palms take a beating from salt spray

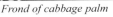

Saw palmetto

Frond of cabbage palm   *Frond of saw palmetto*

239

Earleaf (dune) greenbriar

Earleaf greenbriar showing tendril and fruit

Whitemouth dayflower

Earleaf Greenbriar
and **Whitemouth Dayflower**

Earleaf Greenbriar   *Whitemouth Dayflower*

RELATIVES: These are monocots like the grasses and palms. Greenbriars are in the family Smilacaceae, and day-flowers are in the family of spiderworts (Commelinaceae).

IDENTIFYING FEATURES:

Earleaf (dune) greenbriar *(Smilax auriculata),* 6.5 ft (2 m) in clumps, is a perennial, woody, climbing vine with prickles, tendrils, and dark-green ear-shaped leaves. Mature berries are dark purple.

Whitemouth dayflower *(Commelina erecta),* 2 ft (61 cm), a perennial, grows with erect or reclining stems bearing alternate lance-shaped leaves. Its flow-ers (May–October) have bright yellow anthers, two upper petals of sky blue, and a tiny, whitish lower petal.

HABITAT: Earleaf greenbriar frequently covers shrubs on the salt-pruned dune face. Whitemouth dayflower grows in dune slacks (p. 10).

DID YOU KNOW? Greenbriar is a thoroughly edible plant. Its shoots are tender and nutty flavored, and its roots can be made into flour, soup thickener, and jelly. Related plants, referred to as sarsaparilla, provided the roots for the original root beer. Leaves and stems of dayflowers are also edible when cooked as a pot-herb.

Crested Saltbush
and **Russian Thistle**

RELATIVES: These dicot plants share the family Chenopodiaceae with glasswort, sea blite, beets, and spinach.

IDENTIFYING FEATURES:

Crested saltbush *(Atriplex cristata),* 3.3 ft (1 m) high, is a bushy annual with scaly, silvery leaves that often curl and point upward.

Russian (saltwort) thistle *(Salsola kali),* 3.3 ft (1 m) high, is a bushy annual with short, sharp-tipped, spiky leaves. Its lower stems and leaves may be bright red. Dried bushes in winter take on the familiar look of **tumbleweeds** (which they are).

HABITAT: Both of these annuals burst into growth during summer and die back by the winter. Crested saltbush grows throughout the dune. Russian thistle grows at the dune base and out onto the open beach.

DID YOU KNOW? Crested saltbush has edible, pre-salted leaves. Russian thistle is an invader from Russia's Ural Mountains. As its brown skeleton rolls about on the beach, it releases hundreds of thousands of tiny seeds. These tumbleweeds cause the largest problems out west where they happily take over what once was prairie. On our beaches, this thistle competes with our native sea-rocket (p. 248).

Crested saltbush

Russian thistle

A beach tumbleweed from a Russian thistle

241

Virginia glasswort in September, with tiny flowers

Sea blite in late summer, with flower buds

Seabeach amaranth

Glasswort, Sea Blite, and Seabeach Amaranth

| Glasswort | Sea Blite | Amaranth |

RELATIVES: Glasswort and sea blite share the family Chenopodiaceae with crested saltbush and Russian thistle. Sea-beach amaranth is in the family Amaranthaceae.

IDENTIFYING FEATURES:

Virginia glasswort *(Salicornia virginica)*, 12 in (30 cm), is a perennial with erect, green, unbranched stems and leaves that are only fleshy sheaths. Tiny, pale flowers (August–October) are sunken into the stem joints. The plant turns wine-red during cold months.

Sea blite or annual seepweed *(Suaeda linearis)*, 6 in (15 cm), is a perennial south, and an annual north. The plant has slightly woody branching stems and dark green lance-shaped leaves. Greenish flowers bloom September–October.

Seabeach amaranth *(Amaranthus pumilus)*, 20 in (51 cm), has reddish prostrate stems with fleshy leaves. Yellow flowers are obscure, but many seeds are produced in July.

HABITAT: Virginia glasswort and sea blite grow near saltmarsh. Seabeach amaranth only grows in barren overwash areas near the dune base.

DID YOU KNOW? Glasswort concentrates toxic salt in its branch tips, which turn brown and fall off. Seabeach amaranth is disappearing and is protected as a federally Threatened species.

Indian Blanket Flower and Dune Sunflower

RELATIVES: These dicots share the family Asteraceae with daisies and the tall flower of sunflower-seed fame.

IDENTIFYING FEATURES:

Indian blanket flower or firewheel *(Gaillardia pulchella),* 18 in (46 cm), is an upright annual (north) or biennial (south) with alternating fuzzy leaves. Its long-stalked flowers come in yellow, orange, red, and two-tone combinations, and bloom repeatedly summer through fall. The frilly "Yellow Plume" variety of blanket flower is a cultivar that is widely planted in coastal gardens.

Dune (cucumberleaf) sunflower *(Helianthus debilis),* 2 ft (61 cm), is a sprawling perennial that shows long-stalked, yellow flowers with brown centers. The flower-base leaflets (bracts) are hairy, as are the alternating, stalked, triangular leaves. The plant is an annual throughout most of the Carolinas but often persists through Georgia's winters.

HABITAT: Each lives in sunny areas with sandy soils and throughout the dune.

DID YOU KNOW? In these asters, the "flower" is a composite head of many florets. Petals come only from the outer florets, which are sterile. Both flowers can be propagated by seed or by rooting small plants and watering them for a few weeks. After that, they do best when ignored.

Indian blanket flower

Indian blanket flower with seed heads

Dune sunflower

243

Sea oxeye daisy

Camphorweed flowers

Cottony goldenaster

Sea Oxeye Daisy, Camphorweed, and **Cottony Goldenaster**

RELATIVES: These plants share the family Asteraceae with Indian blanket flower and dune sunflower.

IDENTIFYING FEATURES:

Sea oxeye daisy *(Borrichia frutescens),* 3 ft (91 cm) high, is an upright, shrub-like perennial with fleshy gray-green leaves. Its yellow flowers bloom May–August, and dark brown seed heads follow in the fall.

Camphorweed *(Heterotheca subaxillaris),* 18 in (46 cm) high, is a biennial with thick, roughened, wavy-edged leaves and long-stemmed all-yellow flowers (summer–fall). Crushed leaves smell strongly of camphor.

Cottony goldenaster *(Chrysopsis gossypina),* 18 in (46 cm) high, is a biennial with a cottonlike fuzz to its leaves and flower base. Yellow flowers bloom September–October.

HABITAT: Each lives in sunny areas with sandy soils on low dunes. Sea oxeye daisy is also common near salt marshes.

DID YOU KNOW? Camphorweed's pungent smell comes from special leaf glands and dissuades grazers with a mixture of at least 41 volatile terpene compounds. This plant has been spreading north and is an example of how global climate change is affecting distributions of plants and animals.

Beach Marsh-elder

Beach marsh-elder

RELATIVES: Beach marsh-elder shares the family Asteraceae with other composite flowers including Indian blanket flower, dune sunflower, and daisies.

IDENTIFYING FEATURES:

Beach (dune or seacoast) marsh-elder *(Iva imbricata),* 39 in (1 m) high, is a perennial, shrubby herb with fleshy, alternating leaves. Some lower leaves may be opposite. Lower stems are woody. In late summer the plant's branches are festooned at their tips with green, pealike flowers, whose fruits turn brown in the fall along with the outer tips of the branches.

Leaves are sessile (attached broadly without petiole)

HABITAT: Beach marsh-elder grows from the dune crest out onto the open beach and is one of the Southeast's most salt-tolerant, woody plants.

DID YOU KNOW? This plant's specialized adaptations for avoiding salt pruning (p. 13) include leaves that have a waxy cuticle and that join to the stem solidly without a petiole. The cuticle and sessile leaf attachment work together to prevent salt damage during wind whipping. Because beach marsh-elder collects wind-blown sand, has such a tenacious root system, and can survive occasional saltwater inundation, this plant fosters many dunes and helps to stabilize them as they mature. For those sold on their value, plants can be easily started from transplanted suckers and cuttings.

Beach marsh-elder is highly salt tolerant

Green, pealike flowers appear in late summer

245

Canadian horseweed

Seaside goldenrod

Arching flower stalks of seaside goldenrod

Canadian Horseweed
and **Seaside Goldenrod**

Canadian Horseweed

Seaside Goldenrod

RELATIVES: These plants share the family Asteraceae with sunflowers and daisies.

IDENTIFYING FEATURES:

Canadian horseweed *(Conyza canadensis),* 5 ft (1.5 m), is an annual that begins as a rosette with irregularly margined paddle-shaped leaves. Mature plants have branched stems bearing smaller, thinner, occasionally crowded leaves without petioles. Tiny white flowers (June–October) dry pink-orange and mature into white-bristled seeds.

Seaside goldenrod *(Solidago sempervirens),* 3.5 ft (1.1 m), is a perennial with a tight clump of narrow, evergreen leaves at its base, topped by erect leafy stalks that may arch due to sea breezes. The flowering heads (August–November) are dense with deep-yellow flowers.

HABITAT: Both species grow in dune slacks as well as other sandy coastal areas.

DID YOU KNOW? Beachcombers with allergies take care; some get a reaction by handling horseweed. Grazing animals seem to ignore this plant because of its bitter taste. Goldenrod is used for the treatment of urinary system inflammations. The plant's genus comes from the Latin word *solido,* meaning to make solid (whole) or heal.

246

Pink Purslane and Sea Purslane

Pink Purslane

Sea Purslane

RELATIVES: Pink purslane is related to succulent herbs in the family Portulacaceae. Sea purslane is in the carpetweed family, Aizoaceae.

IDENTIFYING FEATURES:

Pink purslane (kiss me quick) *(Portulaca pilosa),* 3 in (8 cm) high, is a fleshy-stemmed annual arranged with alternating, fingerlike leaves, many with hairs at their base. Its pink flowers have five petals, are slightly smaller than a dime, and appear spring through fall.

Sea purslane (shoreline seapurslane) *(Sesuvium portulacastrum),* 24 in (61 cm) high, is a sprawling, fleshy, perennial herb with inflated, green or red leaves arranged oppositely on the stem. Its starlike, purple-pink flowers are without petals and have five colored sepals. Flowers bloom May through September.

HABITAT: Pink purslane grows on the dune crest and landward, including between the cracks in sidewalks. Sea purslane is a pioneer from the dune face out to the upper beach.

DID YOU KNOW? Sea purslane, sometimes called sea pickle, has edible stems and leaves that taste like salty green beans. In many parts of Asia this plant is sold in vegetable markets and is believed to treat kidney trouble and scurvy. Sea purslane can be propagated simply by poking a cut stem into moist soil.

Pink purslane

Sea purslane, showing reddish leaves and stems

Sea purslane flower

247

American sea-rocket. Lavender flowers (inset)

American sea-rocket fruits

The dried two-stage fruits of American sea-rocket

American Sea-rocket

RELATIVES: Sea-rockets are in the family Brassicaceae and are related to mustards and arugula.

IDENTIFYING FEATURES:

American (northern) sea-rocket *(Cakile edentula),* 12 in (30 cm) high, is a small upright annual that has wide, blunt-tipped, succulent leaves with irregular margins. Its four-petal flowers are either white (most common) or lavender. Both the plant and its dual-segmented fruits turn from green, to yellow, to brown, summer through fall.

HABITAT: Sea-rocket plants blast off with the first rains of spring and are among the first plants to reclaim the open beach that was swept clean by winter waves.

DID YOU KNOW? Sea-rocket greens taste like mild horseradish, similar to its leafy green cousin, arugula, of rocket (roquette) salad fame. Sea rocket's succulent leaves plump after rains to store water for drier times. Each stage of the plant's missle-shaped pods has seeds. The end stage is corky and breaks off to drift at sea, reach distant beaches, and sprout plants in new locations. The base stage stays attached to the dried plant, and when buried by wind-blown sand can start local plants.

Walter's Ground-cherry
and **Poorjoe**

Walter's Ground-cherry   *Poorjoe*

RELATIVES: Ground-cherries are in the tomato family, Solanaceae, and Poorjoe is in the coffee family, Rubiaceae.

IDENTIFYING FEATURES:

Walter's (sand) ground-cherry *(Physalis walteri),* 12 in (30 cm) high, is a perennial herb with fuzzy leaves and stems. Its yellow flowers appear spring through fall and its drooping fruit is a berry within a papery sac.

Poorjoe (rough buttonweed) *(Diodia teres),* 12 in (30 cm) high, is an annual herb with erect stems and opposite, sessile, lance-shaped leaves. The four-lobed, pale lavender flowers (June–October) have bristles at their base.

HABITAT: Walter's ground-cherry grows in sunny areas including the dune face. Poorjoe grows from the dune crest landward in sandy soil.

DID YOU KNOW? Walter's ground-cherry is closely related to a tasty, commercially grown ground-cherry called the tomatillo *(P. philadelphica)*. Poorjoe gets its name from the poor soils where it grows. Because beach dunes present difficult germination conditions for this plant, its coastal populations have evolved larger seeds than plants of the same species growing inland.

Walter's ground-cherry on a dune face

Walter's ground-cherry fruits and flower

Poorjoe. Flower (inset)

249

Tread softly. Stinging bristles (inset)

Seabeach evening primrose on the dune crest

Wilted (L) and open (R) dunes evening primrose

Tread Softly (Stinging Nettle) and Evening Primroses

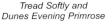

Tread Softly and Dunes Evening Primrose — *Seabeach Evening Primrose*

RELATIVES: Tread softly is related to the spurges, family Euphorbiaceae. Seabeach evening primrose is in the family Onagraceae.

IDENTIFYING FEATURES:

Tread softly (stinging nettle or **finger rot)** *(Cnidoscolus stimulosus),* 12 in (30 cm) high, is an erect perennial with three- or five-lobed leaves. The plant is covered with stiff, stinging hairs. Pure-white flowers bloom spring through fall.

Seabeach evening primrose *(Oenothera drummondii),* 12 in (30 cm) high, is an upright, woody, bushy, or sprawling biennial with thick, fuzzy, smooth-edged leaves. Its flowers (2 in, 5 cm wide) appear in summer and are yellow, turning orange-pink as they wilt. The similar **dunes evening primrose** *(O. humifusa)* has flowers half the size.

HABITAT: These plants grow on and behind the dune crest.

DID YOU KNOW? The irritating bristles of tread softly are hollow and filled with compounds that cause an intense burning itch when the brittle hairs break off in sensitive skin. Carefully, one can harvest this plant's edible seeds and tap root, which tastes like pasta. Evening primrose flowers bloom at night and are visited by hawk moths and other nocturnal pollinators.

Silver-leaf Croton and **Seaside Sandmat**

Silver-leaf Croton

Sandmat

RELATIVES: These plants are spurges in the euphorb family, Euphorbiaceae.

IDENTIFYING FEATURES: These spurges have a milky sap and fruits that consist of three-lobed capsules.

Silver-leaf croton (beach tea) *(Croton punctatus),* 3 ft, (90 cm) high, is a perennial shrubby herb with fuzzy, gray-green leaves on rusty branches. The fruit is a fuzzy, three-lobed capsule seen all year.

Seaside sandmat *(Chamaesyce polygonifolia),* 4 in (10 cm) high and sprawling, is a matlike annual herb with opposite, supple leaves on reddish branches. Its tiny flowers appear in summer.

HABITAT: Both plants grow throughout the dune and on the dune face.

DID YOU KNOW? The fuzz (pubescence) covering leaves of the silver-leaf croton traps humidity to conserve water. Milky sap from these spurges contains a latex that can cause vomiting, nausea, and diarrhea if ingested, and severe inflammation upon contact with eyes or open cuts. In small doses, these euphorbs are well known for their medicinal utility. The family is named for Euphorbus, a Greek physician who practiced during the first century A.D.

Silver-leaf croton

Silver-leaf croton with fruits

Seaside sandmat

251

Virginia creeper in a dune clump. Leaves (inset)

Virginia creeper with fruits

Beach pennywort

Virginia Creeper
and **Beach Pennywort**

Virginia Creeper   *Beach Pennywort*

RELATIVES: Virginia creeper is in the grape family, Vitaceae. Beach pennywort shares the family Apiaceae with parsley, fennel, celery, and dill.

IDENTIFYING FEATURES:

Virginia creeper *(Parthenocissus quinquefolia)* is a climbing, creeping, clumping, woody perennial vine with palmately compound leaves of five leaflets. Greenish flower clusters appear in summer and berries ripen blue-black in fall. Foliage is bright red during cold months.

Beach (largeleaf) pennywort *(Hydrocotyle bonariensis),* 8 in (20 cm) high, is a perennial herb with creeping, underground, lateral stems and circular, scallop-edged leaves. Its white flower clusters appear spring through summer.

HABITAT: Each of these plants grows in sunny dune areas, but beach pennywort also spreads onto the upper beach.

DID YOU KNOW? Virginia creeper berries are poisonous to humans, causing nausea, drowsiness, and profuse sweating. Yet, the birds love the grapelike fruits. Beach pennywort plants growing on tall dunes become isolated and genetically different from those in low swales. The plants on dune tops express a trait for larger leaves in comparison to beach pennywort populations in low areas.

252

Prickly-pear Cacti

RELATIVES: Prickly-pears are related to other cacti in the family Cactaceae.

IDENTIFYING FEATURES: Prickly-pears *(Opuntia* spp.) are perennial cacti with succulent, branching, oval pads (stems), and occasional sharp spines (modified leaves). The spines protrude from eyes (areoles) that also have tufts of tiny barbed bristles. Large, yellow flowers appear in spring.

Eastern prickly-pear (devil's tongue) *(Opuntia humifusa)*, 2 ft in (60 cm), has compressed, glossy pads and spines that are gray, white, or brown.

Cockspur (dune) prickly-pear *(Opuntia pusilla)*, 12 in (30 cm), has small, barrel-shaped pads and large gray spines that give the plant the appearance of a homicidal balloon animal. The inflated pads turn red in the fall.

HABITAT: These cacti grow throughout the dune.

DID YOU KNOW? When the crowded stamens in the center of a prickly pear flower are touched, they writhe with circular movement. This animation helps cover visiting insects with pollen. Cockspur prickly-pears have barbed spines and detachable pads that root in bare sand to form new plant clones. These traits aid dispersal by large animals (like us), but the cactus also spreads when hurricanes break up plants and wash them throughout the dune.

Eastern prickly-pear with flowers

Eastern prickly-pear fruits are called tunas

Cockspur prickly-pear

253

Railroad vine leaves and flower

Beach morning-glory vines on the upper beach

Beach morning-glory leaves and flower

Railroad Vine
and **Beach Morning-glory**

Railroad Vine   *Beach Morning-glory*

RELATIVES: Railroad vine and beach morning-glory are allied with other morning-glory flowers in the family Convolvulaceae.

IDENTIFYING FEATURES:

Railroad vine (bayhops morning-glory) *(Ipomoea pes-caprae),* 6 in (15 cm) high with beach-length stems, is a shiny-leaved perennial vine that runs more than climbs. Its flowers are purple to pink and bloom spring through fall.

Beach (fiddle-leaf) morning-glory *(Ipomoea imperati),* 6 in (15 cm) high, is similar to railroad vine but has shorter runners (often buried) and more leathery leaves, often with three lobes. Its flower is white with a yellow center.

HABITAT: These vines grow among other plants on the dune crest and dune face. By late summer, railroad vine may have its "tracks" stretched to the tide line.

DID YOU KNOW? Extracts from these plants have been shown to reduce inflammation, with railroad vine demonstrating a particular effectiveness for reducing dermatitis caused by jellyfish stings. Railroad vine is found on warm, sandy beaches all over the world. Its seeds float and are spread widely by ocean currents.

Beach Heather and Marsh Pink

Beach Heather   Marsh Pink

RELATIVES: Beach heather is in the rock-rose family, Cistaceae. Marsh pink is in the gentian family, Gentianaceae.

IDENTIFYING FEATURES:

(Woolly) beach heather *(Hudsonia tomentosa),* 1.5 ft (46 cm) high, is a semi-woody evergreen with small, oval leaves held tight to the stem. Its numerous yellow flowers bloom in spring, each open for only a single day.

Beach heather

Marsh pink (slender rose gentian) *(Sabatia campanulata),* 24 in (61 cm) high, is an herb that grows from an erect, branched, perennial stem that is mostly underground. Plants in winter are a low rosette with short oval leaves. In spring, they grow into asymmetrical, thinly leaved branches and bloom with pink solitary flowers. The base of each petal is yellow bordered by a red line.

HABITAT: Beach heather grows atop low dunes. Marsh pink lives in wet dune swales (p. 10).

DID YOU KNOW? Like many dune plants, beach heather has nitrogen-fixing nodules on its roots and adds nutrients to the soil where it grows. On northern beaches in our area, it is one of the only green dune plants in winter, although it has become significantly rare. Marsh pink is pollinated by bumblebees and sweat (metallic green) bees. The plant forms capsules containing up to 700 tiny seeds.

Marsh pink growing in a back-dune swale

Marsh pink flower

255

Partridge pea

Trailing wild-bean

Flowers and seed pods of the trailing wild-bean

Partridge Pea
and **Trailing Wild-bean**

RELATIVES: These plants are in the family Fabaceae with peas, beans, and other legumes.

IDENTIFYING FEATURES:

Partridge pea *(Chamaecrista fasciculata),* 24 in (60 cm) high, is an annual herb with alternate, compound leaves, each with about a dozen leaflet pairs. Its yellow, five-part flowers bloom in summer.

Trailing wild-bean *(Strophostyles helvula),* 3 ft (1 m) high and sprawling, is an annual herbaceous vine with compound leaves of three. Its winged flowers are pinkish and have a dark-purple, upturned, sickle-shaped beak. Both the flowers and the elongate seed pods often occur in pairs.

HABITAT: Partridge pea and trailing wild-bean grow throughout the dune.

DID YOU KNOW? Partridge pea flowers are either right- or left-handed based on the direction that their stamens bend. During water stress, this plant's leaflets fold up tightly to minimize dehydration. Snow geese wintering near North Carolina's barrier islands depend on trailing wild-bean "peas" for food. The importance of this plant for migrant birds on "Pea Island" justified the name of this Outer Banks refuge.

256

Groundsel Tree and Wax Myrtle

Groundsel tree. Unique leaf shape (inset)

RELATIVES: Groundsel trees are tree-like members of the sunflower family, Asteraceae. Wax myrtle is in the family Myricaceae with eucalyptus and guavas.

IDENTIFYING FEATURES: Both plants are woody-stemmed evergreens that grow into large bushes or trees.

Groundsel tree (sea-myrtle, eastern baccharis, salt bush) *(Baccharis halimifolia),* 10 ft (3 m) high, has alternate, thumb-sized, thickened, deeply toothed, silver-green leaves. Yellow male flowers and white female flowers appear on separate plants in early fall. The feathery pappus of the female flower is retained by the seeds, which disperse in the winds of late autumn.

White pappus fruits of the female groundsel tree

Southern wax myrtle *(Morella cerifera),* 10 ft (3 m) high, has leathery, serrated, olive-green leaves that have a spicy fragrance when crushed. Waxy, pale-blue berries occur on female plants in winter.

HABITAT: Both plants occupy similar areas in low dunes and swales (p. 10).

DID YOU KNOW? Groundsel trees in the toughest growing locations are most likely to be males, with females doing best in wetter, less crowded areas. American colonists boiled wax myrtle berries to render their paraffin for fragrant "bayberry" candles, which are still used in old-fashioned Christmas decorations.

Southern wax myrtle. Leaves (inset)

Waxy berries of the female southern wax myrtle

257

Beach vitex dominating a South Carolina dune face

Beach vitex flowers (L) and dried fruits (R)

A female yaupon holly with ripe fruits

Beach Vitex and Yaupon Holly

Beach Vitex   *Yaupon Holly*

RELATIVES: Beach vitex shares the verbena family, Verbenaceae, with many ornamental plants. Yaupon is in the family Aquifoliaceae with other hollies.

IDENTIFYING FEATURES:

Beach vitex (roundleaf chastetree) *(Vitex rotundifolia)*, to 1 ft (30 cm) high with long runners, has rounded, oppositely arranged, gray-green leaves with dense, grayish hairs on their underside. Purplish flowers appear in May, and the blackish fruits ripen in summer. Leaves drop in fall, leaving a tangle of stems over the winter months.

Yaupon holly *(Ilex vomitoria)*, 10 ft (3 m) high, is a shrubby evergreen tree with small, alternating, elliptical, dark-green leaves with wavy-toothed margins. Female plants have pea-sized berries that mature from green to red in fall.

HABITAT: Beach vitex is an alien invader from Asia and the Pacific Rim. In the US, the plant pushes native grasses out of dune-front habitats. Yaupon holly often forms a low canopy throughout the dune and can live in a severely salt-pruned form (p. 13) on the dune face.

DID YOU KNOW? Beach vitex was planted on Southeastern dunes in the 1980s to stabilize beaches. In less than ten years, the plant invaded other sites and began smothering the native dune flora. A battle to stop its spread is currently under way.

Live Oak and Tough Buckthorn

A salt-pruned live oak covering a low dune

RELATIVES: Oaks are together with beech trees in the family Fagaceae. Tough buckthorn is related to the chicle (chewing gum) tree in the family Sapotaceae.

IDENTIFYING FEATURES:

Live oak *(Quercus virginiana)*, grows less than 10 ft (3 m) high on exposed dunes, double that in back-dune forests, and much larger inland. This evergreen tree has a thick corky bark and dark green alternate leaves with margins that curl under. Its acorns form in fall.

Live oak leaves

Tough buckthorn (bully) *(Sideroxylon tenax),* 10 ft (3 m) high, is a thorny tree with dense growth between dead, salt-pruned branches. Its new stems and leaves are covered by a coppery fuzz, which remains beneath the older leaves. Small white flowers appear in spring and dark berries mature in summer and fall.

HABITAT: Both grow throughout the dune to its crest.

Tough buckthorn

DID YOU KNOW? The live oak is Georgia's state tree. Among America's large trees, the live oak is our most hurricane resistant, due to its fracture-resistant wood, spreading root system, and salt-spray tolerance of mature foliage. The US Navy considered the live oak to be of strategic importance for ship-building, which relied on the tree's strong, arching trunk for the stems, sterns, and ribs of our wooden sailing ships.

Tough buckthorn fruits

259

Southern redcedar

The blue waxy cones of a female southern redcedar

Saltcedar growing on the upper beach

Saltcedar branches

Southern Redcedar
and Saltcedar

Southern Redcedar

Saltcedar

RELATIVES: Southern redcedar is a conifer in the family Cupressaceae. Saltcedar is an angiosperm (flowering plant, not a cedar) in the family Tamaricaceae.

IDENTIFYING FEATURES:

Southern redcedars *(Juniperus virginiana)* grow to 30 ft (9 m) behind protective dunes but are taller inland. Dune trees have short trunks and spreading branches. The bark shreds easily and the entire plant has an aromatic smell. Leaves are blue- to dark-green, mostly sharp needles in juveniles, and mostly scalelike in adults. The female trees bear blue, berrylike cones in summer.

Saltcedars *(Tamarix* spp.), 15 ft (4.6 m) high, are scrawny evergreen shrubs with gray-green scalelike leaves. Young plants have smooth reddish bark, and older trunks are brown and furrowed. Its pale pink flowers extend from branch tips in fingerlike clusters.

HABITAT: Low dunes and dune slacks.

DID YOU KNOW? Dune southern redcedar is a different variety from inland trees. Saltcedars are invasive aliens from Asia, introduced in the 1800s as ornamentals and windbreaks. The tree sends down a tap root about as deep as the tree is tall and can tolerate salty soils and extended drought.

260

Pines

Slash Pine

Loblolly Pine

RELATIVES: Pines are conifers related to cedars and are in the family Pinaceae.

IDENTIFYING FEATURES: Pines are evergreen trees with thick, scaly bark and leaves (needles) bundled in clusters called fascicles. Their male and female cones develop on the same tree.

Slash pines *(Pinus elliottii),* 60 ft (18 m) on the coast, have either 2 or 3 needles per fascicle and bear purplish pollen cones. The mature seed cones are a lustrous chestnut brown, bear short, stout prickles, and are attached by distinct stalks. From central South Carolina northward, slash pines are replaced on the coast by the similar loblolly pine *(Pinus taeda).* This pine has 3 (sometimes 4) needles per fascicle and has yellow-brown pollen cones. The mature seed cones are dull brown with sharp, thick prickles, and are on stubby stalks.

HABITAT: Slash pines find themselves near the ocean where beaches have eroded into coastal pine forests and there is little active dune system. Loblolly pines near the beach grow in dune slacks.

DID YOU KNOW? The Outer Banks had extensive stands of loblolly pine before most of the trees were logged in the late 1800s. Although the trees were small and the lumber was marginal, logging them became attractive after mainland forests disappeared.

Slash pines behind an eroding dune

Slash pine branches

Seed (L) and pollen cones (R) of a slash pine

Hollow green weed anchored to a surf shell

Hollow green weed on a rock jetty

A large sheet of sea lettuce stranded on the beach

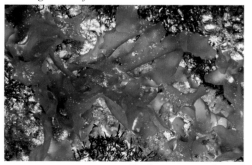

Sea lettuce in a tide pool

Green Algae
(Hollow Green Weed and Sea Lettuce)

RELATIVES: Green algae (green plant division Chlorophyta) are closer to land plants than to the brown and red algae. Sea lettuce and hollow green weed are together in the family Ulvaceae.

IDENTIFYING FEATURES:

Hollow green weed *(Ulva intestinalis,* formerly *Enteromorpha* spp.) forms strands of narrow, limp, deflated cylinders when up to 6 in (15 cm) long in protected areas, but is more hairlike and short where it is exposed to waves.

Sea lettuce *(Ulva* spp.), 2 in (5 cm) wide straps, is a bright, apple-green alga with wavy edges. Its slick, translucent sheets begin attached but are easily torn free.

HABITAT: Both grow in the intertidal zone. Hollow green weed covers hard surfaces in the wavewash, especially jetties and downed trees. Small plants are often found in the surf originating from a single bit of shell. Sea lettuce grows on jetty rocks and submerged logs during calmer summer months and is common in fresh wrack after the first rough warm-season weather.

DID YOU KNOW? Sea lettuce is yummy either raw or boiled in soup. Hollow green weed can grow where it is only submerged at high tide. This way, the plant avoids grazing by marine animals.

Green Algae
(Green Fleece and Hair Algae)

RELATIVES: All are green algae (green plant division Chlorophyta). Green fleece is in the family Codiaceae. Hair algae are within the family Cladophoraceae.

IDENTIFYING FEATURES:

Green fleece algae *(Codium* spp.), 12 in (30 cm) long, looks like forked, spongy, dirty-green fingers attached at a single holdfast. In the water its dense branches form a domed clump.

Hair algae vary in shape but are always composed of thin, green, hairlike filaments. ***Chaetomorpha*** (mostly *C. melagonium)*, 12 in (30 cm) long, is a coarse, wiry, unbranched alga with its individual cells visible to the naked eye. ***Cladophora*** (hair algae of various species), 12 in (30 cm) long, has densely branched hairlike filaments. It can come in the form of wispy, dark-green clumps or dense, cottony balls up to 2 in (5.1 cm) in diameter.

HABITAT: These algae grow in rubble out to 50 ft (15 m). Puffy balls of *Cladophora* grow in protected waters, are sometimes found floating at sea, and occasionally strand in the wrack line.

DID YOU KNOW? The beached green balls formed by hair algae are tough enough to stay cottony for many years, although they quickly bleach white.

Green fleece

The filamentous green seaweed Chaetomorpha

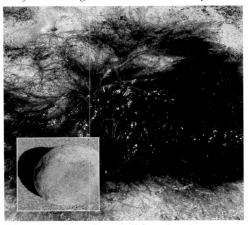

Cladophora, *hair algae. Ball form (inset)*

263

Knotted wrack

Bladder wrack

Dictyota

Padina

Brown Algae *(Knotted Wrack, Bladder Wrack, Dictyota, and Padina)*

Knotted and Bladder Wrack	Dictyota and Padina

RELATIVES: Brown algae (class Phaeophyceae) are more closely related to single-celled diatoms than to green and red algae. Knotted wrack and bladder wrack are allied within the family Fucaceae. Dictyota and padina are in the family Dictyotaceae.

IDENTIFYING FEATURES:

Knotted wrack *(Ascophyllum nodosum)*, 12 in (30 cm), has olive-green to reddish-brown fronds, each bearing several inflated air bladders.

Bladder wrack *(Fucus vesiculosus)*, 6 in (15 cm), has flattened, olive-green fronds bearing pea-sized air bladders that are often paired on forked branches.

Dictyota *(Dictyota dichotoma)*, 12 in (30 cm), has flat, olive-brown fronds with smooth margins and blunt tips that fork into even branches of two. The plants largely disappear in cold months.

Padina *(Padina gymnospora* spp.*)*, 6 in (15 cm), has greenish-brown, fan-shaped fronds with an in-rolled outer margin.

HABITAT: Knotted wrack and bladder wrack attach to rocks and other hard surfaces between the tide lines. Dictyota and padina also attach to rocks but prefer calmer waters out to 15 m deep.

DID YOU KNOW? Divers rub dictyota inside their mask. The algae's slippery coating prevents fogging.

264

Brown Algae
(Sargassum Weed and Turbinweed)

Pelagic sargassum

RELATIVES: These brown algae are in the family Sargassaceae.

IDENTIFYING FEATURES:

Pelagic sargassum (sargasso) *(Sargassum* spp.), 16 in (40 cm) clumps, forms golden bunches with tooth-edged leaves, air-filled bladders, and no central holdfast. *Sargassum fluitans* has smooth bladders and *Sargassum natans* has spurtipped bladders. Both turn dark brown on the beach. Its dark, BB-sized bladders are common within the tide line.

Old (L) and newly stranded (R) pelagic sargassum

Attached sargassum *(Sargassum filipendula),* 16 in (40 cm) long, has smooth, brown, elongate, leathery leaves covered by tiny, faint dots. Branches connect to a tough holdfast. The longest plants have air bladders.

Turbinweed *(Turbinaria turbinata),* 6 in (15 cm), beach as golden bouquets of pyramid-shaped fronds. The algae live attached and float when torn free.

HABITAT: Pelagic sargassum drifts on oceanic currents. Attached sargassum grows anchored to hard surfaces in waters just below the low tide line. Beached turbinweed likely drifted from rocky coastal waters farther south.

Attached sargassum

DID YOU KNOW? As pelagic sargassum drifts at sea, it provides a habitat life raft for hundreds of species of animals. Many of these creatures become stranded along with the algae.

Turbinweed

265

False agardhiella

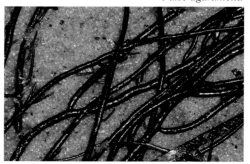

False agardhiella

Graceful redweed

Gracilaria tikvahiae, *beached yellowish-green*

Red Algae *(False Agardhiella and Graceful Redweed)*

RELATIVES: These are red algae (phylum Rhodophycophyta) in the family Gracilariaceae. Red algae are only distantly related to green algae.

IDENTIFYING FEATURES:

False agardhiella *(Gracilaria verrucosa),* 18 in (46 cm), has brown branches like al dente spaghetti. Branches have occasional spiky branchlets and only a slight taper to their base. The similar Agardh's redweed *(Agardhiella tenera)* has fleshy, thick (3/16 in, 5 mm) branches that taper dramatically at their base.

Graceful redweed *(Gracilaria folifera),* 12 in (30 cm), has greenish to reddish, flattened, forked branches, like sinuous clumps of linguini, ending in thin tips. Various stranded species of **Gracilaria** fade yellowish to clear.

HABITAT: False agardhiella grows in inlets and sounds below low tide. Graceful redweed attaches to intertidal rocks, occasionally in the swash zone, or may drift free along the bottom in coastal shallows. All are most common in warm months.

DID YOU KNOW? Red algae have a photosynthetic pigment that reflects red light and absorbs blue light, which allows these plants to live at greater depths than green plants. Many red algae are farmed as seafood and are an important part of the Asian and Asian-food-lover's diet.

Red Algae *(Hooked Weed, Hypnea, and Turf Algae)*

A stranded clump of hooked weed algae

RELATIVES: These *Hypnea* algae are in the family Hypneaceae. Turf algae include many species, but are dominantly species of *Gelidum,* family Gelidiaceae.

IDENTIFYING FEATURES:

Hooked weed algae *(Hypnea musciformis),* 12 in (30 cm) long, grow in wiry, tangled clumps and up-close appear yellowish to brown. Branch tips frequently end in sickle-shaped hooks.

Hypnea *(Hypnea cervicornis)* is similar in color and growth form to hooked weed, but has numerous, pointy branchlets and no hooks.

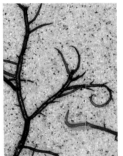

Hooked weed algae   H. cervicornis

Turf algae, 2 in (5.1 cm) high, grow in dense, burgundy and green pom-poms on rocks exposed to surf or currents. Like a weedy lawn, multiple species intertwine in the turf, but species of *Gelidium* are most common.

HABITAT: *Hypnea* species attach with holdfasts to rocks below the low tide line. Turf algae grow on rock jetties in the intertidal wave-splash zone.

Turf algae on a rock jetty

DID YOU KNOW? Algae growing in a turf receive less light due to crowding, but resist dehydration at low tide. If a scrap of turf is transplanted to a calm tide pool, its constituents will grow into elongate forms, but elongate forms of the same species are not able to form turf on wave-washed rocks.

Turf algae, mostly Gelidium

267

Eelgrass

Sun-bleached eelgrass

A clump of shoal grass

Shoal grass blades

Eelgrass and Shoal Grass

Eelgrass   *Shoalgrass*

RELATIVES: These seagrasses are vascular, flowering plants, not algae. Eelgrass (family Zosteraceae) and shoal grass (Cymodoceaceae) are distantly related to various aquatic plants.

IDENTIFYING FEATURES:

Eelgrass (seawrack) *(Zostera marina),* 39 in (1 m) long, has ribbonlike blades, mostly 1/4 in (6 mm) wide, that grow from tubular sheaths connected by rhizomes a little thinner than the blades.

Shoal grass (shoalweed) *(Halodule wrightii [beaudettei]),* 8 in (20 cm) long, is similar to eelgrass but has thinner blades, only 1/16 in (1.5 mm) wide.

HABITAT: Eelgrass grows in subtidal meadows within bays and sounds. Shoal grass grows in shallower water, including sandy areas exposed at low tide. Eelgrass grows most in spring and fall, and becomes dislodged during warm summer months when large clumps strand on the beach.

DID YOU KNOW? These plants bloom with tiny greenish flowers under water and reproduce by sharing pollen carried by currents. Eelgrass fruits look like grains of rice and contain a single seed. The fruits ripen in summer and dislodge when much of the exposed vegetation dies off. After floating for some time, the dispersed seeds sink to begin new plants.

Plant Drifters—Seabeans and **Driftwood**

A **seabean** is a fruit or seed that has made a sea voyage. Some drift to disperse their genes, and others are lost, having floated far from where they could hope to grow. By design or by luck, these drifters end up on particular beaches during selective times. The seabean season is roughly September–March, when tropical storms and winter weather give persistent winds that blow drifters out of sea-currents and onto beaches. Seabean season minus travel time may also correspond to the period when tropical seeds enter the world during the annual Amazonian flurry of flood-season fruiting. Seabean hot-spots are where the Gulf Stream current is closest to shore, but tropical cyclones can drop bounties of seabeans on any beach. Driftwood describes stems, trunks, and other plant parts that have drifted from afar or that have eroded from local forests.

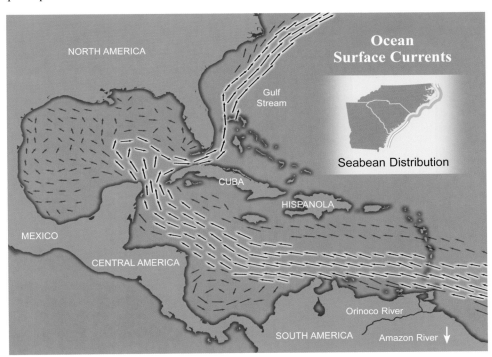

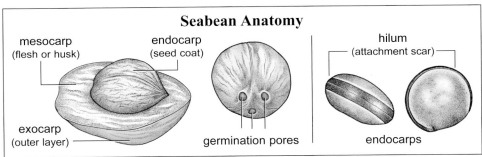

269

Coconut, max 15 in (38 cm)

Coconut endocarp, max 7 in (18 cm)

Sea coconut seeds, max 3 in (7.6 cm)

Coconut and Sea Coconut

RELATIVES: These fruits come from palms, family Arecaceae.

IDENTIFYING FEATURES:

Coconuts *(Cocos nucifera)* strand on beaches as either mature football-sized fruit, immature fruit, endocarp, or husk. Some shriveled immature forms may look unfamiliar. The three-pored mature endocarp, if fresh, contains a layer of fleshy white meat and is partially filled with liquid.

Sea coconuts *(Manicaria saccifera)* grow on the bussu palm in singles, twos, or threes within a brown, lumpy husk. The sea often erodes free the spherical seeds, which have a single scar like a bellybutton and are covered by a brownish, glossy, endocarp occasionally obscured by flaky layers of fruit. They may be weathered to a tan or gray.

ORIGIN: Coconuts grow on warm beaches all over the wider Caribbean. Sea coconuts drop from bussu palms growing near the rivers of the American tropics.

DID YOU KNOW? In the coconut, the Portuguese recognized the surprised face and fibrous hair of a coco (monkey) staring back at them, which is how the fruit got its name. The three germination pores are where the developing root exits. A coconut takes a year to mature on the parent tree. After falling into the sea, it can drift for more than 30 years. The sea coconuts of the bussu palm roll downhill, float, and are dispersed by tropical floodwaters. The palm grows in swampy areas as a slender-trunked palm with enormous fronds to 26 ft (8 m) long.

Starnut Palm, Red Mangrove, and **Tropical Almond**

RELATIVES: Starnuts share the family Arecaceae with coconuts. Red mangroves are in the family Rhizophoraceae. Tropical almonds are in the family Combretaceae and are not directly related to commercial almonds.

IDENTIFYING FEATURES:

Starnut palms (*Astrocaryum* spp.) have seeds with hard, black, tear-shaped endocarps. The nut's rounded end has 3 pores that may look like stars because of some remaining fibrous husk. Old starnuts are weathered brown.

Starnut palm endocarp, max 2 in (5 cm)

Red mangroves *(Rhizophora mangle)* produce seeds that sprout on the parent tree and eventually drop as variously curved propagules that look like flamboyantly long, green writing pens. The root-end is brownish and may have begun sending out rootlets before reaching the beach.

Tropical almonds *(Terminalia catappa)* beach as corky fruits in various stages of disintegration. Black or brown fruits with the familiar almond shape may not have drifted very long. More weathered fruits are bleached and fibrous, and the oldest drifters are deeply pitted.

Red mangrove, max 12 in (30 cm)

ORIGIN: Starnut palms grow in the lowland rainforests of Central and South America. Red mangroves live in coastal areas of the American tropics north to the middle Florida peninsula. Tropical almonds fall from a large-leaved tree, native to Asia, that grows throughout the wider Caribbean.

DID YOU KNOW? Starnuts can be polished to a high gloss and are often used in jewelry.

Worn tropical almond seeds, max 2 in (5 cm)

271

Laurelwood, max 1.5 in (3.8 cm)

Railroad vine seeds, max 3/16 in (5 mm), with split pod

Mary's-bean, max 1 in (2.5 cm)

Laurelwood, Railroad Vine, and **Mary's-bean**

RELATIVES: Laurelwood fruits come from a tree in the family Clusiaceae. Mary's-beans and railroad vine seeds come from morning-glory flowers in the family Convolvulaceae.

IDENTIFYING FEATURES:

Laurelwoods (Santa-maria) *(Calophyllum* spp.) bear spherical, green fruits that weather into a brown or tan, eyeball-like sphere. Most beached fruits are smooth with a small nub surrounded by short fibers.

Railroad vine seeds *(Ipomoea pescaprae)* mature within a papery pod that splits to liberate fuzzy, brown, angular seeds with a circular hilum (attachment scar). Those surf-washed enough to lose their fuzz are glossy and hard (see plant, p. 254).

Mary's-beans *(Merremia discoidesperma)* look like a scorched hot-cross bun. They are black or brown, stony seeds with an oval hilum and a distinct, indented cross.

ORIGIN: Laurelwood seeds likely come from stands of trees in the West Indies. Most railroad vine seeds are probably local, although these plants grow all over the wider Caribbean. Mary's-beans grow on the coast of Central America.

DID YOU KNOW? Mary's-bean, a rare find, is named for the Virgin Mary. The seed gets its cross indentation from a narrow strap that secures it in its pod. Possessing a Mary's-bean can provide a believer with good luck in avoiding evil, in easing childbirth, and recovery from snakebite or hemorrhoids.

Gray Nickarnut, Bay Bean, and Sea Heart

RELATIVES: These seeds come from legumes, family Fabaceae. Well-known relatives include the garden pea.

IDENTIFYING FEATURES:

Gray nickarnuts *(Caesalpinia bonduc)* are hard, grayish beans that look like swollen ticks. The endocarp typically has faint fracture lines encircling the seed.

Bay beans (beach peas) *(Canavalia rosea)* are hard seeds in the classic bean shape and have an elongate, oval hilum. They have a slightly dark mottling to a background of tan, brown, or red.

Sea hearts *(Entada gigas)* are hard, compressed, circular or heart-shaped seeds with an inconspicuous hilum in their indentation. Beneath any crusty sea-growth, they are a glossy purple-brown or dark mahogany.

ORIGIN: Gray nickarnuts grow along the coastlines of the wider Caribbean. Most bay beans may come from plants on Florida beaches, although the plant grows throughout the Caribbean. Sea hearts tumble from the long, twisting pods of the monkey ladder vine, a woody canopy-climber from the rainforests of Central and South America.

DID YOU KNOW? These seeds can be polished to a lustrous shine. The sea heart's monkey ladder vine has the longest bean pod in the world. These seabeans are famous as beach finds as far from their tropical origin as northern Europe. The discovery of a sea heart floating in the eastern Atlantic helped inspire Columbus' search for land to the west.

Gray nickarnut, max 3/4 in (2 cm)

Bay bean, max 3/4 in (2 cm)

Sea heart, max 2.25 in (5.7 cm)

273

Sea purse, max 1.5 in (4 cm)

Red hamburger bean, max 1.2 in (3 cm)

Brown hamburger bean, max 1 in (2.5 cm)

Sea Purse and Hamburger Beans

RELATIVES: These seabeans are in the legume family Fabaceae.

IDENTIFYING FEATURES:

Sea purse beans *(Dioclea reflexa)* are stone-hard, glossy seeds with a flattened side. They are orange-brown and darkly mottled with a thin, dark hilum outlined in orange, wrapping all but the flattened side.

Red hamburger (oxeye) beans *(Mucuna urens)* are circular, stone-hard seeds with a thick, black hilum encircling three fourths of their circumference. Colors are generally on the red side of brown with occasional mottling, and the light border of the hilum is yellowish.

Brown hamburger (horse-eye) beans *(Mucuna sloanei)* are difficult to separate from red hamburgers but for subtle difference in shape and color. Brown hamburger beans tend to be more rotund and gray-brown. Their hilum is thicker with a border more gray than yellow.

ORIGIN: Sea purse beans develop with 2–4 sibling seeds in short, plump sausagelike pods on tropical rainforest vines. The vine is thought to be native to all of the world's tropics, in part due to the seed's impressive survival at sea. Hamburger beans develop within spiny pods hanging on long stems from tropical rainforest vines native to the American tropics and the West Indies.

DID YOU KNOW? These beans are rich in an alkaloid called L-Dopa, which is used in treating the tremors from Parkinson's disease, but in high doses causes hallucinations, delirium, and other ills. These seabeans polish to a brilliant shine.

Blisterpod, Crabwood, and Oaks

RELATIVES: Blisterpods (family Humiriaceae), crabwood (Meliaceae), and oaks (Fagaceae) are not directly related.

IDENTIFYING FEATURES:

Blisterpods *(Sacoglottis amazonica)* look like WWII-era hand grenades because of their woody, air-filled, bulging blisters. Worn pods have open blisters, but internal air pockets surrounding the single, inch-long seed remain to keep the pod floating.

Blisterpod, max 2 in (5 cm)

Crabwood seeds *(Carapa guianensis)* are dull gray-brown and flattened on two sides and rounded on the other. An elongate, distorted hilum scar is opposite the rounded side.

Oak acorns *(Quercus* spp.) are glossy nuts that may or may not have the familiar scaly cap. Some may have a cap completely enclosing the nut. Shapes vary between species from spherical to elongate.

ORIGIN: Blisterpods fall from small trees native to the Amazon and Orinoco River basins. Crabwood is a type of mangrove tree living on coastlines from Central America through the Caribbean to Brazil. Acorns fall from oaks all over North America. They may have traveled down rivers entering the Atlantic or the Gulf of Mexico before riding the currents that ferry them to our beaches.

Crabwood, max 1.75 in (4.5 cm)

DID YOU KNOW? The bubble-wrapped seed of the blisterpod is exquisitely adapted to flotation dispersal within the periodically flooded forests of the Amazon, but the seed does not remain viable after ocean voyages.

Oak acorns of varied species, max 0.8 in (2 cm)

275

Water hickory, max 1 in (2.5 cm)

Pignut hickory, max 1.5 in (3.8 cm)

Bitternut hickory, max 1 in (2.5 cm)

Hickory *(Water, Pignut, and Bitternut)*

RELATIVES: These nut trees are allied with pecan and walnut trees within the family Juglandaceae.

IDENTIFYING FEATURES:

Water hickory nuts *(Carya aquatica)* beach as brownish, lumpy, slightly compressed shells with encircling ridges and a variably pointed apex.

Pignut hickory nuts *(Carya glabra)* often come ashore with their charcoal, tear-shaped, 4-part husk intact. The nut within is similar to the water hickory.

Bitternut hickory nuts *(Carya cordiformis)* look like water hickory nuts but are smoother, without encircling ridges, and have pronounced apex-points if they are not worn.

ORIGIN: These nuts fall from trees distributed over the Southeastern US. Their upstream source is likely to be the major rivers emptying into the Gulf of Mexico and Atlantic.

DID YOU KNOW? These are true nuts: a dry fruit with a hardened ovary wall not attached to the seed within. All nuts are seeds, but not all seeds are nuts. Edible, oil-rich hickory nuts have been used by Americans for about 9000 years. The Powhatan people of Virginia believed that spirits traveling to the rising sun could only complete their afterlife journey after a drink of *pokahichary* served by a goddess. The drink, made from hickory nuts pounded with water, gives us the name for the tree and its fruit.

Pecan, Mockernut, and **Black Walnut**

RELATIVES: These nut trees are allied with other hickory trees in the family Juglandaceae.

IDENTIFYING FEATURES:

Pecans *(Carya illinoinensis)* are similar in shape to the store-bought variety but tend to have thicker shells and a wider range of size and color. Runts may be as small as 1 in (2.5 cm) and color ranges from mahogany to tan.

Pecan, max 1.5 in (3.8 cm)

Mockernuts *(Carya alba)* have rounded ridges and a thick shell, often split at the pointed apex.

Black walnuts *(Juglans nigra)* are brownish-gray with a roughly wrinkled surface. They are bluntly pointed at one end and rounded at the other, and are occasionally heart-shaped.

ORIGIN: Pecan and mockernut trees grow around the Southeastern US. Black walnut trees are most common north of Georgia, but range west to Texas.

DID YOU KNOW? Few of these edible hickory nuts are viable or even contain seeds following a lengthy drift at sea. Pecan trees have been cultivated as a food crop, but wild trees still remain. These native trees have been vastly reduced due to damming of rivers and development of floodplains. The genes of these wild trees are valuable in that they carry traits not present in agricultural trees, such as resistance to pests. Commercially grown pecans are often genetically uniform monocultures of cloned plants. Black walnut trees have been heavily logged for their prized wood.

Mockernut, max 1.25 in (3.2 cm)

Black walnut, max 1.5 in (3.8 cm)

Bamboo cane revealing hollow compartments

Bamboo rhizome and base of culm

Common reed rhizome bundle

Bamboo and Reed

RELATIVES: Bamboos are really big grasses in the family Poaceae, shared with their smaller cousins, the reeds.

IDENTIFYING FEATURES:

Bamboo (tribe Bambuseae, many species) beaches as sections of hollow, compartmentalized cane (the grass's culm), often with its associated rhizome, and commonly with cut marks or other signs that it has been used by people. Bamboo canes put to structural use are commonly introduced Asiatic species of *Bambusa*, although hundreds of species are native to tropical America. Canes are often 6 in (15 cm) in diameter and 30 ft (9 m) or longer.

Common reeds *(Phragmites australis)* beach as bundles of finger-thick rhizomes bound by dense roots. The bundles stay together after lengthy sea travel even when the mass has sun-bleached to a light gray (see plant, p. 233).

ORIGIN: Bamboo has a wide range between North and South America, and introduced species are ubiquitous. Common reeds are native to the Americas. Recently, they have exploded in abundance along Mississippi marshes and are common throughout river banks in the Southeast.

DID YOU KNOW? Bamboo is used to make houses, furniture, boats, bicycles, bridges, music, and dinner, among hundreds of other useful and artistic things.

Beach Tangleballs
and **Saltmarsh Grass Stems**

Beach Tangleballs *Saltmarsh Grass Wrack*

RELATIVES: Tangleballs involve parts of many kinds of dune plants. Marsh grasses are in the family Poaceae.

IDENTIFYING FEATURES:

Beach tangleballs are spherical clumps of intertwined plant parts. These parts vary but commonly include stiff roots, rhizomes, pine needles, and thin twigs. These sea-woven balls keep their shape long after being beached.

Saltmarsh grass stems are browned remnants of the tubular reeds supporting smooth cordgrass *(Spartina alterniflora,* see plant, p. 235). Occasionally, fresh plants also strand.

ORIGIN: Beach tangleballs are woven from coarse plant fibers eroded from the dune by storms. Fibers dense enough to collect on the seabottom are snowballed together by the rolling action of breaking waves. A saltmarsh sheds its dead grass stems during winter storms. The floating stems exit inlets, wash in with the tide, and remain on the upper beach until they decay or are buried by sand.

DID YOU KNOW? Tangleballs form in large lakes and seas all over the world, wherever erosion and waves occur. They are unique conversation pieces and are occasionally sold to tourists as "whale burps."

Beach tangleballs, max 10 in (25 cm)

Fresh (L) and old (R) saltmarsh grass wrack

Saltmarsh grass stems covering the upper beach

279

Saw palmetto trunk, max 12 ft (3.7 m)

Root end of a cabbage palm trunk, max 50 ft (15 m)

Greenbriar tuber, max 24 in (61 cm)

Saw Palmetto, Cabbage Palm, and Greenbriar

Saw Palmetto
and Cabbage Palm

Greenbriar

RELATIVES: Saw palmettos and cabbage palms are together in the palm family (Arecaceae). Greenbriar is a distantly related monocot in the family Smilacaceae.

IDENTIFYING FEATURES:

Saw palmetto *(Serenoa repens)* trunks are rough, curved, less than a foot in diameter, and composed of densely packed fibers. Some trunks retain roots and frond boots that give them the appearance of a giant shrimp (see plant, p. 239).

Cabbage (sabal) palm *(Sabal palmetto)* trunks tend to be straight and are more than a foot in diameter. Roots remain either as stiff, radiating dreadlocks or as a worn bulbous knob (see plant, p. 239).

Greenbriar *(Smilax* spp.) tubers are reddish or dark brown, multi-lobed masses with occasional wiry roots remaining (see plant, p. 240).

ORIGIN: These trunks and tubers are eroded from the dune during severe storms. Palm trunks may be worn by the surf, revealing the densely packed fibers that form them, leaving only a shadow of their former shape.

DID YOU KNOW? Greenbriar tubers are the starchy, underground, energy reserves used by the plant for resprouting after the loss of above-ground growth.

Boneyard and Driftwood Pines

Boneyard Pine

Driftwood Pine

RELATIVES: Pines are conifers related to cedars and are in the family Pinaceae.

IDENTIFYING FEATURES:

Boneyard pines *(Pinus* spp.) left standing on eroding beaches (p. 14) have trunks like straight columns and are supported by deep tap roots. The roots that radiated out at the former ground level typically bend downward at right angles (see plant, p. 261). Pines that have washed out to sea are considered true **driftwood.** When the trunks wash up onto the beach, branches and roots normally have been worn away by surf action, but stumps may remain from multiple branches that angled upward at the same node. Dry pine driftwood is soft enough so that a fingernail can easily press into it. Interior wood retains its pine-resin smell. Cypress *(Taxodium* spp.) logs provide a similar soft, resiny driftwood, but are recognizable by the wide buttress at their base.

ORIGIN: Pines become exposed and fall into the sea when beach erosion intersects with barrier-island forests. Cypress and some pines may also wash down coastal rivers.

DID YOU KNOW? The most persistent parts of a pine log are the resin-saturated heartwood knots that made up its early branches.

Boneyard pine roots show former ground level

A fallen boneyard pine with bark remaining

Driftwood pine log

Boneyard redcedar, max 30 ft (9 m)

Interior wood of southern redcedar

Southern redcedar driftwood

Boneyard and **Driftwood Cedar**

Boneyard Cedar

Driftwood Cedar

RELATIVES: Southern redcedar is a conifer in the family Cupressaceae.

IDENTIFYING FEATURES:

Boneyard redcedar stumps *(Juniperus virginiana)* eroded from dunes have snaking roots that spread widely from the base of the trunk. Bleached wood has a foxy gray exterior, but interior wood is reddish. Even old interior wood retains its aromatic smell. The outer wood is soft enough to depress with a fingernail. True **driftwood,** which has been worn by the surf, has a lumpy exterior and eroded pockets where softer wood was sanded away (see plant, p. 260).

ORIGIN: Forests of southern redcedar in dunes near eroding beaches.

DID YOU KNOW? Aromatic oils in cedar wood are antibacterial, antifungal, and inhibit decay. Cedars outcompete many plants, but unlike pines, cedars are vulnerable to fire. Protection from fire creates conditions for dense stands of southern redcedar near many Southeastern beaches, often where erosion is moving the beach into low, dune-field forests. These areas bear numerous redcedar skeletons.

Boneyard Oak
and **Tropical Driftwood**

Boneyard Oak

Tropical Driftwood

A boneyard oak showing its arching trunk

RELATIVES: Oaks are in the family Fagaceae. Tropical hardwoods come from trees of many families.

IDENTIFYING FEATURES:

Boneyard live oaks *(Quercus virginiana)*, are typically less than 20 ft (6 m) high and have arching trunks with dense, widely spreading root masses. The wood weathers gray and often has abundant sinuous furrows.

Identification of **tropical driftwood** is tricky and requires laboratory detective work. On the beach, educated guesses can be made after looking at a smoothly cut cross-section end-on. Most tropical hardwoods have a tight grain and many are dark or reddish under their sun-bleached exterior. Those haunted by persistent driftwood mysteries can send a 1x3x6-inch sample to the USDA Forest Service, Center for Wood Anatomy Research, Forest Products Laboratory, One Gifford Pinchot Drive, Madison, WI 53726-2398.

A boneyard oak with sinuous furrows

ORIGIN: Live oaks erode from dune forests. Tropical driftwood comes from rivers, either by bank erosion or from loss of felled timber. Many tropical species are resistant to rot and may drift at sea for years.

DID YOU KNOW? Much of the tropical driftwood reaching Southeastern beaches is usable for woodworking.

A reddish tropical hardwood with marine boreholes

283

Beach-worn surfwood

Peat lumps

Dune brittlestem mushrooms. Open gills (inset)

Surfwood, Peat Lumps, and **Dune Brittlestem Mushroom**

Surfwood and Peat   *Dune Brittlestem*

RELATIVES: Surfwood comes from palms, conifers, and hardwoods. Mushrooms are fungi in the order Agaricales.

IDENTIFYING FEATURES:

Surfwood is found as smooth, rounded wood pieces, generally hand-sized or smaller. Many pieces are too soft to reveal their grain, but occasionally, conspicuous clues can be seen, such as the coarse fibrous wood of a palm tree.

Peat lumps are fist- to boulder-sized masses of dark vegetable matter (pp. 15–16) smoothed by surf-sanding.

Dune brittlestem mushrooms *(Psathyrella ammophila)*, 2 in (5 cm), have brown caps that open upward to reveal distinct gills.

ORIGIN: Surfwood may be the last remnants of surf-sanded driftwood or the smoothed pieces of logs pounded into chunks by the sea. Peat is a composite of very old but only partially decayed vegetation. Dune brittlestem is the fruiting body (agaric, mushroom) of a fungus that lives within the upper beach.

DID YOU KNOW? The dune and beach are extensively inoculated with species of fungi, but few form mushrooms on the open beach. Dune brittlestem is a unique, obligate dune fungus that is tolerant of salt and lives on decomposing dune grasses.

BEACH MINERALS

What are Beach Minerals?

Beach "minerals" are loosely defined here as the natural, nonliving, solid parts of the beach. Most of the beach's framework falls into this general category, which includes sand, gravel, and underlying rock, clay, and mud. Other minerals scattered throughout beaches include pieces of the beach's rocky foundation, and fossils (mineralized animal parts) that have been uncovered by erosion.

True minerals have a homogeneous crystalline structure with a particular chemical composition and set of characteristics like color and hardness. Quartz, which makes up most of our local beach sands, is a true mineral, as are the metal oxides and gemstones that also decorate Southeastern sands. Another common mineral, calcium carbonate, makes up limestone, which includes rocks that are essentially a sand-and-seashell granola glued together with calcite (the most common and stable form of calcium carbonate). As you'll see, a wide variety of animal parts can become rock. It is evidence of the living nature of beaches that even their inanimate parts are intertwined with the remnants of former lives.

Perhaps the most important aspect of beach minerals is how they reveal a beach's geological history. Sands, gravel, rocks, and fossils describe what beaches were like hundreds, thousands, even millions of years ago. The descriptions tell how beaches were assembled, what forces have kept them in their constant state of change, and what their future may hold.

A closeup of "pea gravel" from an Outer Banks beach that was once a water-worn river bed

Southeastern Beach Sands

WHAT ARE THEY? Sand is pulverized mineral rock and shell. The Southeastern **beach-sand sampler** to the right shows variety in color, grain-size, and composition. The most common light grains are quartz, which is a crystallized silica. Smaller, tawny, angular grains are feldspar. Shell bits vary in size and are light, rust, or dark. Shiny black, rounded specks are mostly iron-titanium oxide (ilmenite) and iron oxide (magnetite; yes, it sticks to a magnet). Occasionally, gemstone minerals (p. 288) and mica (p. 289) can be seen.

SIZE: "Sand" is finer than gravel and coarser than silt, with grains between 0.06 and 2.0 mm. Our beach sands average about 0.3 mm, but there is much variation among and within beaches. Finer sands predominate on Sea Island beaches, during summer, in dunes, and in offshore bars. Coarser sands occur on many Outer Banks beaches, during winter, and on the lower beach.

ORIGIN: Tens of millions of years ago, minerals that eroded from Appalachian rocks washed down rivers and have been pushed around by coastal currents ever since. As this sand moves north to south, more fragile mineral grains disintegrate, which is why feldspar is most common on northern beaches. Carbonates from shell came from marine animals. The sea is still making this material, and dissolving it.

DID YOU KNOW? We're running out. Sand that formerly washed out rivers becomes trapped behind dams, and seaward flow through artificially stabilized inlets pushes sand into deep water.

Corolla, NC

Cape Hatteras, NC

Cape Romain, SC

St. Simons Island, GA

Little Cumberland Island, GA

Tiny gemstones within sand from a dark deposit

Tiny Gemstones

WHAT ARE THEY? Gemstones on beaches are tiny pieces of pretty minerals scattered among the heavier, darker elements of beach sand. Even in these darker grains, the most common gem is quartz, whose grains under a hand lens look like foggy, raw diamonds. Rarer grains include epidote, which are rounded and translucent yellow-green, and garnet, which are polished pink, reddish, or burgundy. Rarer still are grains of zircon (clear, flat-sided crystals), kyanite (occasionally elongate, deep blue crystals), and tourmaline (smooth bright grains, watermelon-pink to dark green).

SIZE: These gems average less than 0.3 mm. A jeweler's loupe is key to exploring this world, but a microscope is needed to truly appreciate these treasures.

ORIGIN: Erosion of the Appalachian mountains and their foothills (the Piedmont). These gems are scattered throughout the beach but become concentrated by heavy wave action.

DID YOU KNOW? Successful microgem hunters focus on placers, the beach's layers of dense, dark sand (p. 18). These layers occasionally form broad bands following storms. Within the layers, grains segregate according to density. Thin, burgundy bands along the margin of a darker area contain garnet, and similar green bands contain epidote.

Mica and Fulgurite

Mica

Fulgurite

WHAT ARE THEY? Mica is a silicate mineral that separates into sheets and crumbles into glittery flakes. Because of its fluttery form, mica concentrates where light, turbulent current pushes it, like within the troughs of antidunes (p. 23) on the lower beach. **Fulgurites** are petrified footprints of lightning bolts. Most are hollow silica (glass) tubes with a rough, drab, gray-brown exterior; a glassy smooth interior; and a straight or rootlike shape. Specimens from the surf have their exterior worn smooth.

SIZE: Mica flakes are typically less than 0.5 mm, but together can line extensive areas of the lower beach. Fulgurites are generally less than 10 in (25 cm) long with an inner tube diameter of a pencil or less.

ORIGIN: Mica eroded from the Appalachians and their foothills. Fulgurites form where lightning strikes the dune. With the strike, temperatures of more than 3500° F (1900° C) instantaneously melt the quartz sand and expand the air within it, pushing the liquid glass to the outside of a tube around the bolt. The tube cools to a solid in about a second. Fulgurites accumulate over millennia and erode from dunes when wind and water move their sands.

DID YOU KNOW? One of the largest collections of fulgurites is housed at the Nellie Myrtle Pridgen Beachcomber Museum, Nags Head, NC.

Mica glitters in the trough of an antidune

Bright sun reveals tiny mirrorlike mica flakes

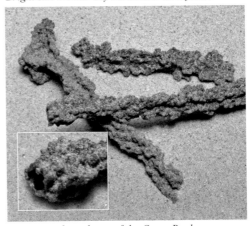
Fulgurites from dunes of the Outer Banks

A pea-gravel beach, Nags Head, NC

Gravel, pebbles, and shell bits on the lower beach

Pumice is a glass-foam rock that floats at sea

Gravel, Pebbles, and Pumice

Gravel and Pebbles

Pumice

WHAT ARE THEY? Beach **gravel** and **pebbles** are broken bits of mineral rock, typically worn smooth by surf action (see gravel beaches p. 19). Most of this material is quartz that varies in color from translucent to brown. Rose quartz is rare. Elongate pebbles are often rounded bits of thick shell. Other hard stones are occasional, such as granite, a rock of many minerals. **Pumice** is a rock formed during explosive volcanic eruptions. These are rocks of frozen foam, infused with gas bubbles held by fragile volcanic glass. Colors vary widely. Pumice floats and can drift at sea for many years.

SIZE: Technically, gravel and pebbles range from 2 to 64 mm. Anything bigger is a cobble. Pumice that reaches the beach is generally less than 1 ft (30 cm) in diameter.

ORIGIN: Gravel and pebbles tumbled down rivers long ago when sea level was much lower, became buried, and were uncovered by erosion as beaches migrated back landward. Pumice floats down rivers, drifts at sea, and could come from many volcanic sources, like the Lesser Antilles and southern Mexico.

DID YOU KNOW? Pumice is cut into blocks as a building material in Mexico and Central America. Some beached pumice rocks bear cubical shapes and smears of mortar as signs of this practice.

Clayballs and Mudballs

WHAT ARE THEY? Clayballs are globs of clay, which is a dense compaction of very fine-grained silicate minerals. The balls are squishy and hold the shapes they are molded into. Colors range through green, gray, brown, and red. Beach **mudballs** are gray-brown globs of mud, which is a semi-solid mix of clay, sand, and organic debris, such as peat (pp. 15–16, 284).

SIZE: All are generally less than 1 ft (30 cm) in diameter.

ORIGIN: Clay- and mudballs come from deposits layered under the beach and just offshore. Storms frequently erode the beach and expose formations of clay (p. 16). The eroded clay rolls in the surf and is sculpted into balls by the circular movement of water within the waves. Balls of dense mud that have enough clay to hold them together can form the same way. Pumping sediment for artificial beach projects (p. 231) is another way that offshore clay and mud can end up on beaches. These mistakes sometimes form beaches that are more mud than sand.

DID YOU KNOW? Mudballs that roll in shell become armor-plated by the flat shell bits sticking to them. These armored mudballs last longer before they disintegrate in the surf. Mudballs buried by beach sand remain for years until they are freed by a storm's erosion.

Clayballs

Mudballs

Peaty mudballs from an eroding formation

Coquina limestone formed of cemented pebbles

Coquina limestone formed of cemented shell hash

Coquina with accompanying fossil bivalves

Coquina Limestone

WHAT ARE THEY? Coquina lime-stone is rock made of cemented fossil shell, sand, and occasionally, pebbles. Coquina is Spanish for little clams, which are common within the rock. The rocks are roughened, with or without shell, and are pale, tawny, rust, or dark.

SIZE: Detached rocks range from the size of a large dictionary to thumb-sized pebbles. Coquina slabs, some the size of a driveway (image, p. 285), can be seen on the beach within the exposed Neuse Formation near Ft. Fisher, NC. Under the barrier island sands, this formation runs north-south, about 9 miles (15 km) long, 2 miles (3 km) wide, and up to 9 feet (3 m) thick, with the main formation east of the beach.

ORIGIN: Our beach coquina comes mostly from the Neuse Formation described above. The rocks formed about 30,000 years ago during the Late Pleistocene, but they contain older "reworked" fossil shells from the Triassic period, 245 million years ago. Coquina formed from buried shell hash (p. 11) that sat near the water table. As the shells partially dissolved, they were bathed in water saturated with calcium carbonate, which cemented the sand-shell mix.

DID YOU KNOW? The formation at Ft. Fisher is vastly reduced from its original size following mining of the rocks for building material in the 1930s.

Fossils

Giant Oyster

Worm Stone and Vertebrates

Shell Fossils and Shark's Teeth

WHAT ARE THEY? Fossils are parts of living things that have been dug up (the Latin *fossus* means a hole in the ground). On beaches, the surf does the digging. Although there is no age requirement, most fossils are pretty old and have been buried long enough to become mineralized or surrounded by rock.

Extinct **giant oysters** *(Crassostrea gigantissima)* are gray, massively thick bivalve shells that wash ashore from ancient reefs. **Fossil venus clams,** larger than our modern quahog (p. 125), lived in estuaries where the beach is now. **Worm stones,** colored beige, rust, or gray, are fossilized chunks of reef built by a polychaete tube worm of the genus *Dodecaceria* (family Cirratulidae). Some of the most familiar vertebrate fossils from coastal deposits are shark's teeth. Rarer vertebrate fossils include alligators, turtles, deer, and whales.

SIZE: Most beach fossils are hand-sized or smaller. Giant oysters are up to 2 ft (60 cm). Whale earbones are fist-size cobbles. The smallest shark's teeth fragments are the size of coarse sand grains.

ORIGIN: Because beach dynamics mix many ages of material together, beach fossils may span ages from recent times to many millions of years. Most beach fossils are from the Pleistocene Epoch (10,000 to 1.8 million years ago). During this time, our Southeastern coastline

Giant oysters, extinct cousins of modern kinds

Fossil venus clams

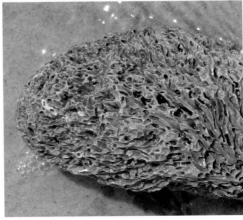
Fossilized worm stone

293

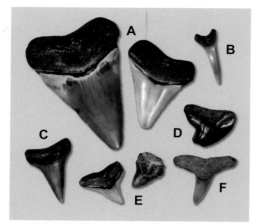

Fossil shark's teeth, max shown, 2.5 in (6.4 cm)

A fossil mix of animals, both aquatic and terrestrial

Whale earbones

advanced and retreated with four major changes in sea level, each corresponding to an ice age. "Young" fossils include worm stones from tube-worm reefs made less than 4000 years ago. Some of our oldest fossils of animals that lived locally are giant oysters, which made up reefs off Topsail Island, NC about 25 million years ago. However, ancient rivers washing material from the Piedmont has sprinkled beaches with some fossils from the Castle Hayne Formation, about 35 million years old, and other formations as old as the Triassic Period, 200–250 million years ago.

Vertebrate beach fossils:

A. Great white shark's teeth
   (Carcharodon carcharias)

B. Sand shark tooth *(Odontaspis)*

C. Mako shark tooth *(Isurus)*

D. Tiger shark tooth
   (Galeocerdo cuvier)

E. Requiem shark teeth *(Carcharhinus)*

F. Lemon shark tooth
   (Negaprion brevirostris)

G. Alligator skin-bone (osteoderm)
   (Alligator mississippiensis)

H. Pufferfish teeth *(Diodon)*

I. Garfish scale *(Lepisosteus)*

J. Horse molar *(Equus)*

K. Deer leg bone *(Odocoileus)*

L. Pond-turtle carapace bone
   (family Emydidae)

Whale earbones tumble free in the surf. Those pictured are from baleen whales.

DID YOU KNOW? Our beaches have no local dinosaur fossils; the barrier islands are too young.

HAND OF MAN

What Have We Had a Hand In?

A lot. Humans are arguably one of the most important elements of a living beach. We contribute to, consume, manage, and shape many of the other elements of the beach. Even on remote beaches, the synthetic crumbs of our existence are ubiquitous. Just as beaches record connections between the "natural" components of continents and seas, coastal sands also receive our own well-traveled discards.

The acquaintance we have with many of the items that follow (after all, we made them) makes this section different from the others in this book. But even recognizable things can have unfamiliar stories. Questions about these beach-finds abound: Who made it? Where did it come from? Why are there so many of such an odd item? How did it get here?

In some ways, the human influence on beaches can be heavy-handed. One of our most profound effects seems to arise from our desire for a permanent presence on the beaches we love. Living persistently on beaches has required battle against the perpetual forces that shape the shore. These skirmishes have brought about both drastic measures and unintended consequences.

And yet, it is the peaceful beauty of beaches that beguiles us. Visitors taken by the joy of the beach often feel compelled to leave testament of their spiritual experience. And further, many actively respond to a sense of obligation to conserve what pleases us.

Evidence of past visitation—an old Bromo-Seltzer bottle erodes from a dune

Beach Shrines and Sand Art

WHAT ARE THEY? Beach shrines are human traces that commemorate beach visits. Some shrines receive visits from many artists over multiple seasons. An example is the **Kindred Spirit mailbox,** which contains notebooks chronicling inspired thoughts from years of visitors. Shrines often use local flotsam and sea shells incorporated into artistic collages. Evidence from memorial ceremonies at sea, such as flowered **wreaths,** occasionally reach the beach. **Sand art** takes the form of elaborate sculptures, but includes the simple classic sandcastle. Shrines and art are limited by daylength, work ethic, and location relative to the tide.

HOW COME? Why did the Druids construct Stonehenge? Perhaps, because they could . . . or perhaps because they had time to kill? Like Stonehenge, the cultural significance of beach shrines may remain a mystery. One hypothesis is that a trip to the beach can bring about a sense of whimsy in just about anyone.

DID YOU KNOW? Shrines we've seen have included the creative use of sea shells, underwear, seaweed, sponges, doll heads, fish heads, mismatched flip-flops, mummified stingrays, and a plethora of colorful plastic drift-toys—all common beach-finds. Sandcastles formed of moist sand are typically on the lower beach, which makes their average lifespan about six hours (see tides, page 38).

Kindred Spirit mailbox, Bird Island, SC/NC line

Whelks adorn a communal driftwood shrine

A memorial wreath

An octopus bejeweled with shells awaits high tide

297

One Spanish coin can start a lifetime search

Cob coins of gold (A) and silver (B,C)

An unfired Civil War bullet, Williams Cleaner type

Treasure and Artifacts

Cob Coins

Civil War Artifacts

WHAT ARE THEY? Rare finds of silver and gold come from Spanish treasure fleets, and possibly, pirates. Notable treasure ships wrecked on the treacherous Outer Banks include the 1750 fleet—7 vessels driven ashore by a hurricane, scattering coins, gold bars, diamonds, and emeralds into the surf. **Gold (A)** and **silver (B-C) cob coins** are rough-margined disks, spilled by the Spanish or (rumored) buried by pirates. Silver pieces-of-eight *(ocho reales de plata)* are greenish or blackish when found **(C)**; cleaning reveals their stamps and dates **(B)**. Other artifacts include Civil War relics, such as **bullets**. Battles near the beaches of South Carolina often found soldiers dumping their heavy loads of unfired bullets as they ran at or from the enemy.

HOW COME? The Outer Banks marked a critical turn eastward for ships sailing to Spain from the Caribbean. This, with extensive inshore waters for hiding, presented a favorable neighborhood for pirates. During the Civil war, soldiers were stationed near numerous coastal forts and encampments.

DID YOU KNOW? Cob coins were struck from the end (cabo) of a bar and hand-trimmed. Famous pirates seeking and losing treasure in the Carolinas included Edward Teach (Blackbeard), Anne Bonney, Mary Read, and Jack Rackham (Calico Jack).

Shipwrecks

WHAT ARE THEY? Beaches punctuate the final voyages for many vessels and their parts, which lie buried under beach sands until erosion reveals them. Parts of a wooden ship exposed in the top image are the **hull planks** attached to **ribs** by **wooden pegs. Bronze bolts** (top, inset) once held heavy timbers like the keel (ship's backbone), stem (bow support), and sternpost (stern support). In the middle image, the supporting **keelson** sits atop **ribs.** Curved stems, sternposts, and knees (90° supports) are commonly of live oak timbers (p. 259). In steamship wrecks, massive **steel boilers** can persist for 150 years or more.

HOW COME? Thousands of ships have wrecked off Georgia and Carolina beaches. Outer Banks waters have been particularly treacherous, in part due to the convergence of currents from the north (Labrador) and the south (Gulf Stream). The colliding currents shift shoals and fuel severe storms. This "Graveyard of the Atlantic," has one of the highest densities of shipwrecks in the world. Many are visible on beaches, especially in winter. Most are from the late 1800s and early 1900s. Many wrecks not splintered by the pounding surf wait buried under the sand.

DID YOU KNOW? The earliest known shipwreck in the area was the British ship *Tiger,* which grounded on Ocracoke Island in 1585.

Ribs and hull planks of an Outer Banks wreck

Steamboat Magnolia, *1852, Jekyll Island, GA*

Boiler of the steamer Oriental, *1862, off Pea Is., NC*

299

Wooden pallet

Dunnage lumber

String-wound water filter cartridge

Foam polyurethane

Dunnage and Boat Parts

WHAT ARE THEY? Pallets are disposable, flat supports for heavy goods during their transport, as on ships. The open bottom allows the load to be moved by forklift. **Dunnage** lumber serves as packaging boards for heavy cargo, and includes skids, braces, and chocks (wedges). The lumber secures heavy shipping freight and is generally rough, tropical or North American hardwood, like oak, which has a high compression strength. **String-wound water filter cartridges** are used for filtration aboard ships. **Foam polyurethane** is used as flotation in boats and has a long life at sea.

HOW COME? These items are jettisoned or lost from the many international cargo ships and offshore platforms upstream from our beaches. A reason for a discard is often seen in dunnage timbers, which are commonly broken. Filters are but one of many consumable items that reach the end of their useful life at sea, where an unfortunate maritime tradition dictates their disposal.

DID YOU KNOW? Tropical hardwood and oak dunnage can provide beautiful material for small woodworking projects, like picture frames. The function of this lumber did not require a straight grain, so much of the wood is nicely figured. Some boards can be used in original condition—sun-bleached gray and peppered with interesting "worm holes" (p. 131).

Buoys, Beach Science, and Sondes

Buoys and Sondes

CRAB

WHAT ARE THEY? Navigational buoys float at sea and mark things that are important to ships. Most are green or red and mark opposite sides of channels. The odd, angular shape of the towers on many buoys enhances their reflection of a ship's radar. The science of beaches is sometimes undertaken with odd contraptions like the **CRAB,** which stands for Coastal Research Amphibious Buggy. The vehicle is used for surf surveying by the US Army Corps of Engineers research facility in Duck, NC. **Balloon radiosondes** measure and broadcast atmospheric data on their way up to 100,000 ft (31,000 m), and often have shreds of the balloon that carried them. **Dropsondes** are GPS and atmospheric computers that broadcast data during their fall from hurricane-hunter aircraft.

HOW COME? Buoys reach beaches when their anchoring chain breaks, often following storms. Large buoys are very difficult to remove. The CRAB is a unique solution to vehicular movement and data collection in surf, even during storms. Radiosondes and dropsondes are disposable instruments extensively deployed to forecast hurricanes and other weather. Each reaches the sea, floats, and is brought to beaches by many of the forces they are designed to study.

DID YOU KNOW? Beacons and sondes contain relatively expensive electronics, but are not worth much on eBay.

A beached radar-reflecting channel buoy

A "CRAB" measures beach profile

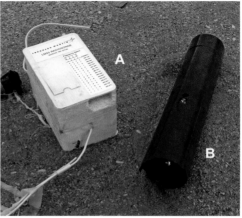

Balloon radiosonde (A) and dropsonde (B)

301

A shredded latex balloon

Mylar balloons tell of inland festivities

Hand grenade smoke bomb (A), firework tips (B)

Shotgun shells (A) and plastic wadding (B)

Balloons, Fireworks, and **Shotgun Discards**

WHAT ARE THEY? Balloons that reach the beach were formerly filled with enough helium to keep them aloft. Latex balloons are often shredded, but **Mylar plastic balloons** are generally intact. Both typically have ribbons or strings attached. Plastic tips of many colors come from launched **fireworks**. Black-plastic hand grenades are spent **smoke bombs**. Plastic **shotgun shells** are generally missing their brass head and are merely a plastic casing. The shells fire a **plastic wadding** along with the lead shot.

HOW COME? Most things going up must come down. Balloons burst or leak their helium in the thin upper atmosphere and then fall to Earth (or to sea). In this way, the joy of an inland birthday party can be transmitted for hundreds of miles. Unfortunately, the sentiment is lost on the sea life harmed by this litter. Fireworks end up in the ocean due to the common belief that water provides a safe location for ballistic revelry. Shotgun shells are discarded by waterfowl hunters in bays and sounds. At sea, most shooting is at clay pigeons (skeet targets) launched from cruise ships. Both the shot wadding and the ejected casings float for many years.

DID YOU KNOW? Environmental concerns and passenger casualties have begun to curtail the use of shotguns on cruise ships.

Sea Heroes (Drift Toys) and **Seaglass (Beach Glass)**

Sea Heroes

Seaglass

WHAT ARE THEY? Sea heroes are plastic, once-cherished, childhood friends set adrift on the open seas. These little synthetic figures often bear evidence of their lengthy voyage—sun-fading, lost limbs, and accumulations of fuzz, crust, and barnacles. **Seaglass** pieces are broken bottle shards that have been rounded, smoothed, and etched by sand and surf.

HOW COME? Sea heroes may be either lost or discarded. Seaglass shows the sea's way of making common and unwanted items into interesting and beautiful objects. Although seaglass has human origins, it ends up on beaches the same way seashells do—by tumbling within waves and currents. A piece of seaglass may move on and off the beach for many decades.

DID YOU KNOW? Variations on the classic plastic army man seem to be the most common sea heroes. We've collected hundreds, and no two are the same. Many may be from developing countries upstream, with styles that have lost favor with sophisticated American kids. Seaglass colors from most to least common are (generally) brown, green, white, light green, dark green, light blue, dark blue, lavender, yellow, and red. Lavender glass was likely in use 1860–1915 when makers added manganese for clarity. After a century in the sun, this glass turns purplish.

A sampling of sea heroes and drift toys

Seaglass arrives along with shell hash

Brown seaglass is common, lavender is rare

Foil balls, 2 in (5 cm), tell of human foibles

Roll-on balls, typically 0.4–1.4 in (1.0–3.6 cm)

Light bulbs, 1–39 in (2.5–100 cm)

Clay pebbles

Nurdles

Balls, Bulbs, and Nurdles

WHAT ARE THEY? Aluminum **foil balls** are buoyant elements of galley waste. **Roll-on balls** are hollow plastic spheres that top the common underarm deodorant applicator. **Light bulbs** range from thumb size to elongate tubes. **Expanded clay pebbles**, 0.5 in (1.3 cm), are a construction material used to make lightweight concrete block. They are also used as growing media in plant hydro-culture. **Nurdles** is the colloquial name for industrial resin pellets of HDPE (high-density polyethylene). The pellets, 0.2 in (5 mm), are precursors for plastic products.

HOW COME? These items are tough, floating elements of trash thrown overboard. Foil balls are symptoms of two common habits—wadding up used cooking foil and tossing trash into the sea. Roll-on deodorant containers are part of the worldwide circulation of discarded plastic. The balls are the most persistent part of the deodorant package and may float for decades. Light bulbs are glass capsules that seem fragile on land but are highly resistant to the sea's intense sun, waves, and biological/chemical decay. Clay pebbles and nurdles are spilled from ships during mass transport at sea.

DID YOU KNOW? Little turtles eat nurdles, although the plastics are bad for them. About 90% of small loggerhead sea turtles washed ashore on Southeastern beaches have ingested plastics.

Container Seals and **Packaging**

WHAT ARE THEY? Container seals record that shipboard containers are unopened. Containers (isotainers) are the international, semi-trailer-sized boxes that haul most every product on the planet. These products have their own individual **packaging**, most often plastic. Attempted incineration results in **melted plastics. Bite marks** demonstrate that this debris is an ingestion hazard to marine life. Triggerfish (family Balistidae) leave diamond-shaped holes.

HOW COME? Plastic floats for decades. Beached container seals reveal both the tradition of overboard discard and the astounding volume of goods shipped in containers. Plastic packaging is multinational, which may indicate its most common source: international shipping. Inhabitants of Caribbean islands dispose of waste by burning, which can result in partially melted plastic at sea. Open-sea animals live in a virtual desert of rare opportunity where any novel item might be food. Their feeding evolved in a world without plastics.

DID YOU KNOW? Household (and shipboard) plastic packaging enters the ocean at an estimated rate of 6.4 million tons per year, reports the National Academy of Sciences. This is ten times what gets recycled. Most plastics become brittle in sunlight after several years and break into tiny shards. These remnants are ingested by many sea animals.

Plastic container seals

A variety of international plastic packaging

A melted plastic bottle, possibly from a burn pile

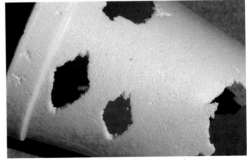

Triggerfish bites in a formerly floating foam cup

Stone crab (A) and lobster (B) floats, 8 in (20 cm)

Deep-water floats, 6 in (15 cm)

A longline "bullet" buoy, 18 in (46 cm)

Hand-made floats from old foam and flip-flops (inset)

Fishing Discards *(Floats)*

WHAT ARE THEY? Styrofoam **stone crab pot floats (A)** bear an X-number, and **spiny lobster pot floats (B)** bear a C-number. Commercial blue crab floats are can-, sphere-, egg-, or doughnut-shaped. They are lime green (GA), or varied in color (FL, SC, NC). Maine lobster floats (rare) are foam bullets with an inserted PVC buoy stick. Hollow, hard-plastic spheres are **deep-water floats** used for longlines (fish hooks strung on long lines) and trawl (vessel-towed) nets. PVC-foam **bullet buoys** are used for surface longlines. Primitive, **hand-made floats** may be fashioned from reused flotsam like polystyrene blocks, plastic jugs, or used flip-flops.

HOW COME? Floats reaching beaches may be casualties of broken lines and stormy seas. But most fishing gear at the end of its useful life gets disposed of at sea. Because floats float, they are among the most common types of fishing gear on beaches. Stone crab and spiny lobster pot floats drift from Florida via the Gulf Stream. Handmade floats are probably from developing countries where various kinds of beach flotsam are welcome raw materials for fishing supplies.

DID YOU KNOW? The most traditional artisanal floats are club-shaped logs. Glass fishing floats formerly used by the Portuguese are rare now. Most sold in curio shops are reproductions.

Fishing Discards *(Floats)*

WHAT ARE THEY? Inflatable **poly-form floats,** to 2 ft (61 cm), are used as markers for longlines, pots, and traps. Even larger buoys of this type are used as fenders (boat bumpers). **Foam bullet floats** are used to keep varied lines afloat and to mark pots/traps. A **high flyer** is a float with a long pole through it, typically with flags or an angular aluminum radar reflector. Floats that have sunk show bay **barnacles** (p. 144) or have become **compressed** as small, hardened versions of their former shapes.

HOW COME? Lost or discarded, floats record their functional lives and experiences at sea. Mesh envelops valuable floats to reduce chances of a single line breaking to free it. Frayed lines often indicate when this tactic did not work. High flyers fly high to make them easier to see in the open ocean. Some floats attached to lost nets sink to great depths where they are crushed by the tremendous pressure. Still buoyant, they are presumably freed when the line holding them disintegrates.

DID YOU KNOW? Depth-compressed floats often have seabottom animals growing on them, indicating that they were once sunken. A typical four-inch (10-cm) diameter can-float dragged to 100 ft (31 m) has about 1,600 lbs (730 kg) of pressure on it.

Polyform floats (lower) and foam bullet (upper)

A beached high flyer, 12 ft (3.6 m)

A foam float that spent time under water

Compressed PVC foam fishing floats

Lid latch employed on a stone crab pot

Spiny lobster and stone crab pot lid latches

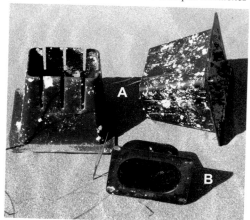

Spiny lobster (A) and stone crab (B) funnels

Fishing Discards *(Trap Parts)*

WHAT ARE THEY? Traps capture crabs and other seafood targets. Pots are traps that are set and left unattended. The black-plastic pot (trap) parts here come from stone crab and spiny lobster fisheries in Florida waters. **Lid latches** (laths) hold lids closed on both plastic and wooden pots. **Pot funnels** are entrances to pots that allow the crustaceans to enter but not escape. Spiny lobster funnels end in a rectangle, and stone crab funnels end in an oval. Beached **traps** (pots) are constructed of wood, plastic, or wire mesh. Each pot has (or had) a funnel entrance, latchable lid, marker float, and rope.

HOW COME? Beached pots are evidence of the power of storms to move even deep objects over long distances. These Florida pot parts come from the Gulf of Mexico and south Florida, upstream within the currents that flow northward (pp. 40, 269). Lid latches are fastened with a corrodible nail that eventually releases the lid after the pot is lost. This design reduces the time that lost pots imprison their target crustaceans. Wood pots slowly disintegrate, freeing their floating, highly persistent parts, including latches, bait cups, and funnels.

DID YOU KNOW? Plastic fishing gear is black because of the color's resistance to degradation in sunlight.

Fishing Discards *(Trap/Pot Parts)*

WHAT ARE THEY? Stone crab bait cups hold the bait (usually fish heads or pigs' feet) within traps (pots) set for stone crabs in Florida. Pots for crab, eel, seabass, spiny lobster, and American lobster are required by state natural resource agencies to have identification **tags,** which occasionally detach and drift. These plastic tags are orange plastic (common), colored by year, or take varied other forms, each with a fisher's license number and contact information. **Octopus pots** are open plastic jugs set to catch octopodes (p. 137).

Stone crab pot bait cups

HOW COME? Bait cups are one of many trap parts freed when traps break apart. Trap tags are traceable trash, typically giving state (and often person) of origin. Names and numbers help track down owners of derelict gear. Most common tags originate locally and from upstream (Florida). Counter-currents sometimes bring American lobster pot tags from the northeast and Canada. Octopus pots that beach are without the concrete or stone that originally lined their flattened side. The pots may come from Mexico where nearly 40 thousand pounds (18 metric tons) of octopodes are caught for food each year.

Trap tags

DID YOU KNOW? Our east-coast trap tags commonly end up stranding on beaches in England.

Octopus pots are usually found battered and worn

A beached, PVC-coated wire crab pot

Escape rings, often float free of corroded pots

Plastic door-latch hook

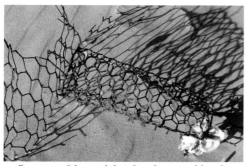

Remnant of the mesh bait box from an old crab pot

Fishing Discards *(Trap/Pot Parts)*

WHAT ARE THEY? Blue crab pots are most commonly made of PVC-coated wire mesh and are yellow, black, or green. Parts floating free from corroded pots include plastic **escape rings** and **door-latch hooks**, with securing shock (bungee) cord. The **bait box** is a recognizable feature of most pots.

HOW COME? Blue crabs (p. 153) are the target of a valuable commercial fishery that utilizes pots (traps left to fish alone). Pots are most commonly set in shallow waters of bays and sounds, but can be carried to sea by storm-driven currents. Pots corrode, fall apart, and liberate their persistent plastic parts. Plastic escape rings are required on pots to allow small crabs to get out. A stretchy cord attached to a door-latch hook closes the door through which fishers retrieve their catch.

DID YOU KNOW? Crab pots often entrap terrapins (p. 178), which drown trying to escape. Turtle excluder devices (TEDs) have been designed to allow these turtles to free themselves. The device is a plastic rectangle, just large enough for a terrapin, affixed to the pot's entrance funnel. These TED pots have been shown to catch crabs at rates equivalent to pots without TEDs. The devices are not yet required in our local pots.

Fishing Discards *(Nets and Line)*

WHAT ARE THEY? Fishing nets are made of synthetic twine or nylon mono-filament and are designed either to strain things from the water or to tangle them up. Shrimp trawl nets strain things, are made of stiff twine, and have meshes generally too small to get a fist through. Fish trawl nets are similar but may have larger meshes. **Gill nets** are either thin twine or monofilament and typically have a distinct **float line** (with floats) and a lead-cored line called a leadline. **Trap/pot rope** attaches floats to traps and can be of the sinking **nylon** type or **floating polypropylene** variety.

HOW COME? Shrimp and fish trawls are heavy nets dragged along the bottom by steel cables. Although the nets are strong enough to scrape up corals, sponges, and relatively large chunks of encrusted hard bottom, they occasion-ally encounter items too heavy to tear away from the sea floor, such as ship-wrecks. Nets torn free of their tow ves-sels are subsequently moved by storms. Gill nets generally float at the surface and are either lost or discarded at sea. Trap rope that floats is most likely to end up on the beach. The black color resists deterioration in sunlight.

DID YOU KNOW? These nets often entangle interesting marine life during their drift at sea and retain skeletons of these encounters following their beach stranding.

Derelict netting with ensnared animals

A beached gill net showing its float line

Nylon rope formerly used for trap fishing

Black polypropylene is a common floating rope

311

Monofilament fishing line retaining reel spool coils

Fishing glowsticks, 3–6 in (8–15 cm)

Seafood basket, 2 ft (60 cm)

Shrimp-heading gloves

Fishing Discards *(Miscellaneous)*

WHAT ARE THEY? Nylon monofilament line is used in both recreational and commercial fishing. Coils often linger, recording the line's use on a fishing reel. **Fishing glowsticks** (lightsticks) are transparent plastic tubes containing chemicals that glow when activated. They have various attachment clips and rings. **Seafood baskets** are used on fishing and shrimping vessels to temporarily hold the catch. Latex **shrimp-heading gloves** are used by shrimpers as they pick shrimp from their trawl catch.

HOW COME? Most seafood baskets are damaged, indicating that they may have been discarded rather than lost. Shrimp-heading gloves and glowsticks are disposable items with a limited life. Glowsticks mark fishing buoys at night and are used as lures on commercial longline hooks set to catch swordfish. Because they last only one night of fishing and the Atlantic longline fleet uses millions of hooks, glowsticks are one of the most common fishery items on the beach.

DID YOU KNOW? Glowsticks are activated to glow after an internal vial of hydrogen peroxide is broken, creating a reaction with cylume chemicals that cause dyes to fluoresce blue, green, yellow, white, or pink. Discarded monofilament line often entangles birds, and is a danger to swimmers and scuba divers.

Wax, Coal, Tar, and Oil

Surf-wax and Coal   *Carnuba Wax and Tarballs*

WHAT ARE THEY? Surf-wax is soft, pale, and often smells like coconut. When rubbed in lumpy layers, the wax gives surfers foot-traction on an otherwise slippery board. **Carnauba wax** is beached as hard, grayish or brownish chunks. **Coal** washed onto beaches is found as fist-sized, black, shiny lumps. **Tarballs** are the sticky, semi-solid leftovers from weathered petroleum.

HOW COME? Surf-wax is rubbed onto boards at the beach, where Murphy's law dictates it will get dropped in the sand. The wax is not much good after that. Discarded, it washes in and out with the tide. Carnauba wax is harvested from fronds of the wax palm *(Copernicia cerifera)*, a native fan palm of Brazil, is transported in mass quantities by ship, and occasionally falls overboard. It is used in making varnishes, polishes, car wax, and candy. Coal comes ashore from the many shipwrecks (p. 299) off our Southeastern beaches. The US Minerals Management Service reports that tanker-transported heavy fuel oils and tanker sludge discharges are the principal sources of oceanic tarballs. Riding currents flowing out of the Gulf of Mexico (p. 269), tarballs from the massive BP oil spill there (2010) have the potential to appear on the beaches of North Carolina and beyond.

DID YOU KNOW? Sunscreen assists a good first effort in removing tar from feet.

Surf-wax (A) and carnauba wax (B)

Coal chunk

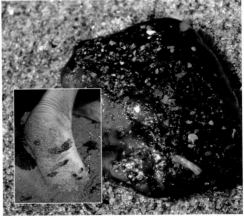

Tarballs come from many sources

313

Cape Lookout, NC

Bald Head Island, NC

Morris Island, SC

Hunting Island, SC

Tybee Island, GA

Lighthouses

WHAT ARE THEY? Lighthouses are towers of brick and steel topped with a rotating light-source, typically focused with a fresnel lens. Twenty-seven lighthouses stand along the Georgia and Carolina coastline, with several visible from the beach, including:

Little Cumberland Is., GA, (1838, p. 9)

St. Simons Is., GA (incarnations in 1810 and 1872, p. 295)

Tybee Is., GA (1736, 1742, 1773, 1866)

Hunting Is., SC (1859, 1875, 1889)

Morris Is., SC (1767, 1830s, 1876)

Cape Romain, SC (2 towers, 1827, 1858)

Oak Is., NC (1849, 1879, 1903, 1958)

Bald Head Is., NC (1795, 1817)

Cape Lookout, NC (1812, 1859)

Cape Hatteras, NC (1802, 1870, 1999)

HOW COME? Lighthouses were built to aid navigation around shoals and capes and through inlets. Most of these lighthouses have been rebuilt in multiple incarnations due to the destructive effects of beach erosion, hurricanes, earthquakes, and warfare. Many were intentionally blown up by retreating armies during the Civil War.

DID YOU KNOW? In 1880, the Morris Island Lighthouse stood 2,700 feet (820 m) from the water. The surf reached the structure in 1938, and today the lighthouse base is its own island about 1600 feet (500 m) offshore.

Life-saving Stations, Instrument Towers, and Piers

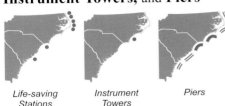

Life-saving Stations | Instrument Towers | Piers

WHAT ARE THEY? Life-saving stations formerly housed crews who stood by to rescue shipwrecked sailors. Most are on the Outer Banks, but none function now. Of these, the **Oregon Inlet Station** remains as a historical structure near the beach. **Instrument towers** erected on Topsail Island collected data on flybys from early jets, 1946–1948. Dozens of **fishing piers** extend out from Southeastern beaches. Many pier pilings from derelict remnants also stand offshore.

HOW COME? The Great Carolina Hurricane of 1854 killed many coastal sailors and highlighted the need for life stations. The US Life-Saving Service (Treasury Dept.) ran these before evolving into the US Coast Guard in 1915. About this time, weather forecasting improved; self-propelled, steel ships could broadcast distress by radio; life-saving needs diminished; and stations were gradually abandoned. Topsail towers are evidence of the Navy's 2-year takeover of the island to test early supersonic missiles and jets during top-secret Operation Bumblebee. Beach piers allow access to numerous fish outside the surf.

DID YOU KNOW? In its 225-year life, the Oregon Inlet Station has been moved due to erosion, destroyed by a storm, rebuilt in 1898, and modernized in 1934. Additional restoration began in 2008.

Oregon Inlet Life-saving Station, est. 1874

One of 8 original Topsail Island instrument towers

Nags Head fishing pier, NC

1898 gun battery, Wassaw Island, GA

Surf-worn brick

An iron chunk corroding over cemented shells

Granite cobble

Asphalt concrete

Historical Remnants

WHAT ARE THEY? Forts and **gun (artillery) batteries** linger on the coast, like the concrete slab of a Spanish–American War battery on the north point of Wassaw Island, GA. Surf-tumbled **bricks** on the beach testify to more than two centuries of buildings lost to the sea. **Iron** pieces could be from ship-wrecks, abandoned cars, or other losses. **Granite cobbles** (10 in, 25 cm) on beaches were brought by man and may be construction material (p. 320) or ship's ballast stones. Asphalt concrete is from roadways originally behind the dune.

HOW COME? Forts and gun batteries defended coastlines and inlets. Although these are the sturdiest of edifices, they are no match for the sea. Bricks are the last remnants of less sturdy buildings. Iron rusts and accumulates concretions of shell that belie its original shape. Granite originated far inland and was heavy enough to stabilize wooden sail-ing ships. Erosion continually overtakes our coastal roads.

DID YOU KNOW? The Spanish–American War (1898) lasted 10 months and gave the US Cuba, Puerto Rico, Guam, and the Philippines. Massive Fort Macon (NC) is one of many coastal fortifications strengthened following the War of 1812. Iron masses can be X-rayed to reveal their original shape, which may be from spikes, bolts, fittings, or cannon shot.

Beach Grooming and Driving

Beach Grooming

Beach Driving

WHAT ARE THEY? Grooming (raking, cleaning) is a practice that mechanically flattens the beach and removes the wrack (p. 17). Public **beach driving** is the use of beaches by private off-road (typically 4-wheel-drive) vehicles.

A beach-grooming machine

HOW COME? Beach-grooming is regulated and occurs only at a few resort beaches. Debate over the practice outlines divergent expectations. One is that beaches should be clean surfaces free of litter and biological material, even if their removal means the loss of shorebirds, beachcombing finds, and other aesthetics. An alternative expectation is that true litter can be plucked by hand, leaving beaches as functioning habitats where beachhoppers (p. 146), seabeans (269–277), bird life (180–220), and natural sand sculpturing (20–22) are well worth any inconvenience they cause. Public beach driving is not permitted in Georgia, South Carolina, and many areas of North Carolina. Where driving is permitted, it is controversial. Beach-driving benefits access by visitors with recreational equipment or who do not wish to walk. Drawbacks include beach changes that threaten aesthetics, wildlife, and enjoyment by pedestrians. Presently, driving in NC is allowed under rules meant to balance access and resource protection. The rules receive scorn from both sides of the debate, which may indicate their wisdom.

Beach driving, Cape Hatteras, NC

The heavily driven beach of Corolla, NC

Beach-driving boundary, Outer Banks

317

Sand fencing and Christmas trees, Corolla, NC

Sand gathered at dune grasses and sand fence

A groyne of granite rock and wood

A geotextile tube groyne traps up-drift sand

Battling Beach Change
(Sand Fencing and Groynes)

Sand Fencing

Groynes

WHAT ARE THEY? Sand fences are posted lengths of plastic mesh or vertical wooden slats held together by wire. They are believed to collect wind-blown sand. Other items thought to fill this role include old **Christmas trees** and other yard waste. **Groynes (groins)** are walls of rock, steel, wood, or sand-containing textile (geotextile tubes) that extend into the surf perpendicular to the beach.

HOW COME? Sand fences are used to keep wind-driven sand (p. 5) on the upper beach and foredune and to prevent human access. They are semipermeable, causing sand-transporting wind to slow and drop its load. In this function they seem only slightly poorer at attracting sand than beach plants. Isolated rows of sun-bleached sand fence in the dune add a pleasant human touch to a beach scene. But following storms, extensive stretches of sand fence become tangled into masses of splintered wood and rusted wire. Groynes halt longshore sand movement in the surf (p. 32, 41), building sand on one side while starving the other.

DID YOU KNOW? To reduce interference to sea turtle nesting (p. 176), sand fencing is sometimes placed in multiple, obliquely angled sections. A groyne's dual effect on erosion and accretion can be seen in the saw-tooth pattern they leave on the shoreline.

Battling Beach Change
(Buildings, Structures, and Roads)

Threatened Houses or Roads

Beach moves beneath houses at Nags Head, NC

WHAT ARE THEY? Threatened buildings, piers, and **roads** are the *casus belli* in our war with erosion. In defense of these assets, we've improvised numerous battle tactics. **Sandbags** are common in North Carolina, whereas harder armoring (p. 320) is seen in South Carolina and Georgia. Evidence of lost battles include derelict houses and **piers**. Battles under way include the continual bulldozing of sand off **Highway 12**, the dune road linking the islands of the Outer Banks.

In our battle with the sea, sandbags replace dune

HOW COME? We underestimate beach erosion and movement. When buildings outlive our ability to forecast beach change, they become threatened. At this point we either fight or adapt. Examples of adaptation often occur in North Carolina, where buildings left on the beach by erosion, or damaged beyond the majority of their value, are rebuilt at safer, landward locations.

Casualty of war—derelict pier, Topsail Island, NC

DID YOU KNOW? We can't win. But at significant cost, we can prolong our battles to forestall loss. We can also strategically avoid losing battles by selecting only the safest ground. The good news is that as individuals we are becoming much smarter about forecasting conflicts. The bad news is that collectively, we are much slower to make difficult decisions, especially on tactics to fight battles begun decades ago.

High tide floods Highway 12, Outer Banks

319

Granite jetty, Masonboro Inlet, NC

Jetties holding sand at bay, Murrells Inlet, SC

Sta-pods front a granite revetment, Fort Fisher, NC

House with a rock revetment, Sullivans Island, SC

Battling Beach Change
(Jetties, Walls, and Revetments)

Jetties

Armoring

WHAT ARE THEY? Jetties are typically piles of rock lining channels into inlets. **Coastal armoring** includes walls, **revetments** (rip-rap, rock piles), and sandbags (p. 319) placed so that they reduce the movement of sand on the upper beach and dune. Some revetments include engineered structures such as **Sta-pods,** which look like a giant set of concrete jacks.

HOW COME? Jetties interrupt the longshore sand flow and reduce the amount of sand that gradually fills an inlet channel. Similar to groynes (p. 318), jetties cause sand starvation and net erosion on their down-drift side. Coastal armoring could be considered the "nuclear option" in the war on erosion, in that these hardened structures sacrifice the beach in favor of the threatened dune property. Because of its damaging effects on adjacent beaches, new coastal armoring is rarely permitted in the Carolinas.

DID YOU KNOW? The majority of Georgia's developed shoreline is armored, mostly with granite revetments. In South Carolina, these hard structures cover about a quarter of developed beaches. Of the three states, North Carolina is least armored. Recently management of developed beaches has favored sand pumping (p. 321) over armoring.

Battling Beach Change
(Artificial Beaches and Dunes)

Artificial Beaches

Artificial Dunes

Pipes move sand from sea to land

WHAT ARE THEY? Artificial beaches come from the accretion of beaches by artificial means. Most commonly this involves pumping sand from inlets or offshore shoals in a water slurry onto the beach. The process is known as beach nourishment (renourishment), beach restoration, and dredge-and-fill. Artificial dunes are piles of sand on the upper beach, generally assembled by **bulldozers**.

Water drains into the surf and the sand is spread

HOW COME? These projects take place where there is an unsatisfactory sand buffer between our coastal development and the sea. Artificial beaches are wider, flatter, and harder than beaches assembled naturally. In comparison to natural dunes, bulldozed dunes have poorly sorted, less stratified sands (pp. 9, 11) and a less diverse assemblage of dune plants.

A newly engineered beach

DID YOU KNOW? Creating a living beach is difficult. Artificial beach/dune projects smother existing swash-zone animals, dune plants, and their seeds with sterile sand that takes at least a few years to re-colonize. In the 1930s, extensive stretches of sand along Outer Banks Hwy. 12 was piled into artificial dunes by the Civilian Conservation Corps (CCC). Some of these dunes have been naturalized over the years, but dunes fronting development are still re-bulldozed following breaches by storms.

Bulldozers move sand into an artificial dune

321

American oystercatcher with bands and radio

Signs indicate areas requiring special protections

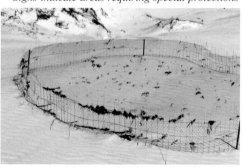

A predator exclosure to protect plover chicks

An old tern-chick hut at the end of the season

Conservation *(Shorebirds)*

WHAT IS IT? Researchers apply numbered and colored **bands** to birds in order to track their movements and fates. Some larger bands can be read with binoculars. Birds are also tracked with tiny **radio transmitters** and a trailing antenna. **Posted shorebird nesting areas** are sections of beach where entry by humans or dogs could cause birds to abandon their eggs and chicks. Not all nesting areas are posted. Circling or agitated birds is a sign that one's presence is unappreciated. **Predator exclosures** are cages that allow plover chicks (p. 193) to enter an area where foxes, fish crows, and other predators cannot. To increase survival of least tern chicks (p. 214), rangers set out shade in the form of miniature Quonset **huts** (black plastic septic pipe).

HOW COME? Banded and tracked birds reveal important information to resource managers trying to reduce threats to their populations. Posted shorebird nesting areas protect birds from foot traffic and disturbance, as long as the signs are heeded. Predation and sun exposure are important sources of chick mortality that can be managed. Exclosures and plastic huts are a substitute for concealing, shading, vegetation.

DID YOU KNOW? Careful behavior allowing birds their space brings about successful shorebird nesting even near highly developed areas.

Conservation *(Sea Turtles)*

WHAT IS IT? Sea turtles (pp. 176, 177) are endangered and depend on beaches for their reproduction. Conservation activities on beaches include **protection of nests** from predators (spring–fall), **morning nest counts** (spring–summer), and special **screening of nests** to prevent disorientation of hatchings by artificial lighting.

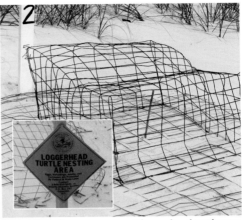

An anti-predator cage over a loggerhead turtle nest

HOW COME? Managers cage nests to reduce egg predation, mostly from raccoons and foxes (pp. 222–223). Sea turtle nest surveyors often use small all-terrain vehicles (ATVs) with low-pressure balloon tires to do this work. Their careful use leaves minimal ruts and does not harm advancing beach plants. Some researchers identify nests with cordons or simple stakes. The conspicuous markers protect nests from human activity and facilitate finding hatched and unhatched eggs for nest-success inventories following the incubation period (about two months). Some beaches have visible lighting that can draw hatchlings away from the sea, killing them. Hiding these lights is the best option, but screened pathways sometimes keep little turtles from wandering landward.

Sea turtle nest counts often require ATVs

DID YOU KNOW? Loggerhead turtles nesting on the beaches of Georgia and the Carolinas are genetically unique. Their tendency to nest on beaches where they hatched has separated them from populations in Florida.

Screens to prevent disorientation from lights

Beach Quests

Although many beachcombers delight in the beach itself, others are driven by quests. These are the searches for uncommon finds whose prospects reinforce the beach-combing addiction. The rarest items can prompt legendary pursuits and become the symbolic excuse for a lifetime of beach adventures.

The facing page briefly outlines tactics for **where**, **when**, and **how** to target some of the many potential quests on Georgia and Carolina beaches. These tactics are the most likely times and places among many opportunities that are more fully described in the referenced pages. Even more research may be helpful. Knowing "habits" and having a complete "search image" are critical to recognizing rare opportunities. But the most important element in fulfilling a quest is persistence. Beaches are places where every footstep and every tide brings something different. An adequately persistent and prepared beachcomber will be able to fulfill all of these beach quests, and even casual combers will find a few. Good luck!

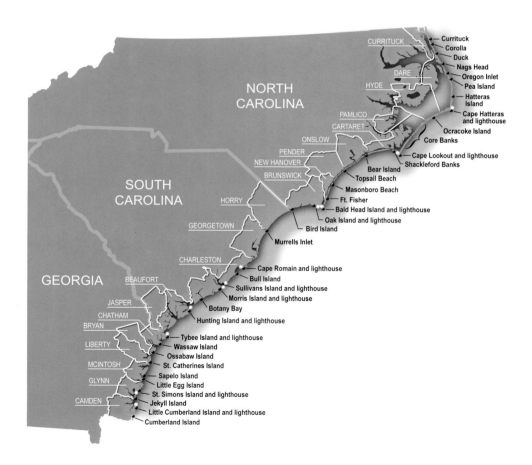

Boneyard Skeletons

Northeastern ends of Georgia and South Carolina Sea Islands, most accessible at low tide, **page 14**

Mushroom Pedestal

Core Banks, NC, during persistent winds, search overwash areas at the base of the dune, **page 21**

Queen Helmet

Bear Island, NC, on a calm day following a storm, search high and low, **page 96**

Blue Glaucus

Cape Hatteras, NC, fall season following strong northeast winds, search the recent tide line, **page 101**

Royal Sea Star

Exposed shoals at inlets, summer during a spring-tide low, **page 164**

Nesting Loggerhead Sea Turtle

Jekyll Island, GA, June and July, attend a night walk guided by the Georgia Sea Turtle Center, **page 176**

Piping Plover

Cape Lookout National Seashore, April–August, bring binoculars and admire from a distance, **page 193**

North Atlantic Right Whale

Georgia coast, December–March, ask park rangers about previous sightings, **page 226**

Seabeach Amarynth

Bird Island, SC, in summer, search overwash areas at the base of the dune, **page 242**

Keeper Seabean

Outer Banks, NC, October–December after strong northeast winds, turn the wrack, **pages 272–274**

Fulgurite

Pea Island, NC, following dune erosion from a severe storm, **page 289**

Giant Oyster Fossil

Topsail Beach, NC, fall, on a calm day's low tide following a storm, **page 293**

Blue and Lavender Seaglass

Nags Head, NC, summer during low tide, search areas with shell hash, **page 303**

Lighthouses

Experience them all from a beach vantage point, some are best seen from adjacent islands, **page 314**

Our Future with Living Beaches

A loggerhead sea turtle draws in a gasping breath, closes her eyes, and flings a wispy arc of sand behind her. After each deliberate flipper stroke, she musters the energy to complete her investment—a broad mound concealing her eggs. It is her fourth nest of the summer. The others, varied in fate, incubate within the beach nearby. Her trust lies with a temporarily tranquil, post-turmoil, rolling landscape of sand, now just being lit, as the sea's horizon warms with morning shades of gold.

A nesting loggerhead covers her eggs with sand

"Mommy, it's a sea turtle!" a girl whispers loudly, dragging a lumpy bag of collected trash up the beach before plopping into a crouch near the dune. Peering from a respectful distance, she soaks in the scene. "She must be old," the girl wonders aloud, scrutinizing the loggerhead's worn, barnacle-dotted shell. "How old is she?" The girl's mother catches up, and kneels beside her daughter. "Don't know . . . really old I guess. Can you imagine the things she's seen?"

We can. No doubt, the turtle's world has changed . . . given a plausible loggerhead lifespan, perhaps 80 years' worth. When she was a hatchling, it's likely that both the beach she scrambled down and the surf where she first swam were hundreds of yards seaward. There may have been some modest cottages nearby, but their remnants, along with the sands of the dunes supporting them, have been scattered by breakers and currents. In the decades since the turtle's memory of her natal beach first crystallized, dozens of powerful storms have dissolved the coastal landscape and reworked it into abundant varieties on a common theme.

Despite all this change, or maybe because of it, the beach's life has persisted. It's as if life understands how ephemeral beaches truly are. Burrowers in the swash and denizens of the wrack live expecting imminent change, pursuing lives of haste with reproduction scheduled before periodic upheavals. On the dune, toughened plants risk eventual catastrophe, but are splendidly separated from competitors unable to cope with coastal hazards. And when the sea rears up to end lives, the seeds of the next generation lie ready to be strategically dispersed.

Over millennia, native beach life has tuned itself well to perpetual change. In contrast, we are still learning. Over the life of our loggerhead, our experimentation with a permanent presence on beaches has ended in messy, losing battles. Feckless rock revetments, overwashed foundations, and skeleton pilings stand as testament to these one-sided skirmishes. Our loggerhead too has kept a relationship with beaches throughout the decades of her reproductive life, but as a beach visitor, rather than resident. It seems that briefly entrusting a beach to incubate eggs does not require the beach to be what it isn't. Sea turtles benefit from beaches, not because they can determine their future there, but because they anticipate it.

We can anticipate as well, that the future of our beaches will be as dramatic as the past. Some of this drama will involve rising sea level, barrier islands rolling landward, and the sinking and dividing of sandy shorelines, all with gradual changes punctuated by sudden shifts caused by tumultuous storms. These changes need not be tragic.

A loggerhead hatchling enters the foamy surf for its first swim

Two months after a little girl pondered the experiences of a nesting loggerhead, the nest the turtle left behind shows life, as dozens of tiny hatchlings squirm free of the sand and stream toward the surf. Turtle by turtle, they are caught by waves rushing the beach and are swept toward a future of intertwined fates. In about 30 years, the most fortunate will become adults, ready to match memories of their beach with what the future holds. Our own children will grow up as well. And some of what they learn of their world may come from pondering mysteries on beaches.

When decades pass and the loggerheads return to nest on their beach, our kids will be there. They will be fellow visitors perhaps, still learning . . . about what to determine, when to accept, and how to sustain the most meaningful portions of life.

327

Resources and Suggested Reading

Beach Features

Neal, William J., Orrin H. Pilkey, and Joseph T. Kelley. *Atlantic Coast Beaches: A Guide to Ripples, Dunes, and Other Natural Features of the Seashore.* Missoula, MT: Mountain Press Publishing Company, 2007.

Pilkey, O.H., and M.E. Fraser. *A Celebration of the World's Barrier Islands.* New York, NY: Columbia University Press, 2003.

Beach Animals

Farrand, John Jr., editor. *The Audubon Society Master Guide to Birding: 1 Loons to Sandpipers, 2 Gulls to Dippers.* New York, NY: Alfred A. Knopf, Inc., 1983.

Fussell, J. O. III. *A Birder's Guide to Coastal North Carolina.* Chapel Hill, NC: University of North Carolina Press, 1994.

Hugh J. Porter, Lynn Houser. *Seashells of North Carolina.* Raleigh, NC: North Carolina Sea Grant, 2000.

Lee, Harry G. *Marine Shells of Northeast Florida.* Jacksonville, FL: Jacksonville Shell Club, 2009.

McLachlan, A., and A.C. Brown. *The Ecology of Sandy Shores.* Burlington, MA: Academic Press, 2006.

Morris, Percy A. *A Field Guide to Shells of the Atlantic and Gulf Coasts and the West Indies.* Boston, MA and New York, NY: Houghton Mifflin Company, 1973.

Ruppert, Edward E., and Richard S. Fox. *Seashore Animals of the Southeast.* Columbia, SC: University of South Carolina Press, 1988.

Witherington, Blair E. *Sea Turtles.* St. Paul, MN: Voyageur Press, 2006.

www.jaxshells.org

Beach Plants

Duncan, Wilbur H., and Marion B. Duncan. *Seaside Plants of the Gulf and Atlantic Coasts.* Washington, D.C. and London: Smithsonian Institution, 1987.

Kraus, E., Jean Wilson, and Sarah Friday. *A Guide to Ocean Dune Plants Common to North Carolina.* Chapel Hill, NC: University of North Carolina Sea Grant College Program by the University of North Carolina Press, 1988.

Perry, Ed, IV, and John V. Dennis. *Sea-Beans from the Tropics.* Malabar, FL: Krieger Publishing Company, 2003.

www.seabean.com

Beach Minerals

Pilkey, Orrin H., Tracy Monegan Rice, and William J. Neal. *How to Read a North Carolina Beach.* Chapel Hill, NC: University of North Carolina Press, 2004.

Stewart, Kevin G., and Mary-Russell Roberson. *Exploring the Geology of the Carolinas: A Field Guide to Favorite Places from Chimney Rock to Charleston.* Chapel Hill, NC: The University of North Carolina Press, 2007.

Hand of Man

Clayton, T.D., L.A. Taylor, Jr., W.J. Cleary, P.E. Hosier, P.H.F. Graber, W.J. Neal, and O.H. Pilkey, Sr. *Living with the Georgia Shore.* Durham, NC: Duke University Press. 1992.

Defeo, O., A. McLachlan, D.S. Schoeman, T.A. Schlacher, J. Dugan, A. Jones, M. Lastra, and F. Scapini. *Threats to Sandy Beach Ecosystems: A Review.* East Coast Shelf Science 81:1-12. 2009.

Lennon, G., W.J. Neal, D.M. Bush, O.H. Pilkey, M. Stuz, and J. Bullock. *Living With the South Carolina Coast.* Durham, NC: Duke University Press, 1996.

Pilkey, OH, W.J. Neal, S. Riggs, D. Pilkey, C.A. Webb. *The North Carolina Shore and Its Barrier Islands: Restless Ribbons of Sand (Living with the Shore).* Durham, NC: Duke University Press, 1998.

Entries in **bold** indicate photos and illustrations.